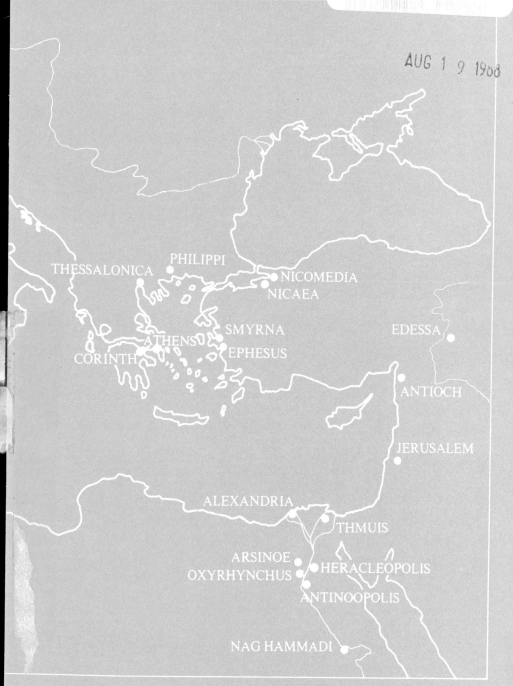

THESSALONICA PHILIPPI
                        NICOMEDIA
                        NICAEA

                                    EDESSA
                SMYRNA
ATHENS
CORINTH   EPHESUS

                                    ANTIOCH

                                    JERUSALEM

            ALEXANDRIA
                        THMUIS

        ARSINOE
OXYRHYNCHUS   HERACLEOPOLIS
            ANTINOOPOLIS

        NAG HAMMADI

The Social Structure of the
Early Christian Communities

The Social Structure of the Early Christian Communities

DIMITRIS J. KYRTATAS

VERSO
London · New York

First published by Verso 1987
© 1987 Dimitris Kyrtatas
All rights reserved

Verso
UK: 6 Meard Street, London W1V 3HR
USA: 29 West 35th Street, New York, NY 10001 2291

Verso is the imprint of New Left Books

British Library Cataloguing in Publication Data

Kyrtatas, Dimitris
   The social structure of the early Christian
   communities
   1. Church history — Primitive and early
   church, ca. 30-600
   I. Title
   209'.015   BR165   60124694

US Library of Congress Cataloging in Publication Data

Kyrtatas, Dimitris J., 1952-
   The early Christian communities.

   Bibliography: p.
   Includes Indexes.
   1. Sociology, Biblical. 2. Bible. N.T. Criticism,
interpretation, etc. I. Title.
BS2545.S55K97 1987 306'.6 87-14993

ISBN 0-86091-163-2

Typeset by Leaper & Gard Ltd, Bristol, England
Printed in Great Britain by Biddles Ltd, Guildford

Contents

Acknowledgements

The original thesis on which this work depends was produced at Brunel University under the supervision and constant encouragement of Professor Keith Hopkins. Valuable suggestions were made by Professor Averil Cameron and Professor J.D.Y. Peel who read the thesis as external examiners and by Professor Robert Browning who kindly read an early version of chapter 6. The idea of publishing this work belongs to Perry Anderson who has in many ways contributed to its improvement. I owe a great deal to G.E.M. de Ste. Croix who patiently enlightened me on several aspects of the topics considered; Ste. Croix read most of the work and saved me from many errors. I am grateful to all the above. Naturally, none of them has any responsibility for the content of the present work. At various stages I received help from a number of friends; I would like in particular to thank Nicos Manolopoulos, Dr. John Peponis, Katia Malachtari and Ino Balta.

D.K.

Foreword

It is very refreshing to find a book on early Christianity, published in Great Britain, which starts out by insisting that early Christianity is today 'an element of ancient history'.

The greatest of English ancient historians, Edward Gibbon, whose *Decline and Fall of the Roman Empire* was published some two centuries ago (between 1766 and 1788), set a precedent which few Anglophone ancient historians have followed: he treated the history of Christianity as an essential part of the history of the Roman empire and gave it the most serious and detailed consideration. Few of his successors have taken the same course. And as universities grew and the syllabuses of their degree courses developed, it was Faculties of Theology which gradually came to monopolize the history of early Christianity. In Britain, ancient history, which in some universities, unfortunately, became a province of Faculties of Classics (or of Latin and Greek), was rarely felt to include early Christianity. In Gibbon's own university, Oxford, where for several generations more students have taken a subject officially called Ancient History than in any other university in the world, the ancient history which formed part of 'Greats' (Literae Humaniores) ended at the latest – and still ends – with the death of Trajan in AD 117. Concentrated as the Greats course has been (though rather less in recent years) on 'prescribed texts', it has been only in Tacitus's brief account of the persecution of Christians in Rome after the great fire of 64, and in the Pliny-Trajan correspondence about the persecution conducted by Pliny in Pontus in *c.* 112, that candidates have actually been obliged to take notice of the existence of Christianity. They might go much deeper, but not many did when I was teaching at New College; and if they wanted to study, for example, the life of Jesus, they would be likely to go to a theologian.

I gather that in some other countries the virtual exclusion of early Christianity from 'ancient history' is less marked, but everywhere in the Western world there seems to be a tendency for the history of early Christianity to be largely abandoned to theologians, who have seldom received much training – some of them none at all – in historical method and research; and of course it is equally true that few ancient historians are able to cope with the theological issues which arise all the time in the study of early Christianity. In March 1986 I gave the 'Gregynog Lectures' at the University College of Wales, Aberystwyth, on 'Early Christian Attitudes to Women, Sex and Marriage'; and for these I had to read a large number of modern biblical commentaries and the doctrinal works, which brought home to me how limited my own previous knowledge had been of the development of Christian doctrine. I have often been shocked, on the other hand, to find a serious incapacity on the part of theological writers to deal with historical issues, even central ones. The problem – insoluble as it is – of the date of the birth of Jesus, for example, which according to Matthew's gospel cannot have been later than 4 BC (the date of the death of Herod the Great) and according to Luke's gospel took place at the time of the 'census of Quirinius' in AD 6, was at last put on a satisfactory footing by two articles by ancient historians: Sir Ronald Syme's 'The Titulus Tiburtinus', in *Vestigia* 17 (1972) 585-601, and even more the magisterial 'Excursus I – The Census of Quirinius, Luke 2: 1-5', in *The History of the Jewish People in the Age of Jesus Christ (175 BC–AD 135)* by Emil Schürer, thoroughly revised and re-edited by Geza Vermes and Fergus Millar (1973) 399-427, which enable the reader to start afresh, in possession of all the important evidence. Again, it was a Classical papyrologist at Oxford, Colin H. Roberts, in the *Harvard Theological Review* 41 (1948) 1-8, who produced what seems to me one of the most important contributions ever made to the understanding of the vitally important concept of 'the kingdom of heaven' (or 'of God') in the teaching of Jesus, by giving a new meaning to a famous passage in Luke's gospel (xvii.21), earlier translated, 'The kingdom of God is within you', or 'among you' – *entos hymōn* in the Greek; *intra vos* in the Latin Vulgate. Roberts showed that in the '*koinē* Greek' of the first century the natural meaning of this expression was likely to be 'The kingdom is *within your power*' ('It is a present reality if you wish it to be so').

In 1964 my own teacher, A.H.M. Jones (who died in 1970), published his great work in three volumes, *The Later Roman Empire 284-602: A Social Economic and Administrative Survey.* This deals at many points with the history of Christianity during the Christian Empire, from Constantine onwards, and in its Chapter XXII gives the best account in any language known to me of 'The Church' *as an insti-*

tution: its organization, clergy and finances. ('Religion and Morals' and 'Education and Culture' are dealt with in separate chapters.) I know of nothing comparable for the first three centuries of the Christian era, when Christianity of course played a far less conspicuous part. Its beginnings and its growth cry out for treatment by those whose interests are both historical and sociological.

In his introductory chapter to this book, 'The Study of Early Christianity', Dr Kyrtatas reviews some of the most important stages in the development of historical writing about early Christianity, paying due attention to the ideological attitudes of the participants in a way that does not come so naturally to most Anglophone historians, who tend to be less interested, perhaps, in formulating explicitly their own philosophical positions and noticing those of others than historians writing in other languages. His position is thoroughly Marxist (as is my own), but entirely without the narrowness of outlook and the sectarianism that disfigure some would-be Marxist writing. (Confronted with work of that kind, I often think of the Emperor Constantine's exasperated remark to a Christian ascetic, a Novatianist, whom he much admired for his holiness but whose excessively strict theological views he found tiresome: 'Fetch a ladder, Acesius, and climb up into heaven by yourself'.) Dr Kyrtatas has thought effectively about methodology, and he shows no trace of the 'reductionism' (if I may call it that) which would interpret religious phenomena exclusively in social or economic terms. He and I may have different opinions at some points, but I much admire his honesty as a historian and his ability to seize upon essentials. It is quite remarkable that his first degree was principally in economics, that he never received formal academic instruction as a historian, and that he had not written historical essays before he started work on his thesis for a doctorate at Brunel University, entitled 'Social Status and Conversion', out of which this book has grown. He has an advantage over most of us in that Greek is not Greek to him as it was to Casca in *Julius Caesar*: I envy his ability to read fluently even the rhetorical flatulence that we all have to endure if we want to become acquainted with authors like John Chrysostom, Hippolytus and Philo. In modern Greek education, Latin naturally plays a far less important role than in western Europe; but here too Dr Kyrtatas has read all the important sources. His command of English, too, is remarkable.

It may be appropriate for me to add a few words about the initial expansion of Christianity, since Dr Kyrtatas has not had occasion to discuss in this book the narrative of the earlier part of the Acts of the Apostles, which with some supplementation from the Epistles and Revelation constitutes virtually our only historical authority for the events it describes, whatever our trust or distrust of its narrative may be. In my book, *The Class Struggle in the Ancient Greek World from the Archaic Age to the Arab Conquests* (1981, corrected 2nd impression 1983), especially pp. 427-433, I have emphasized that Jesus himself lived and taught entirely within a non-urban Jewish-Galilean environment, which was on the fringe of the Graeco-Roman world and of course was dominated politically by Rome but was not in a real sense an integral part of Graeco-Roman civilization and was far from sharing its thought-world, notably its ethics. I must say, to me the most puzzling problem in the rise of Christianity is still (see p. 433 of my book, just mentioned) its rapid transformation from a rural and altogether non-Graeco-Roman religion, a form of Judaism indeed, into a *polis*-religion, one that could flourish in the Greek and Roman *city* which was the prime unit of Greek and Roman civilization.

When the disciples had convinced themselves that Jesus had 'risen from the dead', they began to spread their message, but still at first entirely among their fellow Jews, whether in Palestine or in the nearby Diaspora. Even when they were persecuted by the leading Jews, and many of the earliest Christians had to leave Jerusalem itself, they went (as Jesus had done) only to 'the [country] regions [the *chōra*, the countryside] of Judaea and Samaria' (Acts viii.1), and still preached mainly in the villages (viii.25), although Philip, exceptionally, is said to have gone into the city of Samaria, a predominantly pagan town (viii.5ff), and later to have preached 'in all the cities' as far as Caesarea (viii.40). Even when Paul was converted, and started to preach in Damascus, he spoke 'in the synagogues' to the Jews there (ix.20, 22), before returning to Jerusalem. It is as late as Acts x.45-8 that we first hear of the conversion of a significant number of Gentiles, at Caesarea, the capital city of Roman Judaea. Even in chapter xi we hear at first of preaching in Phoenicia, Cyprus and Antioch 'to none but unto the Jews only' (xi.19); but from verse 20 onwards we begin to find Christians of Cyprus and Cyrene preaching to Greeks at Antioch, with much success (xi.20-1, 25-6). Even after this, the standard procedure for Christian missionaries like Paul and Barnabas was to go first into Jewish synagogues (see e.g. Acts ix.20 with 22; xiii.5, 14-15; xiv.1; xvii.1-2, 10, 17; xviii. 4, 19; xix.8; cf. xviii.7-8, 26). There, they would often find a wider congregation, consisting not only of Jews but also of Jewish 'fellow travellers' (if I may call them that), who are most commonly referred to nowadays as 'God-fearers' (the Greek text calls them, among other things, most often 'God-fearers' or 'God-worshippers': *phoboumenoi* or *sebomenoi ton theon*). Such people appear frequently in Acts, for example in x.2, 22, 35; xiii.16, 26, 50; xvi.14; xvii.4, 17; xviii.7; cf. viii.27-38; xiii.42-43; xiv.1; and xviii.4. It was easier for a 'God-fearer' to become a full member of a Christian community than a-Jewish proselyte; and in particular, if a man, he would not have to undergo circumcision, a necessity for becoming a proselyte.

The methods of evangelization in Acts are principally miracle and the claimed fulfilment of prophecy. The latter was particularly suitable for an audience of Jews, and even of 'God-fearers', many of whom must have had some acquaintance with the Jewish scriptures (cf. Acts viii.27-38)..What were regarded as miracles were evidently a constant feature of Christian missions: in the first ten chapters of Acts alone see i.9-11; ii.4-13 ('glossolalia', with 14ff., also x.45-6; xix.6; and of course I Cor. xii, xiv); iii.2-12 (with iv.8-10, 14, 16, 17-22); iv.30; v.5, 10-11, 12, 15-16, 19-26; vi.8; viii.6-7, 13, 39; ix.3-9, 17-18, 32-5, 36-42; x.1-7 (with 19-22, 30-3), 10-16 (with xi.5ff.). Miracles continued to play a very important role in procuring conversions: see Ramsay MacMullen, 'Two types of conversion to early Christianity' in *Vigiliae Christianae* 37 (1983) 174-92, particularly 184-8, with the notes, 191-2; and also *Christianizing the Roman Empire AD 100-400* (1984) 183, Index, *s.v.* 'Miracles'. And it is still worth reading the whole of the fifteenth chapter of Gibbon's *Decline and Fall of the Roman Empire*, especially on the role of miracles, § III (pp. 28-32 of Vol. II of the standard edition by J.B. Bury, in 7 vols) and the conclusion of the chapter, pp. 69-70.

Most people may perhaps feel that the Christian emphasis on a future life, with its rewards for good Christians and punishment for others, must have played a major part in the process of conversion. I would not strongly dissent from this, although I would point out that most Greek and Roman pagans, especially among the upper classes, seem to have had much less interest than might have been expected in life after death. This was borne in upon me by reading the great work of Erwin Rohde, *Psyche*, which went through eight editions between 1893 and 1920, and of which there is an excellent English translation by W.B. Hillis (1925; 2-vol. paperback edition 1966). The conclusions of this book seem to me to receive further confirmation from funerary inscriptions published subsequently (I will mention only Richmond Lattimore's *Themes in Greek and Latin Epitaphs*, 1962). As Gibbon said, 'We are sufficiently acquainted with the eminent persons who flourished in the age of Cicero, and of the first Caesars, with their actions, their characters, and their motives, to be assured that their conduct in this life was never regulated by any serious conviction of the rewards or punishments of a future state': doctrine of this kind they regarded as 'an idle and extravagant opinion' (*op. cit.* 20). But to my mind the most powerful weapon in the Christian armoury, in multiplying and retaining new adherents, was the remarkable organization of the Christian churches, which was entirely unparalleled in the pagan world. On this question too I would draw attention to Gibbon's fifteenth chapter, § V (*op. cit.* 39-54).

I warmly commend Dr Kyrtatas's book to all those who are interested in the development of Christianity (and indeed to many who may suppose that they are not), all the more so because it is written for 'the general reader' and avoids the kind of learned obscurity and nitpicking that unnecessarily confine the reading of many such investigations to a small circle of scholars. It is interesting from beginning to end.

G.E.M. de Ste. Croix

Introduction

The Study of Early Christianity

In the last few decades interest in the history of early Christianity has undergone a significant revival. Professional church historians apart, an increasing number of ancient historians are including early Christianity in their field of research. Christian sources, such as the New Testament, the sermons of the Church Fathers, saints' lives, are being examined for the evidence they provide in matters not just of religious, but of secular, history. More significantly, religious developments are now being studied through the same methods as other philosophical, political and ideological processes. A new generation of scholars is carrying out a systematic and consistent examination of early Christianity within its historical context, as an integral part of the history of late antiquity. To most historians today early Christianity is indeed an element of ancient history.

Systematic interest in early Christianity has an almost continuous history of more than three centuries. But when this interest first emerged, it fell under a number of distinct headings. Biblical studies were not directly related to church history and the latter was considered independently of the sermons of the early Fathers and of saints' lives. Attention was focused on each subject for different motives: as I see it, historical investigations proper are always preceded and structured by philosophical conceptions of history or by new philosophies of history – of which historians need not always be conscious. The urge to acquire first-hand knowledge of the works of the early Church Fathers – in particular those which had not been handed down through continuous tradition – was felt in the sixteenth century within the intellectual climate of Renaissance humanism: one of the earliest scholars to attempt the publication of such texts was Erasmus. The late seventeenth century witnessed the foundation by Bolland of a school in Antwerp which is still publishing editions of saints' lives. At the Abbey of Saint-Germain-des-Prés, the Maurist brothers Mabillon and Montfaucon set up a systematic programme of publications of the works of church Fathers and other ecclesiastical writers.[1] Educated at Port-Royal, Tillemont began publication in 1693 of a great work on ecclesiastical history which brought together patristic material outlining a history of Christianity down to 513. During the whole of the eighteenth century, other scholars continued to produce critical editions and commentaries which have not lost their value today. In the mid nineteenth century the persistent interest in publishing texts related to theology and church history led to the Migne series, the *Patrologia Latina* and *Patrologia Graeca* still widely used.

Publishing critical editions of texts was one side of the question; the other was understanding the Bible. As is well known, its study was central to Martin Luther and the Protestant movement. The conflict between Catholics and Protestants as to whether or not the Bible could be correctly understood outside the tradition of the church led to endless discussions which brought historical approaches into the field of exegesis. But before a systematic historical reading could be advanced, it was the authority of the Bible itself that had first to be questioned effectively. This was achieved under the influence of Rationalism. The contribution of such philosophers as Hobbes and, above all, Spinoza to a critical examination of scripture was far-reaching. Spinoza was most influential on three major issues. First, he regarded prophets as 'endowed with unusually vivid imagination', but he did not accept that 'knowledge of natural and spiritual phenomena can be gained from the prophetic books'; second, he saw miracles as 'natural occurrences' and argued that they should be explained 'as to appear neither new ... nor contrary to nature'; and third, he put forward as a universal rule in interpreting scripture that nothing may be accepted as an 'authoritative Scriptural statement which we do not perceive very clearly when we examine it in the light of its history'. To Spinoza 'the method of interpreting Scripture does not widely differ from the method of interpreting nature – in fact, it is almost the same'.[2] English Deism's contribution to the study of the Bible was also rationalist in character.[3] John Locke's quest for 'rational Christianity', indeed, was soon to influence the French Encyclopaedists. Once stripped of external authority and examined on its own, the Bible became the object of endless discussions involving not only 'textual criticism' but also, and above all, 'source criticism' i.e. the investigation of the sources of the Biblical texts. Before the end of the eighteenth century another related but quite distinct trend of scholarship evolved, the so-called 'quest for the historical Jesus', which stimulated the most minute investigation of the New Testament from a historical point of view.[4]

A great moment in the study of early Christianity was when all these separate fields of scholarship started to become interrelated so as to produce a continuous account of the Church as part of ancient history in general. The principles of such an endeavour were laid down by the philosophers of the Enlightenment. In 1734 Montesquieu published anonymously his *Considérations sur les causes de la grandeur et de la décadence des Romains*; history was now conceived as governed by natural laws, hence the idea of grandeur and decline. This new historical philosophy enabled the writing of a new kind of history. In 1776 Edward Gibbon published the first volume of his *Decline and Fall of the Roman Empire*. He devoted two chapters to early Christianity, one on the progress of the Christian religion and the other on the conduct of the Roman government towards Christians. Drawing upon a number of sources including Tillemont, the Maurists, their Italian disciples and a few others, Gibbon composed a narrative history of early Christianity, presenting it as a contributory factor to the decline of the Roman world. But above all Gibbon was able to read for himself a vast amount of patristic literature not for its significance in the development of doctrine, but for the clues it contained about early Christian history. One of Gibbon's most important contributions was his conviction that the growth of early Christianity should be ascribed to 'natural' causes. The triumph of Christianity could always be regarded as having been determined by 'the ruling providence of its great Author', but 'as truth and reason seldom find so favourable a reception in the world' it would only be right to consider 'the secondary causes as well'. Such, for Gibbon, were the intolerant zeal of the Christians, the doctrine of a future life, the miraculous powers ascribed to the primitive church, Christians' pure and austere morals and the union and discipline of the Christian republic.[5] With Gibbon, early Christianity ceased to be a field of research confined to theologians and philosophers: it now attracted the interest of ancient historians as well.

In the late eighteenth century the study of early Christianity passed to the German universities.[6] There, under the great influence of Hegel, the understanding of early Christian history was revolutionized. In the age of Rationalism, everything in Scripture contradicting the principles of reason had to be rejected: it was only by peeling off the accidental and historical elements that the universal truths of Christianity could be expected to emerge. Consequently, and perhaps ironically, attention shifted from universal truths to temporal elements. The historical aspects of early Christianity came increasingly under investigation.[7] Inevitably this approach created a contradiction. Truth on the one hand, history on the other – these two elements did not seem to converge. The contradiction was resolved by dialectical philosophy. Hegel argued that religion was an integral part of universal history. Truth, as contained in the dogmas of religion, was not opposed to history; it was a stage in its development. The early Christian community sustained, according to Hegel, a double relation: 'first, a relation to the Roman World, and secondly, to the truth whose development was its aim'.[8] Religion was simultaneously placed within the course of history and subordinated to a higher form of reason, absolute knowledge, the ultimate stage of history.

The idea of universal history's development in terms of stages emerging from contradictions and syntheses turned the attention of historians to the greatly neglected period which preceded the emergence of Christianity. Hellenism was put forward as the intermediary period between classical Greece and Christianity.[9] Christianity first appeared in the world in Judaism but soon came into contact with the world of Hellenism. This approach was taken up by a number of scholars, the most prominent of whom were F.C. Baur, D.F. Strauss and Bruno Bauer.[10] Using the terms of Hegelian dialectics Baur argued that the ancient Church – later called Orthodox and Catholic – was the product of a struggle between Judaizers and Hellenists, a struggle between Jewish and Gentile elements in primitive Christianity. In order to substantiate this insight, Baur carried out a close scrutiny of the New Testament texts. Peter's speech was opposed to that of Stephen in Acts; Paul was opposed to Peter in the Epistles to the Corinthians, and so on. Baur was followed by the German theologians known as the Tübingen School, who were gradually led to even more radical positions, considering the New Testament as a very late product of a synthesis between the competing factions. The principles of this approach have today been modified in several ways but not completely abandoned. What is more important, since Baur many scholars have realized that the New Testament texts – like all other historical documents – can be understood correctly not only when placed in their exact historical context but also when interpreted within a theoretical scheme. Strauss and Bauer, who went much further, raised a storm at the time with their publications, but little if anything in their specific theses has survived criticism. The significance of their work lies in its radicalism and its subjection of all the Gospels' historical content to very close scrutiny. Bauer actually rejected so many of the historical accounts given in the New Testament documents that he was led to place the birth of Christianity, not in Palestine, but in the Hellenistic environment of Alexandria and in Rome a century later than the traditional apostolic age. In the same vein, Christian theology was reduced to Hellenistic philosophy intermingled with Judaism.

In the philosophical sphere the concept of religion was once again revolutionized by another pupil of Hegel's, Ludwig Feuerbach. According to Feuerbach the essence of religion was man himself. God was seen as human nature purified. The whole sphere of the religious was to be understood in the light of this basic truth. Today only a small number of existentialist theologians are turning back to Feuerbach, but in his own time he exercised a liberating effect on the radical Hegelians. As is well known, Feuerbach was at first enthusiastically endorsed by the young Marx and Engels.[11] In their early work Marx and Engels developed a theory of ideology which was based on Feuerbach's conception of religion. At that time the Marxist conception of history was not yet formulated, and neither was concern with ancient history and early Christianity. Early Christianity as we shall see, did not attract Engels, until many years later.

In the meantime German biblical scholarship was spreading to other countries: the Tübingen School and Strauss were influential in Holland, Switzerland and England. In France, German radical criticism was represented by Ernest Renan. Strictly speaking, Renan's work was not only lacking in originality; it actually was a reduction of German criticism to its lowest common denominator, exhibiting literary rather than scientific merits – which does not mean that it did not provoke a storm of objections among theologians when it first appeared. The importance of Renan lies rather in his popularization of the subject. Until then, biblical criticism was confined to specialists; after Strauss and especially Renan it attracted a much larger audience.[12] This audience included the late nineteenth-century socialists, who joined in the debate about early Christianity for their own purposes and gave a new stimulus to research.

Marx referred a number of times to Christianity and its early history. As has now been convincingly demonstrated, the relevance of his work for the study of ancient history in general has been wrongly neglected.[13] But the systematic treatment of early Christianity in particular is in fact to be found in the work of Engels. Engels first dealt with the affinity of social movements to Christianity in 1850 when, in examining the Peasants' War in sixteenth-century Germany, he contrasted the biblical interpretation of Thomas Münzer with that of Martin Luther; he subsequently hinted several times at the revolutionary potential and conservative application of Christianity. In the last period of his long and productive career he turned to the history of primitive Christianity, writing three articles exclusively on that subject. The first was a sort of obituary on the occasion of Bruno Bauer's death in 1882, and addresses itself to a number of problems relating primitive Christianity to 'the historical conditions under which it arose and reached its dominating position'. Relying on Bauer's work, Engels advanced his own view of the problems. His argument ended with a piece of Darwinism: 'Not only Palestine, but the entire Orient swarmed with such founders of religions, and between them there raged what can be called a Darwinistic struggle for ideological existence.'[14] A year later Engels wrote a second article on primitive Christianity in which he dealt with the Revelation of John. On the basis of the work of a Berlin professor he argued that Revelation was the oldest extant Christian text, and that it offered an authentic picture of primitive Christianity as a great revolutionary movement made by the masses. Today the dating of Revelation has been shown to be a far more complex problem than was then thought. But it may be noticed that the popularization of the work of the radical biblical scholars was considered by Engels to be in the interest of the socialist movement. Engels was ready to endorse the following statement by Renan – of whose work he did not otherwise approve:

> When you want to get a distinct idea of what the first Christian communities were, do not compare them to the parish congregations of our day; they were rather like local sections of the International Working Men's Association.[15]

Belief in this comparison motivated Engels's concern with the subject; how far this view has been sustained by current investigations I shall discuss later on in this book. But I would like here to say a few words on this motivation.

The concern of Protestant theologians, from Luther to the Tübingeners, with the life of Jesus, the primitive church and the Christian movement of the first three centuries – Christianity, that is, before Constantine and the First Ecumenical Synod at Nicaea – is not difficult to explain. In source criticism and historical research they found justification for their own views as opposed to the patristic interpretations still held by Roman Catholicism. Trying to understand the Bible 'on its own', Protestant scholars were led to a historical reading, a reading, that is, which carefully considered the culture and historical environment in which the biblical documents emerged. The emphasis by Protestant scholars on the revolutionary and liberating character of early Christianity seemed to justify their efforts to liberate contemporary Christianity from the 'Papal yoke'. Engels had similarly political motives for studying the world of the early Christians. In the third and longest article he published on the topic, less than a year before his death, he declared:

> The history of early Christianity has notable points of resemblance with the modern working-class movement. Like the latter, Christianity was originally a movement of oppressed people. ... Both Christianity and the workers' socialism preach forthcoming salvation from bondage and misery; Christianity

places this salvation in a life beyond, after death, in heaven; socialism places it in this world, in a transformation of society. . . . And in spite of all persecution, nay, even spurred on by it, they forge victoriously, irresistibly ahead. Three hundred years after its appearance Christianity was the recognized State religion in the Roman World Empire, and in barely sixty years socialism has won itself a position which makes its victory absolutely certain.[16]

This last article by Engels on early Christianity was published in a German journal edited by Karl Kautsky. As early as 1883, when Engels wrote his first article, Kautsky had contributed an article of his own on the subject of the 'origin of prehistoric bible history', while two years later he wrote for the same journal another article on the origin of Christianity. In his work of 1895, *Forerunners of Modern Socialism*, Kautsky devoted a section of the introduction to early Christianity. He immediately sent the book to Engels for his comments. Engels replied that the book 'gets better the further one reads', but that 'Plato and Christianity are still inadequately treated according to the original plan'. Fourteen years later, when preparing a second edition of his work, Kautsky felt that subsequent investigations had opened up 'a multitude of new points of view and new suggestions, which expanded the revison of (his) Introduction to the *Forerunners* into a whole book'.[17] This new book, *Foundations of Christianity*, first published in 1908, was in its thirteenth edition when the first English translation was made in 1925. Between 1895 and 1908 Kautsky had the opportunity to read a number of works on Roman history and the history of early Christianity; above all he now had at his disposal Adolf Harnack's *The Mission and Expansion of Christianity in the First Three Centuries* (first German edition in 1902), and Giuseppe Salvioli's *Le capitalisme dans le monde antique* (Paris, 1906). Kautsky's further reading did not alter much of his original thesis; it did help him to add a number of points and to expand and clarify a number of others. It is important, however, to notice the shift in the intellectual climate of the period. During the last decade of the nineteenth century and the first of the twentieth, scholarship had developed new interests, which we may call sociological in order to distinguish them from earlier, more philosophical interests. A major stimulus to this shift was, obviously, provided by Marxism.[18]

The first Marxist after Engels to attempt a large investigation of the ancient world was Ettore Ciccotti. Ciccotti published his *Il Tramonto della Schiavitù nel Mondo Antico* in 1899, but apparently it was not read by Kautsky until a decade later. (Kautsky reviewed the German translation of this book at length in 1910/11.) The next major Marxist scholar to deal with the problems of antiquity was Salvioli; and within a few years a number of Marxists turned their attention to the class struggle in the ancient world. Slavery and the slave system were at the centre of the discussion. It is to this context that Kautsky's work belongs.

It has been argued that 'the preponderance of classical history in early Marxist work may be said to reflect, in some sort, the centrality of classics in literary discourse and higher education ... It may also have been a residue of that older tradition in Radical thought, stemming from Gibbon's *Decline and Fall*, which took the Roman Empire as a supreme illustration of the paralysing force of religion. More pertinent, though, from the point of view of Marxist education was the transparency of social relations in the ancient world, the naked character of class domination ... and the first-order relationships between religion, politics and economics.'[19] All this is certainly correct, but it does not sufficiently explain why the subject became popular among Marxists precisely during the first decade of the twentieth century and was subsequently almost entirely forgotten. To answer this question we have to consider the state of the working-class movement and the aspirations of Social Democracy before World War I. At that time the social revolution and the transition to socialism were the order of the day. The Marxist theorists of the Second International were drafting their programmes of social reforms; they were in need of historical parallels. According to the general Marxist periodization of history, there are but two transitional periods in history comparable to that which is expected to come. The first is the decline and fall of the ancient world (and in particular the decline of slavery), the second the French revolution and similar bourgeois revolutions in other countries, which led to the formation of the modern nation states. The idea of investigating social evolution in history with the purpose of drawing information of use to the imminent socialist revolution (already hinted at in the *Communist Manifesto*) is to be found clearly expressed in a very popular pamphlet of 1902 by Kautsky, called *Social Reform and Social Revolution.* After the war, with the developments in Russia, the European socialist movement had other matters to discuss: above all, it had to discuss the realization of the first attempt to transform a capitalist into a socialist state. Historical parallels did not seem at that time to have much to contribute. The renewed interest among Marxists in the ancient world during recent decades may perhaps be seen in the same light. In Western Europe, especially since the sixties, socialists have become increasingly convinced that they have to discover their own way to socialism, which means that the great transitional periods of the past have to be reinvestigated and perhaps reinterpreted.

The Marxists of the turn of the century, however, were not alone in examining ancient history and the history of early Christianity from a sociological point of view. I have already mentioned that in 1902

Harnack published his first edition of *The Mission and Expansion* in which he dealt, apart from the geographical spread of Christianity, with what he called 'the inward spread of Christianity' among the educated classes, at court, in the army, among women. Two years later Max Weber wrote his celebrated work *The Protestant Ethic and the Spirit of Capitalism*. In this work Weber did not deal with early Christianity, but when Harnack read it on its publication he added a note about it in the second edition of his *The Mission and Expansion* (1906), expressing great admiration. Weber's work was, in Harnack's view, 'A brilliant example of how to treat the lofty problems set by the influence of the moral and religious consciousness upon the material conditions of life, with adequate breadth and insight'.[20] A few years later Weber produced an encyclopaedic article in which he attacked directly the views expressed by Engels and his disciples (although, as usual, he did not give names).

> It is not only mistaken, it is absolute nonsense to maintain theories such as that Christianity was the result of 'social' conditions or was a product of ancient 'socialist' movements. It is enough to point out that, like every redemptive religion, Christianity held that worldly aims were dangerous and so was the wealth which made these aims attainable ...
>
> Indeed, it was just because of the belief in the permanence of Roman rule until the end of time that men felt it was hopeless to strive for social reform and therefore rejected all class struggles; and this was the source from which flowed Christian love – purely ethical, charitable, and transcendental.[21]

Weber, as early as 1896, also attacked Engels' view that early Christianity had attracted a large number of slaves.[22] On this problem (which shall be discussed in the next chapter) Weber and Kautsky more or less concurred. They both accepted the view advanced by Harnack with respect to the urban character of the early Christian movement, though the former regarded it as a movement of the urban petty bourgeoisie, the latter as a movement of the urban proletariat. But for a long time neither view had any significant impact on the study of the question. Belief in the servile origins of the early Christians was predominant until recent years.

In the early twentieth century discussions concerning the origins of Christianity continued in Russian Marxist circles, but were more or less abandoned by Marxists in the West.[23] The same lack of interest in early Christianity characterized the sociologists influenced by Weber, and the whole field was left once more primarily to church historians, many of whom made valuable contributions. Among them a prominent position belongs to Rudolf Bultmann, one of the most important exponents of form criticism. Instead of searching for original sources, form criticism distinguishes between separate literary units within each Biblical document. By tracing the history of each unit this method shed light on the historical setting which gave birth to these units. Bultmann's conclusion was that, though part of the material incorporated in the Gospels goes back to the primitive Palestinian church, the rest of the material, and above all the editing of the Gospels, was the product of the Hellenistic church. This conclusion led to an extreme scepticism about the possibility of approaching the historical Jesus: what Bultmann offered instead was a clear distinction between the Aramaic and the Hellenistic environment in which particular literary units emerged.[24] This extreme scepticism has recently been challenged by Geza Vermes, who has attempted to demonstrate that with a '*real* familiarity with the literature, culture, religion and above all spirit, of the post-biblical Judaism from which Jesus and his first disciples sprang' it is actually possible to reconstruct some basic elements of Jesus' life story.[25] In spite of their obvious difference, the two approaches concur that the world of Jesus was very different from that of the early church. Early Christian history begins with the mission to the Gentiles, not with Palestine.

To the brief and schematic considerations presented above I would like to add a few remarks on some more recent developments. Professional ancient historians are increasingly coming to turn their attention to early Christianity. A.H.M. Jones, in his great work *The Later Roman Empire* (1964), contributed a great deal to the study of a number of topics in early Christianity among which may be singled out church finance. No better testimony is required of Jones' sociological concerns than two articles he wrote in 1959, both of which have been highly influential. The first is called 'The Social Background of the Struggle between Paganism and Christianity', the second 'Were Ancient Heresies National or Social Movements in Disguise?'. Jones' contribution to the field cannot easily be summarized. His approach was not determined by any simple theoretical scheme; its most important characteristic is perhaps its systematic and detailed examination of ancient sources: what Jones was able to establish in the field of Christian history is very difficult to disprove. Clear sociological concepts were to reappear in the study of ancient history in the early seventies; two works have attracted particular attention in the English-speaking world. The first is M.I. Finley's *The Ancient Economy* (1973), which puts forward a creative discussion of Weberian categories; the second Perry Anderson's *Passages from Antiquity to Feudalism* (1974). Anderson's work, though clearly Marxist in general outlook, owes most in its details to non-Marxist historians. Neither Finley nor Anderson have much to say about early Christianity, but they both re-draw the background for a fresh examination of religion in its social context. This survey should also draw attention to the widely discussed book by G.E.M. de Ste. Croix, *The Class Struggle in the Ancient Greek World* (1981). Characteristic of this work is the careful scrutiny of ancient sources combined with the application of rigorously defined Marxist concepts; long sections are devoted to aspects of early Christian history.[26] A number of important points are made, but the book's great virtue is perhaps that in it early Christianity is now being considered within a much wider conception of ancient history than is usual. While the book's title refers to the Greek world, what is actually discussed is much more. In *The Class Struggle in the Ancient Greek World* a new world is beginning to emerge which defies traditional chronological and cultural boundaries.

Scope and Limits of the Present Study

The present work deals with a small number of topics which, in one way or another, have long attracted the attention of students of early Christianity. Above all, it is an attempt to investigate the social origins and the social positions of the early Christians. Recent studies are arriving at the conclusion, contrary to long-held views, that the primitive Christian communities, those which emerge after the first chapters of Acts, did not consist of the 'dregs of the populace'.[27] However, in spite of the important work which is being done on the subject, few of the recent books concerned with such sociological issues go far beyond the New Testament age.[28] What still requires investigation is the composition of the early communities from the first years of the mission to the Gentiles down to the age of Constantine, when large sections of the population, from all social classes, started joining the Christian churches.

Naturally, a re-evaluation of the subject requires a fresh examination of the ancient sources. But this task cannot be performed as if it were a simple and 'innocent' reading of texts. Several decades ago scholars such as Harnack and Cadoux, to name but two, went through almost all the relevant sources in a highly systematic way. So, although new archaeological discoveries are constantly shedding light on the history of early Christianity (mainly in Egypt), most of the important ancient sources are well known, or easily available, to all students of early Christianity. In this book I have tried to reconsider a number of the relevant sources, together with recent finds, in the light of progress made in the field of ancient history. Beyond this, I have departed from more traditional approaches only in one, rather important respect. Ancient historians and church historians are usually very much concerned to establish the dating and authenticity of their documents. But since much of the evidence concerning the social origins and position of the early Christians derives not only from what Christian sources report but also from the mentality of their authors, I felt that I should make use of all Christian documents which fall broadly within my period, including those of uncertain date and authorship. For the same reason, I have not always made a distinction between 'orthodox' and 'heterodox' or 'heretical' groups. For my purposes, all those who considered themselves Christians have been discussed without discrimination. I have therefore generally avoided using the word 'Church' in the sense of a unified body of believers; I commonly refer to 'the Christian churches', a term which I find corresponds much better to the reality of the period. A number of my conclusions are tentative, and I have tried to make this as clear as possible. Given the nature of the inquiry, conclusions will depend, to a great extent, on the interpreter's point of view; and, what is more important, the existing evidence is often so scanty that only the cumulative impression created by a number of sources enables the investigator to formulate plausible hypotheses.

At the outset of an investigation into the social composition of the early Christian communities, a clear statement is required of the criteria of class used to classify the early Christians. The easiest approach would perhaps be to follow one of the modern theories of class. Given the nature of the evidence, however, this is often all but impossible. What I have done is to rely more or less upon what can be called the spontaneous sociology of our informers, for it is in their terms that the evidence has reached us. It cannot be expected that this spontaneous sociology is in any way systematic or uniformly accepted by ancient authors, but a number of social categories defined in legal terms or developed by common sense seem to have been, if not generally accepted, at least generally understood. In such works as Artemidorus' *Interpretation of Dreams*, slaves who enjoy the confidence of their master are distinguished from those who do not; bankers, usurers, men who collect subscriptions, all fall in one group; orators and philosophers in another; people in the service of the emperor constitute a single category and so on.[30] I have found there to be some value in such classifications, but whenever possible I have tried to employ more rigorous concepts.

To conclude these introductory remarks, let me say a few things about the nature of the available sources and draw attention to their limitations.

1. Sociological studies of the early Christian communities are primarily based upon direct statements of ancient authorities. Such statements are,

unfortunately, infrequent. Even when they do exist moreover, they are liable to two types of distortion: (a) the writer's lack of statistical data and of any accurate method of evaluating any such data possessed (ancient writers usually employ approximations); and (b) the author's personal interests and bias.

2. Prosopographic investigations are a further source which sometimes appears more reliable than direct statements. But early Christian sources, and especially legendary and mythological accounts, concentrate, as a rule, on the behaviour of notable persons rather than on the behaviour of the common people. Common people and everyday affairs only rarely attract the attention of commentators.

3. A third source is provided by existing archaeological data. Sepulchral and other inscriptions would seem the obvious place to look. But those of wealth and rank were much more likely to commemorate important events of their lives – and their deaths – than the poor and humble. The same may be expected to hold for personal letters, such as those found among the Egyptian papyri; they are likely to belong to groups of people not necessarily representative of the whole community.

4. Church rules and related material can be used as a further source. Given an appropriate analysis, we could get a picture of the social structure of the Christian communities to which such material applied. It may be objected, however, that church rules did not necessarily reflect the actual composition of a community: rules tend to have a preventative character and do not entitle us to be sure, say, that a particular crime had ever been committed. But, fortunately, this is not the case with early Christian rules. Usually, they were either (easily detectable) repetitions of Judaic legislation or verdicts on problems troubling the churches.

5. Linguistic considerations too can usefully be employed by sociologists. The provincial countryside in several areas had been incompletely Hellenized or Romanized. The usage of vernaculars by early Christians is a sign of Christian penetration into the native and primarily agricultural population. Late antiquity, however, witnessed a revival of traditional vernaculars, which embraced the wealthy and educated as well. The social origins of early Christians can also be traced by the idiom of Greek or Latin used. But once again this is not a very reliable source, because even the uneducated tended to write in the respectable idiom of the learned, rather than in their own spoken, language.

6. Finally, sociological investigations of a period which has left so little reliable evidence must take account of the fact that social status was usually accompanied by wealth and education. Although these three features were by no means universally concomitant, and unreserved conclusions can often be misleading, it is reasonable to expect that a

community with many of the wealthy and educated would also include people of high social status.

* * *

The bulk of this work was originally written in 1980 as a University thesis. Since then an impressive amount of research has been carried out on several aspects of early Christian history. While preparing the work for publication I was able to take advantage of a number of recent books and articles. Without altering the book's original structure I rewrote the whole text, adding a few points and making some minor revisions; but as some important works appeared even after the final revision, I should perhaps add a few words here on some of them. I found it encouraging to realize that on various issues modern scholars are arriving at new, and mainly converging, conclusions. As could be expected, interest has mostly concentrated on the period of the first disciples, when the primitive church emerged, and the period of Constantine, when Christianity was adopted by an emperor who made it his task to begin to convert the empire. Among the most important works written on these two periods I would include Meeks's *The First Urban Christians* (1983) and (for the specialist) Barnes's *Constantine and Eusebius* (1981). Meeks has clearly demonstrated that, even in the age of Paul, Christianity, far from being a movement of the destitute and the most oppressed, represented a cross-section of urban society.[31] Furthermore, a number of the first converts are shown to have had 'high status inconsistency', a fact which probably made them more sensitive to religious experiences than others. Barnes, on the other hand, although himself more interested in the 'external steps by which Constantine's rule was achieved',[32] has strongly argued for the religious sincerity in the emperor's motives. In the behaviour of Constantine, religious experience, as opposed to cynical expectations, has once again been brought to the foreground.

One of the most striking features in late antiquity is the developing religious intolerance which replaced the rather 'enlightened' attitudes of the former periods. In spite of the pioneering work being carried out, the persisting question is still 'Why were the early Christians persecuted?'[33] In view of the complexity of the situation it has even been argued that 'The interesting question is whether the Romans ever knew *why* they persecuted the Christians'.[34] The answer seems now to lie not so much in the behaviour of the pagans, as in the common elements which pagans and Christians developed alike in the Later Empire. As Ste. Croix has argued in an as yet unpublished paper, 'we can understand the origin of this situation far better if we consider the persecution *of* the Christians, in the first three centuries and the early years of the fourth, as well as persecutions *by* the Christians from the fourth century onwards'. For there is clearly an element of continuity in the two periods, namely, 'the deep-seated belief in the necessity to preserve the goodwill and favour of the gods, or of God, which might be endangered by certain kinds of religious misbehaviour'. It may therefore be said that the Romans were led to persecute the Christians for more or less the same (religious) reasons which later made the Christian Church 'the greatest organized persecuting force in human history'.[35]

In studying religion in late antiquity, many scholars are still preoccupied with refuting Dodds's *Pagan and Christian in an Age of Anxiety*, written more than twenty years ago. Dodds' approach, and in particular his concept of 'an age of anxiety', seem objectionable to most contemporary authors. Peter Brown, for example, has found it preferable to describe the period as 'an age of ambition' and others have followed closely.[36] And yet, in trying to understand religious experience in the ancient world, scholars have been pursuing some of Dodds's principles more faithfully than they are ready to accept. Thus, in treating the 'dialogue of paganism with Christianity' it is now more or less taken for granted that it is not doctrinal disputes that interest us most (as they did in the past) but 'those differences of feeling which seem to constitute a psychological dividing line'.[37]

As more and more works are trying to penetrate into 'feelings' it has become clear that much less is still known about pagan views of Christianity and Christian views of paganism than was once thought. This is probably the major reason which has led many scholars to re-examine what fragmented and often unreliable evidence there is. Robert Wilken, for example, went carefully back to the sources in his *The Christians as the Romans Saw Them* (1984) and Stephen Benko made a sober reflection on pagan charges of Christian immorality in his *Pagan Rome and the Early Christians* (1985). Ramsay MacMullen's *Paganism in the Roman Empire* (1981) can be read in a sense as a long introduction to his *Christianizing the Roman Empire* (1984). In this second book, interestingly enough, he neither starts, as usual, with Paul, nor ends, (again as usual), with Constantine. He argues that in AD 312, conversion was far from complete and recourse to coercion and social pressure became essential to make Christianity the religion of the majority. MacMullen has also quite convincingly tried to demonstrate that prior to Constantine, healings, exorcisms, miracles and martyrdoms created more converts than theological or moral doctrines. In fact, contrary to what seemed once self-evident, moral values of pagans and Christians are often shown, on close examination, to have been in many respects almost the same. When occasionally differences in principles may be detected, they are hardly reflected in actual behaviour.[38]

Having learned much more about pagans and Christians, especially about their feelings and religious experiences, the time was ripe for a continuous narrative of the developments from the pagan to the Christian world. This work was very recently undertaken by Robin Lane Fox in his *Pagans and Christians* (1986). Much has already been written about this praiseworthy book. It is a mine of information, it is impartial, and it deals equally with 'hard facts' and feeling, as they are revealed in myths, visions and dreams, as well as literature and inscriptions. Lane Fox is aware that not all that was presented as new in Christianity was really new, that not all Christians observed Christian virtues, that coercion and intolerance did much to ensure Christian success; but he is also interested in pointing out the elements which 'brought a lasting change in people's view of themselves and others', a view which mostly affected relations between the sexes, attitudes to life and death (in particular life after death), and the growing importance of religion, especially belief, in people's lives.[39] Lane Fox is probably wrong in trying to minimize the effects of Christian martyrdoms and exorcisms on conversion, but he must be duly credited for having stressed the most obvious, and yet hardly ever mentioned, path through which Christianity won numerous new friends: everyday social relations at work and in private houses. Contrary to what the early Christians themselves would have us believe, from the times of Paul to the times of Constantine, Christianity appears to have spread primarily informally between individuals with few, if any, traces of more formal missions directed by church leaders. This acute observation helps us keep early Christianity in the right perspective: even at the age after Constantine, Christians were no more than a significant minority in the Roman Empire.[40]

In one respect, however, modern scholarship does not yet seem to have broken completely with more traditional views. The Christian historians of the fourth and fifth centuries, reflecting the ideas of their times, were inclined to record past events only in so far as they had prepared the way to victory. Common people did not count and neither did their beliefs or morals. When Christianity had become official religion, what did it matter who the early Christians were, besides those who had distinguished themselves? This attitude has to some extent determined modern scholarship to our day. The second and third centuries A.D. are mostly examined for their contribution to later developments. Thus, whereas some work has been done to reveal the beliefs, feelings and conduct of the common Christians in the first generation and in the generation of Constantine, for the period inbetween, it is mostly Christian leaders, saints and martyrs who have attracted attention. It is therefore all the more interesting to read in Lane Fox's account a whole section devoted primarily to the social world of the

Christians in the 180s. Unfortunately and unexpectedly, Lane Fox has
found it preferable to accept almost unquestionably the 'orthodox' view
which regards heresy as a late product in the development of Christian
dogma. Besides other drawbacks this unsupported belief has obscured
the understanding of the spread of Christianity in the countryside. It has
been repeatedly stressed by church historians that early Christianity was
by and large an urban religion. This might have been so, but the plain
truth is that we are not sufficiently informed. The fact that 'orthodox'
Christians had little to say about their 'brethren' in the countryside is not
conclusive. It is significant however, that what they actually say suggests
that in the countryside it was mainly heterodox beliefs which prevailed.
When the Alexandrian bishop Dionysius, for example, mentioned the
existence of Christian villagers in Egypt, it was only with the intention to
report how he managed to convert some of them to orthodox beliefs
(certainly not all of them – and not as amicably as Lane Fox, following
the orthodox tradition, would have us believe).[41] Or again, when the
theologian of the Roman church Hippolytus referred to a whole
community of Christian villagers in Pontus (not mentioned by Lane
Fox) it was only to ridicule their doctrines and to record their failure.[42] It
therefore appears that if we take for granted that heresy and heterodoxy
were late products diverting from a more or less continuous mainstream
orthodoxy, we may be led to dismiss large and important sections of
early Christianity, just because their views did not prevail.[43]

Lane Fox has argued much more carefully and convincingly about the
spread of Christianity in the towns where the orthodox groups were
often dominant. It is quite clear that there were few converts in the
highest or lowest classes, as he stresses – though probably not for the
reasons he gives. This scarcity may hardly reflect on the lack of occasion
such people had 'to learn about Christianity from a teacher whom they
could take seriously'. It is also clearly wrong to argue that social mobility
did not help Christians to penetrate into the upper classes because
such mobility in the Greek-speaking towns was limited.[44] The highest and lowest classes were probably under-represented in early Christianity for quite different, perhaps opposite reasons. This problem
can be approached only within the context of the social structure and
social stratification of the Roman world in the first Christian centuries. It
is quite obvious, however, that since the aristocrats represented a very
tiny minority of the whole population, the few Christian aristocrats
attested are much more significant than the few slaves or poor peasants.

In the present work, I have tried to deal with the common Christians
of the first three centuries, not for what they did to preserve or develop
the 'essence' of Christianity for future generations, but for their own
sake. I have dealt with important personalities mainly to distinguish

them from ordinary Christians, certainly not to treat them as representative of their age. I know of course that I have said extremely little about feelings and beliefs, but as we are still much in the dark as to who these Christians were, I have instead attempted to establish their social origins and careers. If this work is done properly (and there is clearly still much to be done), then we may be able to examine their psychology and their conduct better.

PART I

Christianity among Slaves and Freedmen

1

The Oppressed Class Theory

Interest in the social origins of the early Christians and their possible consequences for early Christian doctrines was being expressed as early as the late eighteenth century by Edward Gibbon. The 'community of goods' reported in Acts, together with a few statements from pagan authors preserved by the Christian Fathers, led Gibbon to the conviction that the earliest Christians were recruited from 'the inferior ranks of mankind'; 'the virtue of the primitive Christians,' consequently, 'like that of the first Romans, was very frequently guarded by poverty and ignorance'. Yet Gibbon was too well acquainted with the sources to leave the matter at that. In the first place he observed that the community of goods was only adopted 'for a short time in the primitive church'; he felt, furthermore, that the 'unfavourable picture' given by pagan authors 'though not devoid of a faint resemblance, betrays, by its dark colouring and distorted features, the pencil of an enemy'; he observed, finally, that a number of early Christians were known 'who derived some consequence from the advantages of nature or fortune' (who were, that is, educated or wealthy). According to the testimony of Pliny, which is supported by what is known about the martyrs of Lyons, the early Christians seem to have belonged to 'every order of men'. 'And yet', Gibbon concluded, 'these exceptions are either too few in number, or too recent in time, entirely to remove the imputation of ignorance and obscurity which has been so arrogantly cast on the first proselytes of Christianity'.[1] A century later, when, through the work of Strauss, Bauer and Renan, the history of early Christianity had come to attract a wide lay audience, the subject was being viewed as a matter of successive stages. At first, that is, Christians were poor and insignificant people; later the church was joined by people of education and wealth. What was not entirely clear, however, was how long each stage had lasted. Did the primitive church end when the 'community of goods' ended in the first chapter of Acts, or did it last as long as Christians were persecuted by the Romans; that is, for the first three centuries of the Christian era? When Engels produced his popularization of the work of the German Protestant biblical scholars he favoured the second alternative. The history of early Christianity he argued, had 'notable points of resemblance with the modern working-class movement'. As we have seen in the Introduction, an optimistic conclusion was drawn: 'Three hundred years after its appearance Christianity was the recognized state religion in the Roman World Empire, and in barely sixty years socialism has won itself a position which makes its victory absolutely certain'.[2]

It is not difficult to understand why Marxists turned their attention to early Christianity, accepting the 'oppressed-class' theory advanced by Engels. As Kautsky understood only too well, 'Engels wanted to point out the irresistible and elemental nature of the progress of our movement, which he said owed its inevitability particularly to the increase of its adherents in the army, so that it would soon be able to force even the most powerful autocrat to yield'.[3] On the eve of the October Revolution Lenin compared the socialist movement to 'primitive Christianity with its democratic revolutionary spirit'. Once again, 'primitive Christianity' was Christianity until it was given 'the status of a state religion'.[4] It is interesting to note, however, that in the late nineteenth century the 'oppressed-class' theory was accepted by numerous biblical scholars who were anything but Marxists. The evidence considered by Gibbon had obviously contributed to this view, but it seems above all that a certain reading of the Gospel necessarily pointed towards the oppressed. Jesus was seen as a great social reformer 'who aimed at relieving the lower classes from the wretched condition in which they were languishing', and the Gospel was read as a programme for social reform. Reviewing the nineteenth-century literature on the subject, Harnack noted that 'for years books and pamphlets have been written dealing with the Gospel in this sense'.[5] Harnack himself did not share this view; he agreed that 'if Jesus were with us today he would side with those who are making great efforts to relieve the hard lot of the poor and procure them better conditions of life', but in general, he felt, 'the Gospel aims at founding a community among men as wide as human life itself and as deep as human need'.[6] Besides being a historian of early Christianity, Harnack was also a militant Protestant, and in spite of the fact that his own reading of the Gospel resisted its reduction to a social programme, he was aware of the reasons which were leading so many theologians to reformist ideologies. 'Protestantism', he declared, 'must be understood, first and foremost, by the contrast which it offers to Catholicism, and here there is a double direction which any estimate of it must take, first as *Reformation* and secondly as *Revolution.* It was a reformation in regard to the doctrine of salvation; a revolution in regard to the Church, its authority, and its apparatus'.[7] Belief in the revolutionary character of early Christianity strengthened the case of Protestants against Catholicism. As it can be seen, Protestants and Marxists were, for quite different reasons, led to similar views about early Christianity. But before concluding these remarks I would also like to make brief mention of a third group of people whose cause was leading them to see the oppressed classes as the principal supporters of the early Christian movement.

When Engels developed his 'oppressed-class' theory of early Christianity he was, of course, relying on a very crude picture of Roman society. Following the view of some ancient historians, he regarded the population of the Roman world as being 'sharply divided into three classes, thrown together out of the most varying elements and nationalities: rich people, including not a few emancipated slaves ..., big landowners or usurers or both at once ...; propertyless free people, who in Rome were fed and amused by the state – in the provinces they got on as they could by themselves – and finally the great mass, the slaves'.[8] Early Christianity, consequently was conceived 'as the religion of slaves and emancipated slaves, of poor people deprived of all rights, of peoples subjugated or dispersed by Rome'.[9] Earlier in the same century another line of inquiry was also connecting early Chritianity with the servile population of the ancient world. At a time when the reaction to American slavery was making abolitionism 'a live issue in Europe', interest turned naturally to the decline of ancient slavery.[10] In this field views were radically divergent. On the one hand, there were those who attempted to show that Christianity had contributed to the decline of ancient slavery; on the other, there were those who argued for the opposite view. In 1847, when Henri Wallon produced a major work on the subject which was highly favourable to Christianity, Marx was declaring that 'the social principles of Christianity justified the slavery of Antiquity'.[11] In spite of its weaknesses, the view that Christianity had been opposed to slavery became very popular among scholars. Even F.C. Baur, who had gone carefully through the sources and was aware of early Christianity's unwillingness to advocate a general abolition of slavery, felt compelled in 1853 to argue that,

> And yet we cannot but judge that the abolition of slavery is a requirement of the moral consciousness which agrees with the spirit of Christianity.[12]

But it was not these cautiously expressed thoughts that prevailed. The view that became dominant was that of Paul Allard, who claimed in

1876 that early Christianity was not only opposed to slavery but had significantly contributed to its decline, if only after its ascent to power. Accordingly, many, if not most of the early Christians would be slaves or oppressed people in general. The title of Allard's work is significant and revealing: *Les Esclaves chrétiens*.[13]

It seems, therefore, that by the end of the nineteenth century the theory that early Christianity was a religion of the oppressed classes was becoming dominant. Protestants wanted to liberate Christianity from the Catholic Church; Marxists wanted to find parallels for the awaited socialist revolution; and the abolitionists, some of whom were Catholics, wanted to demonstrate that Christianity was incompatible with slavery. A number of Marxists starting with Ciccotti at the turn of the century, attempted to demonstrate that Christianity was in no way responsible for the decline of slavery. This view was not widely accepted, and even Marxist scholars did not consider it to be contradictory that, in spite of its justification of slavery, Christianity was able to attract large numbers of slaves. As we enter the twentieth century, we find the few exceptions to this general consensus being less and less heeded. It is only in recent years that the tide has begun to turn.

2

Christianity, Slavery and the Slaves

Slavery in the Ancient World

The study of ancient slavery, inaugurated in a systematic way in the eighteenth century, has met with problems, some of which have yet to find satisfactory solutions. Not only are scholars in dispute as to numbers, prices, types of employment, relative profitability (and productivity), reproduction and living conditions of the slaves of classical antiquity; the attempt to locate slavery in society and history has also produced equivocal and controversial claims. True, the first set of questions ultimately aims at breaking the ground for the more general problem of the evaluation of slavery. It would be a serious mistake, however, to believe that slavery as a historical phenomenon could be understood if we merely knew more about the numbers of slaves and so on.[1]

To locate slavery in society is to establish its relation to other types of human subjection and to determine its contribution to economic production. The mere existence of slaves in a given society should not be taken to imply that in that particular society there exists a mode of production based on slave labour.[2] Unfortunately, the distinction between slavery as a form of subjection and as a slave system determining production is absent in Aristotle's influential moral arguments. Aristotle's definition, according to which 'any human being who by nature belongs not to himself but to another is by nature a slave', is a truism; it is also a dead end for philosophical investigation. The problem about whether slavery is natural, as Aristotle believed, or contrary to nature, as some of his contemporaries claimed, is based on the ambiguity of the concept *nature* (and *natural*) and the even greater ambiguity of the concept *soul*, which Aristotle conjures out of the

25

magician's hat to argue that 'it is here (i.e. in the soul) that the natural ruler and the natural subject ... are to be found'.[3] A different tendency in philosophical reasoning on slavery derives from Hegel. In his celebrated passage on masters and slaves, he demonstrated by employing his dialectical method the potential transformation of this type of subjection into its opposite, and hence the relative character of the concept 'natural slavery'.[4] Slavery existed because '... the Greeks and Romans had not yet risen to the Notion of absolute freedom. ...' 'Slavery and tyranny are, therefore, in the history of nations a necessary stage and hence *relatively* justified.'[5] The theory of stages was systematized by Marx and the Marxists who, by making them contingent on production, developed a new basis for historic periodization. It is in the light of this that slavery as a specific mode of production is to be distinguished from slavery as a form of human subjection: the former may only be found in a few historical societies; the latter may be found in virtually any society.

There is no need to discuss here the notion of a slave mode of production and the problems of its application in antiquity. For present purposes it is adequate to repeat Aristotle's observation, according to which the idea of a master lies 'not in his acquiring slaves but in using them'. The significance of the employment of slaves in production is clear. Masters were not just freed from manual labour; they were also able, by employing overseers (often selected among slaves) to 'devote themselves to statecraft or philosophy'.[6] Slavery is demonstrated to be, not an incidental feature of antiquity, but inherently linked to the status of free citizens. In classical Athens, where freedom achieved its highest form, slavery degraded to its basest form, becoming chattel slavery.

* * *

As a stage of human history, slavery has its historic origin. Since Aristotle, the relation between slavery and war has been well known and commonly accepted. Historians have proposed the following causal sequence of the process that led to the establishment of the slave system (in the sense of a mode of production): Through war and conquest the aristocracy acquired vast fortunes, which it invested in land, compelling small landowners – free peasants – to sell their property; as estates grew larger and larger, the aristocracy found it cheaper to employ war captives as agricultural slaves instead of using free workers; the need for slaves consequently led to further wars (slave hunts); and so on.[7] Alternatively, the causal sequence can be inverted: the demand for slaves – Finley has argued – *preceded* the supply. 'The Romans captured many tens of thousands of men, women and children during the Italian and

Punic wars because the demand for slaves already existed, not the other way round.'[8] Of the conditions required for the transformation of captives into slaves, Finley picks out the private ownership of land; a sufficient development of commodity production; and the unavailability of an internal labour supply. It is very difficult to find decisive arguments in support of either theory. Finley's view has in its favour that not all wars in the ancient world led to slavery; the transformation of captives into slaves is no simple matter. The relations between war and slavery, however, are so complex that it is also plausible to think – as Hopkins did — in terms of a closed circuit, in which the supply of slaves created new demands and the demand for slaves led to new wars. It is always dangerous to search for a single original cause for complex social phenomena.

As we pass from the problem of origin to the results of the intrusion of slaves the situation becomes a little clearer, though still highly complex. To speak only of the Roman empire, we observe that gradually its whole social and economic structure changed. The growth of markets was accompanied by an increase in monetization, the influx of booty by investment in land and the formation of large estates. The impoverishment of the peasants – accelerated in due course by lengthy military service – encouraged emigration to the towns and provinces. The population of Rome, by the end of the last century BC, reached perhaps one million people, followed by Alexandria, Antioch and Carthage. Eventually, under the early emperors, the Roman political and legal systems were modified to such an extent that – especially as regards the political system – they only remotely resembled those of the Republic. Many factors contributed to these developments – but slavery clearly played a substantial role.[9]

* * *

Classical legislation depicts all men and women as being either free or slaves. Once again reality proves far more complex. The view expressed by an ancient lawyer that slavery was *contra naturam* and the lengthy discussions by Aristotle illustrate the perplexity which the institution caused the ancients themselves. Scholars have often discussed the legal aspects of the dual conception of a slave as both a person and property. In Juvenal's *Satires* a woman is depicted as demanding the crucifixion of a slave. 'But what is the slave's offence?' the husband asks. 'You must hear his defence: no delay can be too long when a man's life is at stake.' And he gets the following reply: 'So a slave's a *man* now, is he, you crackpot?'[10] In the second century AD the expression 'between slavery and freedom' was applied by a rhetorician to helots, *penestai* and other dependent labourers, all of which had probably disappeared by then.

But the same expression can be used to indicate a form of dependent labour which existed almost everywhere and was in practice considered slavery – debt-bondage.[11]

A further disadvantage to the application of the legal category 'slave' in sociological analysis is that it conceals some of the differences between types of slaves. As we shall see in considering conversions of slaves to Christianity, it makes a great difference whether they belonged to the urban or the rural *familia*. (Such distinctions, regrettably have tended to be neglected in the work of modern church historians.) The financial and living standards of urban slaves may differ considerably: they depend not only on the slaves' own occupations but on their masters' status as well. Even within one household, 'slave' can mean a wretched labourer or an overseer with a family and some property – even a banker or skilled craftsman. Manumission also produced differentiations in the status of slaves: when manumitted by Roman citizens slaves became citizens themselves; in classical Athens, by contrast this hardly ever happened. Scholars are therefore in dispute as to whether all slaves are to be considered as members of the same social class. The problem is further complicated by the fact that no single definition of class has been generally accepted: Weberians consider function in the market as essential, but slaves, as a rule, did not function in the market on their own; for Marxists, position in the relations of production has been seen as the basic factor, but there has been controversy as to whether a common ideology and common political activity is also required. Slaves, it is agreed, brief historic periods apart, were not characterized by ideological homogeneity; and, naturally, they did not participate in political assemblies. Recently, Ste. Croix has demonstrated convincingly that neither class consciousness nor political activity in common are elements necessary to Marx's conception of social classes. Class, then, is defined as a relationship of exploitation – and in this sense slaves in antiquity were obviously one of the classes most easily distinguished.[12] For present purposes, however – whenever the evidence permits it – I shall treat different groups of slaves separately. For not all of them had the same access to the religious beliefs and practices of their masters.

* * *

This brings us to the question whether slaves in antiquity had religions of their own. According to Weber, slaves 'have hitherto never been the bearers of a distinctive type of religion'.[13] This view is apparently confirmed by one of the few pieces of information on the subject given by an ancient writer. Tacitus reports that a senator once exclaimed: '... nowadays our huge households are international. They include every alien religion – or none at all.'[14] It could be that some slaves had no interest in religion whatsoever; but the statement may also reflect the well-known attitude of Roman aristocrats, who, as a rule, called even Christians atheists; Romans called religions they disapproved of superstitions.[15] It is much safer to take Weber literally: Slaves did not have a *distinctive* type of religion. Bömer, indeed, has shown that many of them participated in the religious rites of the free population, and that in religion even slaves became *persons.*[16] From ancient works on agriculture we know that rural slaves observed the religious festivities led by their masters; when their masters turned to Christianity, slaves – at least sometimes – remained pagan and protected their 'idol-religions' by force if necessary, as we shall see. Inscriptional material and evidence from the rites performed for the *lares* demonstrate that slaves served as *ministri* assisting freedmen (usually serving as *magistri*) in the local cults.[17] We know little about the details of religious rites, but we may assume that slaves were normally initiated into new cults along with their masters (the conversion of households to Christianity will be discussed at a later point). A well-documented case is that of the Bacchic cult: Livy, who gives an account of the banning of the cult in 186 BC, virtually asserts that slaves were seduced into observance of these rites.[18] Finally, according to Cumont, Mithraism and several Syrian cults spread to the West as oriental slaves were imported into Italy.[19] In general, we may assume that slaves either retained their traditional religions (especially those they possessed before their captivity) or else were converted to new religions along with the households to which they belonged. There is no evidence that they ever developed any religions of their own.

Christian Attitudes to Slavery

The early Christians never developed an attitude towards slavery which was in any sense opposed to the dominant view of the pagan world. This simple fact should have been clear enough to scholars acquainted with Christian literature. Instead, ever since the early nineteenth century, the question has provoked lengthy discussion and great confusion. There are, in my view, three basic reasons for this confusion. In the first place, slavery has often been considered as part of the more general question of poverty; accordingly, almsgiving, care for widows, orphans and others have found their way into the discussion. But in spite of their similarities poverty and slavery are two completely distinct social phenomena. A complex set of legal procedures restricted slaves in ways that did not affect the poor; to give two examples relevant to our subject, slaves lacked freedom of movement and the freedom to participate in religious practices without their masters consent. On the other hand, the Roman world did contain slaves who were anything but poor, and who had better prospects for social advancement than many of the free. Secondly, the Christian principle of universal equality in the eyes of God has been understood as an implicit call for the abolition of slavery. But this is to conceal the fact that it is *only* in the sight of God that all men were considered equal. The declaration found in the Epistle to the Galatians (3:28) has often been quoted in this context: 'There is no such thing as Jew and Greek, slave and freeman ... for you are all one person in Christ Jesus'. This declaration is of purely spiritual significance: its call for universal equality is of a piece with its call for the elimination of discrimination between men and women; for the same passage also says that there is no such thing as male and female. There is, finally, a third, much more sophisticated, argument to prove the existence of a Christian abolitionism. It has been a common claim ever since Wallon that, according to Christianity, the morality of individuals had to be changed before social reform could be achieved: early Christianity, therefore, focused attention on morality rather than on social reform. This claim at least accepts as a fact that early Christianity had nothing to say about slavery; but it has no sound foundation. For it confuses slavery as an institution with master slave relations. Actually, even if it was left to individuals to emancipate their slaves (and this, as we shall see, was not the case), the institution of slavery as such would remain unaffected. Morally imperfect individuals would always exist, and with them the bonds of at least some slaves. All these attempts to discover an essential incompatibility between slavery and Christianity were products of the nineteenth-century abolitionist movement; and they may have helped to promote it. But by seeking objective justification in history they have brought confusion to a subject illuminated quite adequately in our sources. Christianity – even in its earliest form – though expressing concern for the poor, never questioned the institution of slavery as such.

* * *

The decline of slavery, in fact, had little to do with either Christianity or Stoicism.[20] In the last decade of the nineteenth century the Marxist Ciccotti examined the economic circumstances which brought an end to the institution of slavery. In the mid twentieth century Marc Bloch demonstrated that it was not until the age of Charlemagne that slavery disappeared from most areas. More recently, Finley and Ste. Croix have given their own accounts of the decline of ancient slavery; in spite of their differences, neither attributes it to ideological or religious factors. This much should cause no serious objections today. And yet, since it could still be argued that abolitionism was nevertheless latent in Christianity's aspirations, we should take a closer look at our sources. We must note to begin with that Christianity never formulated any clear declaration about slavery as such. This observation makes reasonable the assumption that the institution of slavery had not been a cause of great concern to early Christian circles. In order to comprehend Christian attitudes to slavery we have to examine incidental remarks. But the whole problem can be better understood if we first look back at the prevailing views on slavery in the Graeco-Roman world.[21]

Aristotle was the first ancient author we know to have formulated systematic views on slavery; but he could hardly have been their inventor[22]; in the *Politics* we get acquainted with a discussion which must have had a long history. The idea of 'natural slavery', that some people are born to be free while others are born to be slaves, was probably known before Aristotle but not universally accepted: in Aeschylus, for example, Fortune, not Nature, is held responsible for slavery. The impulse to find ideological justifications for slavery came from the institution of slavery itself. Ruling classes seldom rule by force alone; existing inequalities, even existing cruelty, must be explained as in some way natural. Aristotle's philosophical arguments however were intended, in my view, to appease the conscience of the intellectual members of the slave-owning classes rather than to persuade slaves of the justice of their fate. What seems to me to have kept many slaves (especially domestic slaves) in submission – besides fear, which must always have remained the principal factor – was a peculiar psychology which led them to identify their personal interests with those of their masters. The words attributed to slaves in the tragic poets, such as 'Master's luck is mine' (*Agamemnon* 33) or 'an honest slave suffers in her own heart the blow that strikes her mistress' (*Medea* 55) are not just the invention of slave-owners.

After Aristotle, the theory of 'natural slavery' was so far as I know, never again seriously advocated. In the Hellenistic and Roman worlds the distinction between Greeks and Barbarians, on which the idea of 'natural slavery' depended, lost much of its value. Once again, the view that Fortune, not Nature, was responsible for slavery became prevalent, and was formulated systematically by the Stoics. Stoicism, like all other ancient philosophies, accepted slavery as something normal: it never questioned it as an institution. On the other hand, through exponents such as Seneca, Stoicism professed that all men were equal, especially in their common fate of death; 'we are born unequal, we die equal', Seneca wrote.[23] Seneca protested against the inhuman behaviour of some slave-owners; and he reminded masters of the power fortune had over all men. Enslavement was a matter of fortune; beneath the appearances of slavery and freedom, all men were in reality equal:

> How about reflecting that the person you call your slave traces his origin back to the same stock as yourself, has the same good sky above him, breathes as you do, lives as you do, dies as you do? It is as easy for you to see in him a free-born man as for him to see a slave in you.

Seneca was obviously addressing himself to slave-owners: when he instructed them to have 'slaves respect you rather than fear you', he was hoping that humane behaviour on the part of masters would lead slaves into voluntary submission.[24] He never addressed himself to slaves directly. Seneca, then, just like Aristotle, was formulating an ideology for masters, not slaves. Christianity, while it borrowed much from Stoicism, developed at this point a peculiar and novel characteristic of its own: Christianity addressed itself directly to slaves as well.

Paul came very close to Seneca when he said that the slave who was called to be a Christian was the Lord's freedman and that the free man who received the call was Christ's slave (1 Cor. 7:22); roles, then, were interchangeable. But Paul's formulation is more absolute, it is not fortune (or Fortune) that is held responsible for a man's position but God himself. In an epistle which, if not Paul's own, clearly belongs to his school, not only masters but slaves themselves become the objects of admonition: 'Slaves, obey your earthly masters with fear and trembling, singlemindedly, as serving Christ' (Eph. 6:5). Formulas such as this became a cliché in subsequent Christian writings. Another New Testament epistle goes into further details: 'Slaves, accept the authority of your masters with all due submission, not only when they are kind and considerate, but even when they are perverse' (1 Peter 2:18). All these formulas were followed by corresponding ones addressed to masters: 'You masters, also, must do the same by them. Give up using threats; remember you both have the same Master in heaven. ...' (Eph. 6:9). This idea of the Christian preacher as mediator is reproduced in the late-first-century text known as the First Epistle of Clement, which was sent from the Roman church to the church of Corinth: 'The strong are not to ignore the weak, and the weak are to respect the strong' (*1 Clem.* 38). In another text of the same period, probably of Syrian origin, called *Didache* (The Teaching), masters were told they should 'Never speak sharply when giving orders to ... slaves', while slaves were told that they should obey their masters 'with respectfulness and fear, as the representatives of God' (*Didache* 4); exactly the same words are repeated in yet another text of the same period which may have been of Alexandrian origin (*The Epistle of Barnabas* 19). It is clear that from an early age

Christian authors started copying from one another, and on this subject felt they had little to change; the continuation of this tradition can be traced through the following centuries (see for example *The Apostolic Constitutions* 4.12, 7.13).

From what we have seen we may infer that Christianity did indeed go further than Stoicism: Seneca had called for the milder treatment of slaves; Christians called slaves to a voluntary submission – even to perverse, even to heathen masters. The call was made in the name of God, and was expected to bring prompt results; it has therefore been claimed, and with reason, that Christianity actually attempted to strengthen the ideological justification of slavery.[25] But the constant and almost obsessive repetition of the same admonitions preserved in our documents throughout a long period bears witness to the meagre results of the attempt.

Luther, Erasmus and Calvin interpreted a Pauline passage in 1 Corinthians (7:21) as an advice to slaves to accept their freedom if they were ever given the chance; but most scholars today accept the very opposite interpretation: 'If you may become free, remain rather a slave'. Since we are concerned with early Christian attitudes to slavery, it is particularly important to note that this second interpretation was the one accepted by the early Church Fathers, and above all John Chrysostom, who was categorical on the subject. With such overwhelming support for the view that Paul and the early Christian preachers called slaves to remain in their state of servitude, even if given the chance to be free, there should have been no need for further discussion. I myself have rehearsed the facts, which have been well presented by Maurice Goguel, only because the widely read New English Bible (first publication 1961) insists on the first interpretation.[26]

Christianity in the philosophical version advanced by the Alexandrian school came close to Stoicism in another respect which deserves attention. In the sophisticated works of Clement of Alexandria in the late second century it is claimed, as in the works of Seneca, that a man is not considered a slave if he does not deserve to be one. According to Stoicism, a man becomes a slave because of his bad character; according to Clement, because of his sins – otherwise, he is not 'really' a slave. 'As slaves', we are told in a work called *Stromata*, 'the Scripture views those "under sin" and "sold to sin", the lovers of pleasure and of the body'.[27] In another work, the *Paedagogus* (The Instructor), Clement, though familiar with the Aristotelian view, did not accept the theory of 'natural slavery'. He considered it preferable from the Christian point of view, and much closer to the reasoning of the times, to adopt the language of Seneca: 'Slaves too are to be treated like ourselves; for they are human beings, as we are.' Only that for Clement the common human nature is demonstrated not by the common fate of death, but by the common God, who 'is the same to free and bound'.[28] Just like Seneca by the way, Clement nowhere in his massive *oeuvre* addresses himself directly to slaves; what he has to say, he says to masters. But we shall have more to say about Clement's attitude in chapter 6. Origen, who continued the Alexandrian Christian tradition, wrote that slaves should be taught how to 'obtain a free mind and receive noble birth from the Logos'[29]; in fourth-century authors such as John Chrysostom we find the same view prevailing.[30]

* * *

Christian attitudes to slavery are also reflected in the Church Orders, which are a kind of legislative document. The first work of a systematic regulative character which contains detailed references to slaves is the *Apostolice Paradosis* (Apostolic Tradition), attributed to Hippolytus of Rome and dated between AD 215 and 217. The first point to note of the *Apostolic Tradition* – and all subsequent Christian legislative texts – is that slavery was accepted as a matter of course. In the section referring to the acceptance of new converts it commanded that detailed inquiries be made about the lives of the persons considered. It was of special importance to check whether the candidate was a slave or a free person: if he was the slave of a believer, the master's permission was required, and slaves whose masters did not 'bear witness' to them were rejected. If the slave's master was a heathen, moreover, then the slave was taught 'to please his master, that there be no scandal (*blasphemia*)'; this rather obscure expression must have meant in effect that such slaves were not accepted. Slaves, again, could not move around freely to join Christian meetings and congregations: if their master was a heathen or even a Christian with 'no understanding', slaves might think themselves entitled to run away or to have their freedom bought for them. In the first case, the result would truly have been a scandal. Christianity would have been accused of advising slaves to run away; this would have been not just bad publicity but detrimental to the interest of Christian slave-owners.[31] There still remained the possibility of emancipating slaves at the Christian community's expense (slaves with enough money of their own would have bought their liberty anyway). (I shall deal with this problem in some detail in chapter 3.) For the time being, suffice it to say that early Christian communities, as a rule, were not concerned with the problem of slave emancipation.

It was in accordance with this general rule that the *Apostolic Tradition* dealt with a number of special cases. A man's concubine, for example, if she were a slave, was allowed to 'hear' (the Christian preaching) on the condition that she had reared his children and that she consorted with no other man. Again a believer who had a concubine should either marry her, if she were free, or leave her and marry another, if she were a slave (unless they already had children together). Finally, a Christian woman who consorted with a slave was rejected by the church if she did not desist.[32] This last regulation was prompted by Christianity's observance of the Roman law; it was subsequently modified under Callistus, bishop of Rome from AD 217 to 221, who thought the clause contrary to the interests of the Christian community and so decided that the church should treat unions between Christian women of rank and slaves as if they were a proper marriage.

The next legislative document to consider is a compilation known as the *Apostolic Constitutions*. This work, unlike the *Apostolic Tradition*, which originated in the west, drew upon various texts most of which were of eastern origin. Its date cannot be fixed: several sections belong to the second and third centuries, others to the third and fourth. The *Apostolic Constitutions*, among other instructions, reproduce all the material on slaves which was found in the *Apostolic Tradition*. In additional sections, which may belong to the fourth century, the *Apostolic Constitutions* established several days during which slaves should be allowed to rest. Leisure days were all Saturdays and Sundays, Holy Week and the week after, Ascension Day, the Pentecost, Christmas Day, Epiphany, the name-days of the Apostles and of Stephen, the first martyr. From the fact that slaves are to be instructed 'who it is that suffered and rose again' we may infer that many of them were still pagans.[33] In a document known as the *Apostolic Canons*, affixed to the *Apostolic Constitutions*, the ordination of slaves into the clergy is not permitted without their masters' consent. Two reasons are given. In the first place, ordination without the master's consent 'would grieve those who owned them'; secondly, such a practice 'would occasion the subversion of families'. This is yet another case in which we see Christianity openly on the slave-owners' side. The *Apostolic Canons* considered a slave's emancipation to be a necessary precondition for his ordination, but left the matter to the master's discretion. In the fifth century the same restriction was extended to slaves who wanted to become monks.[34]

Similar in character to the Church Orders were the Canons of the Church Councils. Most of the Councils held before Christianity achieved official recognition are poorly documented, but from one of them we do get a clear picture of the Christian attitudes to slavery. In the early years of the fourth century, in 305 or 306 according to C.J. Hefele, representatives from the whole of Spain gathered at Elvira in the south of the country and made pronouncements on a number of urgent issues.

Among the representatives was Hosius of Cordova, famous through the Arian controversy and a leading figure in the Council of Nicaea. The Council of Elvira took it for granted that many Christians were slave-owners and some the owners of large numbers of slaves; it was also accepted that these slaves were often pagans (how often we do not know). The urgent matter was not slaves' religion but the protection of their owners from idolatry. Idols were therefore not to be tolerated in the house of a believer; and if a master was unable to keep idols away from his house because he feared his slaves on account of their number he was at least to keep himself at a distance. The same Council dealt with the murders of slaves by their masters. In a manner recalling the Judaic legislation (cf. Exodus 21:20-1) it fixed a penalty of seven and five years' excommunication respectively for any woman who intentionally or 'accidentally' killed her maidservant; by contrast, a woman who left her husband and married again was excommunicated for life.[35]

At this point Ste. Croix has drawn attention to a problem which has been passed over in silence by other commentators. Apart from the above-mentioned Canon referring to the dangers of idolatry, nowhere does Christian literature consider the effects of slavery on the master. Slaves in antiquity were frequently subjected to corporal punishment and torture; they were often the victims of sexual abuse. It is strange, to say the least, that no Christian legislative or moral document ever referred to slavery as the institution which led masters 'into the gravest temptation, to commit acts of cruelty and lust'.[36] This complaint can hardly be overstated. An autobiographical text of the mid fifth century by the Christian Paulinus of Pella gives a picture of what many masters themselves must have felt about the problem. It is worth quoting from it at some length:

> I checked my passions with this chastening rule: that I should never seek an unwilling victim, nor transgress another's rights, and, heedful to keep unstained my cherished reputation, should beware of yielding to freeborn loves though voluntarily offered, but be satisfied with servile amours in my own home; for I preferred to be guilty of a fault (*culpa*) rather than an offence (*crimen*), fearing to suffer loss of my good name.[37]

Nowhere do our early Christian sources refer to this problem, though they go into great detail about other matters of sexual behaviour.

* * *

The idea of slavery was used, from the earliest days of Christianity, as a metaphor of a believer's relation to God or Jesus. We read in a number of documents, by church leaders especially, that Christians referred to themselves as slaves of Christ.[38] It is sometimes thought that this attitude reflects a general tendency to treat slaves as equals. Joseph Vogt writes that 'slaves had been ennobled merely by becoming the symbols of man's place in the kingdom of God'.[39] Closer attention leaves us in no doubt that the attitude is the very opposite of this: Christians thought of themselves as humble in the face of God, as slaves should feel in the face of their masters. 'If in no other way', Chrysostom wrote, 'let us render (God) service at least as our servants render it to us'.[40] In so saying, Chrysostom had no intention of eliminating the differences between slaves and masters; and neither did the hermit-monk Antony (according to his biographer Athanasius). Antony exhorted Christians to behave like slaves in the face of God, but did not intend by this an alleviation of the slave's life.

> With these thoughts let a person convince himself not to grow careless, especially if he considers himself to be the Lord's slave, obliged to do his master's will. Just as a slave would not dare to say, 'Since I worked yesterday, I am not working today' ... so also let us persist daily in the ascetic life ...[41]

The idea of slavery, moreover, was employed in Christian writings to describe the height of moral degeneration, just as the rabbinical writings referred to slaves as idle, thieving and vicious. Traces of this attitude appear with ample evidence to suggest the existence of numerous Christian slave-owners. In the next section I shall deal with a small number of cases in which Christian slaves are reported to have died in persecutions along with their masters. In the mean time, I should like to note a more common phenomenon: slaves were often used, sometimes under torture or the threat of torture, as witnesses for the prosecution of their Christian masters; so we learn from Justin's *Second Apology* (12.4), among other documents. A document preserved by Eusebius gives a vivid account concerning the slaves of the martyrs in Lyons and Vienne (AD 177). The document, which treats it as normal that Christians had pagan slaves, reports that

> There were also arrested certain heathen slaves of our members ... and these ..., fearing the tortures which they saw the saints suffering, when the soldiers urged them, falsely accused us of Thyestean feasts and Oedipodean intercourse ...[42]

A fragment of Irenaeus gives the same information, adding the following explanation:

> these slaves, having nothing to say which would meet the wishes of their

tormentors, except that they had heard from their masters that the divine communion was the body and blood of Christ, and imagining that it was actually flesh and blood, gave their inquisitors answers to that effect.[43]

Furthermore, Tertullian in his *Apology* (AD 197) writes of slaves [*domestici*] as the enemies of Christians by their very nature. A little further on, in more violent vein, he writes that heathens hate the Christians 'like rascal slaves' hate their masters and that they break out against Christians 'like rebels breaking out of slave-pens, jails or mines, or that sort of penal servitude'.[44] The situation remained unchanged until the time of Constantine: Canon 3 of the Council of Ancyra (*c.* AD 314-9) mentioned Christians 'betrayed by their slaves', confirming that the 'very nature' of slaves was still the same.[45] In the circumstances we can understand how men like Origen developed so a low an opinion of slaves as to write that the Christian teacher does not discourse on the Divine Wisdom to the uneducated and to slaves; though, as we saw above, he advised masters to teach them how to 'obtain a free mind'.[46]

* * *

The alleged primitive communism of the early Christian communities is also relevant to the present discussion. In an often quoted passage of Acts (2:43 ff., repeated in 4:32 ff.), the first Christians are reported to have sold their possessions and distributed their wealth to those in need. This behaviour, understood as communism, seems also to imply abolition of slavery; for how could people with no property possess slaves?[47] The problem, however, is far more complicated than might appear: there has been considerable discussion as to whether Luke was reporting a historical fact or an idealistic fiction.[48] (The idea of common ownership in fact was known among the Greeks and was to some extent practised among the Jewish sect of the Essenes.) To judge from the structure of the text itself, it seems unreasonable to believe that its author was making a purely idealistic declaration. But to call it a declaration is misleading: we actually have to do with a passing remark, repeated twice in much the same manner. Luke must have found these remarks in his sources, for he had no reason to invent a practice unknown to his own time, especially since its abandonment would require some kind of explanation, which he does not provide.

I therefore accept the historicity of the account, but not quite in the way most scholars do. In point of fact, it has been believed since the nineteenth century, when the subject attracted much attention, that either the whole idea of communism is fictitious or that it was no more than a passing phase in the life of the early community. 'This maxim' (of common ownership), Hegel thought, 'was well enough suited to the man who had no possessions; but it must have been a serious problem for anyone who had property ... consequently, it was abandoned, whether by dire necessity of from prudential considerations, at an early date'[49]; the 'communism' of the early church Renan felt, could not have been as rigorous as Acts implies[50]; Engels held that 'The traces of common ownership which are also found in the early stages of the new religion can be ascribed to solidarity among the proscribed rather than to real equalitarian ideas'[51]; Kautsky's response was ironical: 'Its necessary presupposition was that at least one-half of society should remain unbelievers, otherwise there would have been no one to buy the possessions of the believers.'[52] It was Troeltsch who went deeper into the matter and pointed out that 'It was a communism composed solely of consumers, a communism based upon the assumption that its members will continue to earn their living by private enterprise ...'[53] By pointing out this feature Troeltsch was challenging the applicability of the notion of communism itself; but I believe we must go even further. To put it bluntly, I would say, following Harnack, that as far as communism is concerned 'nothing of the kind ever existed'.[54] The phenomenon described in Acts did not constitute a unique or passing phase in the history of the primitive Christian communities. It is in another sense that we must understand its historicity.[55]

The practice of common ownership among the early Christians is further attested by the second-century pagan satirist Lucian, who, in his work *The Death of Peregrinus,* gives a vivid description of a Christian community in his own times. Among other information, Lucian writes that

> their first lawgiver persuaded them that they are all brothers of one another after they have transgressed once for all by denying the Greek gods and by worshipping that crucified sophist himself and living under his laws. Therefore they despise all things indiscriminately and consider them common property, receiving such doctrines traditionally without any definite evidence.[56]

If this account is more or less correct, it creates problems that most historians prefer to ignore. For if the story in Acts represents an early attitude which was gradually superseded, how are we to explain its reappearance a century later? (To make no mention of similar practices among the Carpocratians and other heretical groups.) Renan believed that Lucian's story was a mere impression among heathens, Kautsky suggested that it 'may not be taken literally', and many modern writers have preferred to ignore it.[57] In my opinion we must look at the matter in a different way.

The first chapters of Acts, in which the relevant passage occurs, are dominated by anguish in the expectation of the *parousia*. The apostles, in an expression of the agony of the early church, inquire about the establishment of the 'sovereignty of Israel'. Receiving no definite reply, they are left in a state of lasting fear of which we are reminded constantly (1:6-7; 2:43; 5:11; etc.). This is not the well grounded fear elsewhere found – 'for fear of the Jews' (John 7:13) – but a spiritual fear. The story in Acts goes as follows:

> A sense of awe was everywhere and many marvels and signs were brought about through the apostles. All whose faith had drawn them together held everything in common: they would sell their property and possessions and make a general distribution as the need of each required (2:43-46).

This description speaks neither of idealism nor of an organized practice constituting a historical phase. Our information concerns the reaction of people who were trembling before the realization of the eschatological expectation. These people had no concern for social reforms and it never occurred to them to question the institution of slavery. Their donations, as Harnack pointed out, were voluntary, a fact which fits the psychology of people who are expecting the end of the world. Behaviour of this sort is often to be observed among people who are living under intense strain; and we find a close parallel in the behaviour of a Christian group in Pontus in the late second century, when all scholars would agree that the early 'communism' belonged to the past. According to a contemporary witness, a leader (probably a bishop) of a Christian community in Pontus convinced his flock that the 'judgement' would come within a year. Those who heard him prophesying that the day of the Lord was nigh started to pray day and night in great fear. 'And to such a pitch were the brethren worked up by fear and terror, that they deserted their fields and lands, most of them selling off their property.' We can see that this reaction was spontaneous, unorganized and inconsiderate. Those people went on spending their money for as long as it lasted; they lived for a while on anything they could find, and when a year had passed and their eschatological expectations were not fulfilled 'their maidens married and the men went back to their husbandry, while those who had sold off their property in haste were ultimately found begging'.[58] Thus ended the story in Pontus; the similar story related in Acts (and possibly that told by Lucian also) must have had no better ending, and this explains why it goes unrecorded. The alleged communism of the early Christians, then, was an occasional voluntary communism of consumption among frightened people with no resemblance to the institutionalized practice of the Essenes. Even the Essenes, after all, did not live in an egalitarian society; the members of the Qumran sect belonged to punctiliously observed social ranks.[59]

Christianity and the Slaves

A small number of texts, mostly New Testament texts, encourage the view that Christianity had been successful among slaves. The fact that early Christian attitudes to slavery, as we saw above, did not provide an incentive to slaves to join the churches is irrelevant. Christianity had low opinion of women too, but it is quite clear that this constituted no major obstacle to their conversion. Since the nineteenth century most scholars have taken it for granted that slaves were numerous in the early Christian communities: ancient historians and historians of early Christianity are in agreement. There have of course been exceptions: in the late nineteenth century William Ramsay flatly opposed the dominant view, arguing that the first converts were among the educated classes and that it had been the task of these classes to absorb the 'ignorant proletariat'. Today, an increasing number of scholars, among them E.A. Judge, Heinz Kreissig, R.M. Grant and W.A. Meeks, are questioning the oppressed-class theory which views slaves as typical converts. But it is the traditional view that dominates the field still, and we are still told that Christianity 'was notoriously spread by slaves' or that 'Slaves made up a sizeable part of the community'.[60] We shall therefore have to go through the evidence once again and see if we arrive at any firm conclusion.

* * *

For methodological purposes I have grouped slaves in four categories: rural slaves, urban slaves, slave miners and the slaves of the emperor. The last group, which is clearly identifiable and has a special significance, I shall examine in a separate chapter. Slave-miners, too, are clearly identifiable in our sources and present no major difficulty. On the other hand, while the distinction between rural and urban slaves (based on the Romans' distinction between the *familia rustica* and the *familia urbana*) is more or less valid in the case of large and rich households, in other cases it is almost impossible to determine whether a slave was employed as a domestic or an artisan or in agricultural and pastoral labour – in many cases he had a number of different tasks. A good example of the lack of any clear-cut distinction between rural and urban slaves is given in a parable reported by Luke.

> Suppose one of you has a slave ploughing or minding sheep. When he comes
> back from the fields, will the master say, 'Come along at once and sit down'?
> Will he not rather say, 'Prepare my supper, fasten your belt, and then wait on
> me while I have my meal; you can have yours afterwards'? (17:7-8).

As a working definition I have treated as rural slaves only those who
passed most of their day, or their entire day, out in the fields and had
little or no personal contact with their masters; such slaves as the one
described in the New Testament parable I have included with urban
slaves, slaves living in their masters' houses and under their close supervision.

Rural Slaves

To the best of my knowledge, rural slaves are nowhere reported to have
been converted to Christianity throughout our period. The only Christians known to have worked as rural slaves are those who were
condemned to do so during the persecutions. We are told that those
members of the imperial household found to be Christians during the
persecution of Valerian (AD 258) were to be 'sent in chains as
conscripts to Caesar's estates' (some might already have been slaves but
the rescript probably refers to freedmen or freeborn persons, since it
declares that their property should be confiscated).[61] On the other hand,
it is reported that Christian landowners often had pagan slaves, and
sometimes Jews, working on their estates.[62]

The fact that rural slaves are not mentioned in our sources as having
been converted to Christianity does not necessarily mean that this never
happened; early Christians, as a rule, had no interest in reporting such
conversions. It is rather the living conditions of agricultural slaves –
never questioned by Christianity – which justify our scepticism as to
whether such slaves ever expressed congregational interests. Max
Weber, who was the first to make this observation, wrote that

> in the barracks of earlier times Christianity would have made little headway,
> but in the age of St. Augustine the free peasants of Africa were actually
> fervent supporters of a local heresy.[63]

In the Italian vineyards, where slaves were often chained, only overseers
were allowed to live in families; the rest of the slaves lived and worked
under military discipline.[64] From the tombstone of a slave-trader we
gather that in the first century AD it had been common practice to lead
slaves chained together by the neck; chained slaves are also depicted in
paintings and sculptures.[65] At roughly the same period, Pliny the
Younger informed a friend that at a certain place, because chained

slaves could not be employed there, a 'good type of slave' was to be used. The use of unchained slaves was obviously recommended here as an exception[66], and the rescript of Valerian mentioned above confirms that agricultural slaves in the middle of the third century were still often in chains. The inauspiciousness for Christianity of rural slaves' living conditions needs no further comment: what has already been said suggests that no congregational religion stood a great chance of success with this type of slave. After Constantine their conversion was often advanced by force.[67]

Urban Slaves

Let us now turn to the urban slaves: domestics, artisans, unskilled labourers. Some of them, I have assumed, would have been engaged in agricultural or pastoral employments as well, but their conditions of life and their close relation to their masters opened to them prospects of religious participation in their owners' family cult. But we must not exaggerate their privileged living conditions. Though in practice slaves did have families (the so-called *contubernium*), these families were not recognized under Roman Law and could be dissolved at any time by the master's decision.[68] Cato, in his *familia urbana* had established a system of prostitution to cater for the sexual needs of his slaves; a century later, Varro advocated family life for slaves as of greater utility, as did Columella. Columella advocated exemption from work of slave-mothers with three children or more. Varro and Columella were referring to the *familia rustica,* but there is reason to believe that this development was still more common in cities. Yet, even in the later Empire the strong family bonds which seem to have been so essential to all congregational religions such as Christianity were lacking among slaves.[69]

A number of New Testament epistles, however, suggest that some domestic slaves may have been converted at an early age. Paul, as we have seen above, addressed himself to both masters and slaves; the First Epistle of Peter gives advice to slaves alone; similar admonitions are repeated in a number of other early Christian texts. But it is not so clear that the slaves mentioned were Christians, that is baptized members of the congregations: they could just as well have been pagan slaves of Christian households. More concrete evidence is needed to support the view that the early Christian communities included numerous slaves.

On the contrary, another set of documents gives the general impression that the early communities did not include slaves. The first such document is the Slavonic Version of Josephus' *Jewish War.* A number of passages of this Version are omitted from the Greek text and are generally considered as Christian interpolations; authentic or not, they may be taken to reflect the conditions of early Christian life. One such passage runs as follows:

> Many of the common people listened to their preaching and accepted their call – not because they were men of mark, for they were working men, some only shoemakers, others cobblers, others labourers.[70]

The description, clearly concerned with the urban population makes no mention of slaves, though it seems an appropriate context in which to speak of them if any significant number had been converted. Two similar passages occur in Athenagoras' *Legatio* and Tatian's *Oratio*; neither refers to slaves.[71] Minucius Felix, in his apologetic work of the late second or early third century, *Octavius*, confirms the impression. *Octavius* reports a debate between a Christian and a pagan; at one point the pagan accuses Christians of being

> Fellows who gather together illiterates from the dregs of the populace and credulous women with the instability natural to their sex, and so organise a rabble of profane conspirators ...

To this accusation the Christian answers:

> That most of us are reputed poor is no disgrace, but a credit, for the mind is relaxed by luxury, and braced by frugality.[72]

The 'reputed poor' are evidently members of the free population; once again, there is no reference to slaves.

Two further documents have sometimes been put forward as evidence to the contrary. Tertullian's *Apology* contains a passage sometimes understood as referring to slaves. According to Tertullian, one of the reasons for which Christians collected money was for 'iamque domesticis senibus', which can be translated 'for slaves grown old' but which can also mean 'old people confined to the house'. At any rate, Tertullian does not even say that these people are Christians, merely that they were taken care of by Christians. (In *On Idolatry*, Tertullian alludes to the existence of Christian slaves owned by pagan masters, but the expression is highly rhetorical and, perhaps, without historical value.[73]) Explicit reference to the existence of slaves among the early Christians is made by the pagan author Celsus: in his work *Alethes Logos*, written about AD 180, he gives the following picture of some early Christians:

> By the fact that they themselves admit that these people are worthy of their

God, they show that they want and are able to convince only the foolish, dishonourable and stupid, and only slaves, women and little children.

In Origen's view, however, the views mentioned by Celsus belong to people 'who are supposed to be Christians' but who are 'entirely contrary to Jesus' teachings'; and Celsus himself makes it clear that he is only recording a personal impression commenting, in fact, upon the following expression, which he attributes to Christians:

But as for anyone ignorant, anyone stupid, anyone uneducated, anyone who is a child, let him come boldly.[74]

It is to be observed that slaves are not mentioned. It therefore looks as if Celsus' deduction was based on a wish to discredit Christians.

* * *

A small number of slaves did exist in the early Christian communities. In a well-known letter to Trajan reporting on his investigation about the spread of Christianity in Pontus the *legatus Augusti* Pliny refers to two women slaves. (There is no way of telling whether they belonged to an urban or a rural congregation.) In a letter to the martyr Polycarp of Smyrna which will be examined in some detail in the next chapter Ignatius, his fellow bishop and martyr, writes that some Christian slaves were asking for the church's support in buying their freedom. In the Acts of the Christian Martyrs a few slaves are reported to have fallen victims in local persecutions; Eusebius reports that among the martyrs of Palestine there were even some slaves, but gives the name of only one such slave.[75] Unfortunately, the evidence is so fragmentary that no conclusion about numbers can be drawn. What seems certain is that slaves did not constitute a significant minority in the early Christian communities and that those mentioned were in the nature of exceptions. Slaves, at any rate, did not make their presence felt.

Scholars have repeatedly sought to confirm the view that Christianity was particularly successful among the slave population by referring to a small number of Christian slaves of whom some biographical details are known. I have, accordingly, left the discussion of this evidence till last. No one, so far as I know, has pointed out that in almost all these cases the converted slaves had Christian masters. Such was Onesimus, the runaway slave mentioned by Paul in his Epistle to Philemon; such were 'Chloe's people' (if by this expression we are to understand slaves and not freedmen) mentioned in 1 Corinthians (1:11); such the slaves mentioned in Ignatius's letter to Polycarp; Blandina, the slave martyr of

Lyons, who suffered along with her mistress; such Felicitas, catechumen and martyr along with her fellow-slave Revocatus and her mistress; such Porphyry, the slave and fellow-martyr of the presbyter Pamphilus. The same can be said finally of Callistus, a slave who, *after* gaining his freedom – a fact often forgotten – became bishop of Rome. (Callistus, however, may best be considered with the other Christian members of the *Familia Caesaris*.) We know by name of but one slave, Sabina, who had a pagan mistress and was obliged to run away from her.[76]

On the basis of this evidence it cannot be claimed that Christian slaves were, as a rule, being converted along with their masters and mistresses: the number of known cases is, unfortunately, extremely small. But the fact that almost all known cases of slave conversions are of this type points to the plausible hypothesis that slaves who became Christians were normally in the ownership of Christian families. A fugitive slave who found his way back to his Christian master through the new faith; several slaves who voluntarily followed their masters and mistresses into captivity and execution; and a slave who became a banker through the support of his Christian master – all these instances suggest that we are dealing with exceptional cases which are best seen in the light of the privileged relationship some slaves enjoyed with their owners. Such relationships were, if anything, strengthened by Christianity. A mid-second-century Christian Apology presents a clear picture:

> but as for their slaves or handmaids, or their children, if any of them have any, they persuade them to become Christians for the love that they have towards them; and when they have become so they call them without distinction brethren.[77]

Slave Miners and Convicts in Penal Servitude

Working conditions had always been very hard for miners. In the Roman world mines were worked predominantly by slaves and those convicted of serious crimes – though this may not have been the case in small gold- and silver-mines. Having children was almost out of the question for slave miners. Slaves had constantly to be brought to work from outside for fairly short periods 'until through ill-treatment they died in the midst of their tortures'. Diodorus Siculus, from whom I borrow the expression, goes on to give the following account of the conditions of miners in Egypt:

> Consequently the poor unfortunates believe, because their punishment is so excessively severe, that the future will always be more terrible than the present and therefore look forward to death as more to be desired than life.[78]

We learn of not one conversion to Christianity among slave miners; but then our evidence is sparse. Yet when we take into account that, during the persecutions, Christians were often condemned to the mines, it is interesting that, as far as we know, they never succeeded in converting the slave mining population. Tradition has it that the apostle John was condemned to the mines for several years[79]; the same fate also awaited Paul, according to the apocryphal *Acts* that bear his name. These *Acts,* though unreliable as history of the primitive age of Christianity to which they pretend to refer, reflect the conditions of life typical of the mid-second century. Except for an obscure statement that, while in the mines, Paul 'worked fasting, in great cheerfulness, for two days with the prisoners', the *Acts* say nothing about actual conversions.[80] In the second half of the second century, the Roman bishop Soter was known to have sent supplies to Christians condemned to the mines[81]; late in the same century, a number of Christians were condemned to the mines of Sardinia. (Among them we find Callistus, the slave who, after gaining his freedom, became a bishop.) Through the good will of a concubine of Commodus, all condemned Christians except Callistus, were released. (Callistus, we are told, begged that he likewise might be released and was finally emancipated.) No one, however, pledged on behalf of the other convicts.[82] During the persecutions of the early fourth century numbers of Christians were condemned to the mines of Egypt, Thebais and Palestine; similar convictions of Manicheans in Palestine are known. The churches expressed concern for the victims and organized aid as far as possible without, however, making it their policy to attract other miners to the faith.[83] An extant letter of Cyprian to Christian martyrs condemned to the mines encourages the martyrs but says nothing about the heathen miners. Further reference to Christians condemned to the mines appears in Eusebius' *Martyrs of Palestine* (*c.* AD 306-310) and in the *Apostolic Constitutions*, with no other information; Eusebius refers several times to the purple marble mines in Thebais but writes nothing about the miners.[84]

The above is not a complete list, but is sufficient, I hope, to make the point. The fact that slaves were still condemned to work in the mines in the age of the Christian emperor Constantine is the natural outcome of a long-developed policy which had never questioned the institution of slavery, not even in its worst forms.[85]

* * *

To conclude my remarks, I would like to deal briefly with a problem which has remained open since de Rossi's publication of the Christian sepulchral inscriptions. In these inscriptions, de Rossi observed the title 'slave' never occurred; today we know that it does, but only rarely. Several scholars, taking it for granted that slaves had been numerous in the early Christian communities, attempted to explain the contradiction in terms of a desire on the part of the early Christians to do away with social distinctions. Thus J. Bass Mullinger and others after him interpreted the absence of the title 'slave' as 'silent but significant evidence ... of the uniform disregard in the church itself of any distinction between the slave and the free man'.[86]

Harnack, on the other hand, who himself believed that in the Christian communities during the first centuries 'the lower classes, slaves, freedmen, and labourers, very largely predominated', admitted that de Rossi's evidence was not such as to allow us to be certain whether the absence of the title 'slave' was accidental or intentional.[87] In a more recent study, Kajanto, though still mesmerized by the belief that 'Christianity largely began as a religion of the poor and the humble' and that it therefore embraced a 'considerable percentage of slaves and freedmen', rejects the interpretation that Christians wished to do away with social distinctions on the following grounds:

> Tradesmen, doctors and the like did not allow their titles to pass unnoticed, and the different grades of clerical hierarchy were conscientiously recorded. The infrequency of freedmen's and slaves' designations cannot, then, be attributed to a tendency to disregard social differences ...

Even so, Kajanto arrives at the paradoxical and unexpected conclusion that

> It is possible that the rejection of the idea of slavery influenced the etiquette of cemeteries so that it was considered un-Christian to reveal that the deceased was, or had been, a slave.[88]

My own view is that the supposedly 'mysterious' absence of the title 'slave' from the sepulchral inscriptions of a religion 'notoriously spread by slaves' can be solved only by questioning the very premiss, that Christianity spread among slaves.

We are left with a question about whatever happened to the famous equality of the first Christians; for we see clearly that they did in fact observe social and legal distinctions. Some pagans who were willing to take Christianity seriously had the same question in mind. 'Are there not among you some poor, and others rich; some slaves and other masters? Is there not some difference between individuals?' they asked. 'There is none', replied the early-fourth-century Christian apologist Lactantius. 'For since we measure all human things not by the body, but by the spirit, although the condition of bodies is different, yet we have no slaves, but we both regard and speak of them as brothers in spirit, in religion as fellow-slaves.'[89]

Slaves and their Christian Masters

In the earlier sections of this chapter I dealt with Christian attitudes to slavery and the extent to which domestic slaves were Christianized. The basic argument advanced was that Christianity did not question the institution of slavery and that Christians exhibited no particular eagerness in converting slaves. Only a small number of slaves embraced the new religion; and it looks as if those converted were favourites of their Christian masters. I should now like to turn away from this small number of Christian slaves and consider the bulk of slaves. How did these people react to the spread of the Christian movement, and how did they feel about their Christian masters – when they had such masters? Pagan sources give no information about master-slave relations in Christian households; Christian documents have very little to say on the subject, and what they do say is exclusively from the masters' point of view, because, as we have seen, the Christian point of view was the point of view of Christian slave-owners. Not that all or most Christians owned slaves – we know little about the numbers – but the legislative and other extant documents reflect, as a rule, the interests of the slave-owners, whatever their numbers. Our discussion of the topic cannot, therefore, rely upon any clear evidence, but must base itself on inference and estimate.

Almost all research into religious sentiment among the oppressed sections of ancient societies faces a common difficulty: even when there is information about the beliefs of the oppressed – and this is unusual in itself – it is presented from the point of view of the upper classes. This need cause no surprise. Laws were used to secure domination over the oppressed classes, while literary texts were written by people who had not only the required education but also leisure, both the privilege of the dominant classes. True, a small number of ex-slaves managed to acquire a high degree of education; but it was in their new status, the status of an emanicpated slave that they would write, and even they would write for an upper class audience. So even in such cases we do not have, strictly speaking, a slave view. When we read in authors such as Varro of slaves with a 'little education' this means no more than a knowledge of reading and writing notes and bills.

Inferences about the religious sentiments, and the feelings more generally, of the oppressed classes must be based on a reinterpretation of the behaviour of these classes through a critical examination of the views of ancient authors. But such inferences, however plausible, can never be more than speculation. The psychological categories necessarily employed in such investigations derive from modern man, and there is no guarantee that the ancients always felt or reacted similarly. Bearing this in mind, we can proceed to speculate on some aspects of religious sentiments among slaves as it may be seen to derive from slaves' position in society.

We might get the impression, reading the ancient sources, that, though often false and bent on escape, slaves in classical antiquity tended sometimes to accept their position more or less passively. It is true that miners, for example, did not really have much alternative. Their living conditions were wretched and their supervision extremely close; Diodorus wrote that they 'look forward to death as more to be desired than life', and he may not have been far from the truth. Those of the agricultural slaves who laboured in gangs were sometimes in chains, under equally close supervision – though it is hard to believe that cultivation with chained slaves could have been very profitable; other types of slaves are known to have perished under similar or worse conditions. The passivity of such slaves is not difficult to comprehend. But do we get an accurate picture of the behaviour of domestic slaves from classical Tragedy, New Comedy and Roman Comedy, where we read so much about the *servus fidelis*? I shall argue that the idea of the submissive, faithful slave is to a large extent a distortion of the true picture by slave-owners' thinking. But since, to some degree at least, slaves were faithful, an explanation is required.

The prospect of eventual emancipation, often singled out by scholars in this connection, must be considered a significant, though not over-riding reason for submissiveness among slaves. Very little is known about the numbers of manumitted slaves at any given time; even if we did know more about numbers and percentages, it would still be very difficult to determine the effects prospects of emancipation had on a slave's general behaviour. But we can assert with a high degree of certainty that thousands of slaves lived out their lives in slavery, with no prospect or hope of emancipation. Why did so many of them remain passive, and even faithful, betraying no sign of rebellion? In answering this question we can learn from similar cases examined by modern psychologists.

It has been observed that subjects living in conditions of almost total dependence upon others – such as children, or, in our case, slaves – when faced with a strong external threat from authority – be it father or master – tend to identify themselves with the aggressor. A common outcome of such identification is almost total submission to the aggressor's will. Under such conditions, one theory of modern psychology claims, obedience is less unpleasant than it would otherwise have been. The dependent subject who has identified himself with his aggressor, is in a sense only obeying himself when he bows to his lord's desires. Hegel had laid the foundations for this way of thinking when he wrote that the consciousness of the slave cancels itself as self-existent, and *ipso facto* does itself what the consciousness of the master demands. Under these conditions 'what is done by the slave is properly', according to Hegel, 'an action on the part of the master'.[90] But 'this willing obedience obviously only goes to a certain limit, varying with the individual'.[91] If this limit is overstepped, the introjected aggression of the master or father (resulting otherwise in domestic quarrels) turns against masters and fathers. Varro had felt this aggression on the part of slaves, and advised masters to treat slaves more generously so that 'their loyalty and kindly feeling to the master may be restored'.[92] Literary sources such as Juvenal's *Satires*, which are quite revealing about everyday behaviour, suggest that the cruelty of masters was frequently excessive. Fathers, we are told, teach their sons to treat slaves with extreme harshness; nothing pleases some masters more 'than a good old noisy flogging, no siren song to compare with the crack of the lash'.[93] What we read in the *Satires* is confirmed by other literary documents and extant Roman legislation too.

It is almost impossible to penetrate the psychology of slaves. How far slave submission was due to unconscious identification or to conscious fear of punishment we cannot say. What we do know is that the limits of willing obedience were often exceeded and that master-slave relations were not as peaceful as we might believe at first sight. For corroboration of this view we need not go so far as to refer to the slave revolts, the most important of which occurred during brief periods in the late second and early first centuries BC; it is arguable that the great Roman slave rebellions developed under exceptional circumstances, when large numbers of new slaves from the same regions were concentrated in Sicily and southern Italy. Open and violent conflict between slaves and their masters occurred in individual households, as reports of masters murdered by their slaves remind us. We also know of several cases of attempted murder of masters, and we may infer that many other such incidents occurred for which no evidence has survived.[94]

Historical and legislative documents make it clear that slaves escapes were a common feature of everyday life, greatly exacerbated during war and social unrest. Owners used slave collars and turned to the aid of astrologers to recapture their fugitive slaves. Slaves are also known to have conspired, cheated and stolen from masters and masters' friends. Finally, slaves would also react with passive forms of resistance such as idleness, laxness, intentional clumsiness, even lack of discipline and not-so-passive answering-back: 'The tongue is a slave's worse part', some masters thought.[95] An exceptional piece of information about slaves' feelings is provided by Phaedrus, a freedman of Augustus. In the introduction to his fourth book of fables, Phaedrus writes:

> Now I will explain briefly why the type of thing called fable was invented. The slave, being liable to punishment for any offence, since he dared not say outright what he wished to say, projected his personal sentiments into fables and eluded censure under the guise of jesting with made-up stories. Where Aesop made a footpath, I have built a highway, and have thought up more subjects than he left behind; although some of the subjects I chose led to disaster for me.[96]

* * *

In several cases, slaves are reported to have participated in the dominant or established religious rituals such as the Lares (Compitalia and Augusti); the cults of Ceres, Venus, Spes and Mercury Felix; the Bacchanalia and Saturnalia; Mithraism and other Syrian religions; and so on.[97] Some slaves also took part in the religious ceremonies of the families they served, in city and country alike. In order to understand the idea of participation in family cults we must bear in mind the religious character of the ancient family: when the head of a household was converted to a new cult or adopted a new god, the other members of that household too were often initiated. As far as Christianity is concerned, from the days of Paul until the age of Commodus and later, ample evidence (including the significant testimony of the prophet Hermas[98]) suggests that the conversion of the head of a household to Christianity was often followed by the conversion of all the dependent members of that household – though it is far from clear to what extent slaves too were converted. (In chapter 6 I shall discusss this problem in some detail and comment on the conflicting evidence.) It should be stressed, nevertheless, that although slaves did participate in several religious cults, they were never themselves the bearers of a *distinctive* type of religion. This is an important feature of slave psychology which must be considered along with the lack of a distinctive slave consciousness. Slaves, furthermore, are not even known to have adapted any of the religions they embraced to their own class interest: the liberties allowed them during the Saturnalia must be seen as a concession of the slave-owners and the Saturnalia were in no way – as some scholars believe – a slave religion.[99]

Very little is known about the reaction among slaves to the spread of the Christian movement; throughout our period it seems they were normally expected to be pagan. The few Christian slaves considered earlier did not see in Christianity a force that would free them from slavery: the importance they attached to it lay in its promises for the afterlife. The most that Christian slaves might have asked for was financial aid from their Christian community towards manumission. (As we shall see in chapter 3, even this aid was denied them by church leaders.)

One striking fact is that slaves did sometimes turn against their Christian masters in a more violent way than would normally be expected. Canon 41 of the Council of Elvira supposed that some Christians owned large numbers of heathen slaves, and forbade Christian masters to tolerate idols in their houses. But if masters feared their slaves 'on account of their number', slaves could be left to worship their idols, so long as Christian masters kept their distance from their slaves and watched out against idolatry.[100] It is not hard to see that behind this enactment lay the strong resistance of at least some pagan slaves to their masters' attempts to convert them to Christianity. Further evidence suggests an even more hostile attitude of slaves towards their Christian masters: pagan slaves – it is attested in several documents – had been used as witnesses for the prosecution of their converted masters. Those Christian authors who provide the information obviously felt uneasy about it and attempt to present the slaves' behaviour as the result of torture or the fear of torture. We cannot reject this explanation; but there are undoubtedly cases in which slaves accused their masters spontaneously. Slaves knew perfectly well, furthermore, that by denouncing their masters they often risked further torture and even the death penalty.[101]

An interesting story in this connection is related in the third-century *Acts of John.* A certain Callimachus, 'prominent citizen of Ephesus', bribed the slave of a Christian couple to be allowed to 'dishonour' the body of the dead Christian mistress. By divine intervention the slave was killed, while Callimachus was prevented from performing his necrophilistic act. The apostle John converted Callimachus but realized that the 'accursed' slave was hopeless. Having been brought back to life, the slave said: 'O, what end is there to the powers of these terrible men! I did not want to be resurrected, but would rather be dead, so as not to see them (i.e. all these Christians).' Needless to add that by divine intervention the slave was struck dead a second time. There is obviously no truth in the story, but the class prejudice of the third-century Christian compilers is as clear as the slave's expected reaction.[102]

Let us to back to our original question: are they any grounds for postulating that Christianity had a distinctive appeal to slaves? Judging from the evidence given above, scanty and fragmentary as it may be, it seems not. The new religion imparted to slaves no sense, vision or expectation of liberation. Similarly, there are no grounds for assuming that when a master was Christian he normally succeeded in developing a special relationship between himself and his slaves. As far as we know, very seldom did a slave view submission to his master's will as the discharge of moral obligation to obedience and humility. Such instances as there were of a close bond of affection between master and slave, resulting in the voluntary martyrdom of the slave along with the master or mistress, as well as the opposite phenomenon the vindictive denunciation of master by slave, should not, I think, be attributed to any particular moral or social feature of Christianity. They were rather manifestations of the typical ambivalence of slaves' feelings towards their masters, as we have seen with reference to pagan masters. I would therefore insist that the psychological aspects of master-slave relations were always complex and ambivalent. By the selection of examples we can prove almost anything we like; and to conclude from the existing evidence that master-slave relations among Christians were characterized by greater humanity or affection is as arbitrary as to conclude that the *servus fidelis* was typical of pagan slaves.

3

Christianity, Manumission and Freedmen

Manumission

Tacitus asserts, in a famous passage, that freedmen and their descendants 'are everywhere':

> They provide the majority of the voters, public servants, attendants of officials and priests, watchmen, firemen. Most knights, and many senators, are descended from former slaves. Segregate the freed – and you will only show how few free-born there are![1]

Scholars are divided as to how seriously this statement should be taken. It is generally agreed, nevertheless, that, especially from the Principate onwards, the number of freedmen – and their descendants – increased considerably and that some, at least, managed to acquire great fortunes and even to enter the highest ranks in the Roman hierarchy. Narcissus, Pallas, Nymphidius, the father of Claudius Etruscus, are the best known cases; but the list could go on to include senators, such as Larcius Macedo, or (possibly) the emperor Pertinax, who were sons of ex-slaves.[2] To understand the position of freedmen in Roman society, we must first turn briefly to the history and legal forms of manumission, and go on to discuss some psychological features peculiar to freedmen.

The History and the Motives of Manumission

We shall understand Roman manumission better if we take a brief look at the earlier history of manumission. The practice of liberating slaves was almost as old as slavery itself. In the course of history, manumission and slavery developed and changed, both in form and in social function. In Greece manumission had formally been established by the fifth century B.C., and from that point on we can trace its history alongside the history of slavery.[3] Manumitted slaves in Athens normally became, not full citizens, but metics, unless granted manumission as a reward for special services. Originally metics were foreigners who had settled in Athens on payment of a tax and did not enjoy civil rights; there is no way of distinguishing immigrant metics from ex-slave metics or their descendants and, though it has been suggested that the number of freedmen among metics was far from negligible, the plain truth is that we have no idea.[4]

Sparta's case was different and serves as a warning not to treat all forms of dependent labour as being one and the same thing. In Sparta forced labour had been imposed upon the original inhabitants, the helots. Helots and similar social groups elsewhere were distinguished from chattel slaves in several ways: first, they were of the same nationality (or perhaps of two nationalities) and had fixed social relations; secondly, their property was much more substantial, and different in legal terms from that of slaves; thirdly, they outnumbered overwhelmingly the free population; and fourthly, they were owned by the state, not by individuals. Their social position differed accordingly, the major peculiarity being their frequent revolts. Helots therefore, by contrast with slaves, were not subject to manumission, except by the state on those occasions where they were needed to assist the Spartiates against a grave external threat.

In the East (certainly in Asia Minor, probably in Egypt and Syria as well) where conditions of production are not well attested before the Hellenistic period, it seems that, in spite of what is commonly believed, chattel slavery was not unknown. In the Hellenistic and Roman periods, slavery saw further development, not least for domestic purposes and mining; though many domestics were probably employed in agriculutral work as well. References to slavery in the cities of the Hellenistic East are rare and of dubious value, but suggest that slavery did exist.[5] It can be assumed that, though less common than in the later Roman period, manumission was frequently practiced in the Hellenistic world following a pattern similar to that of Greece. In the Roman period, slavery and manumission became more common in the East; even in Egypt, *pace* Westermann and others, it is increasingly believed that slavery was not that uncommon in production. Alexandria in the imperial age gives the impression of being the centre of a slave market spreading all over Egypt. A major difficulty in discussing slavery in Egypt, however, is the ambiguity of the non-technical terms for slaves used in Egyptian papyri; but even in this field progress is being made.[6] Inscriptions deriving from the Roman and Jewish minorities on the North Euxine shore suggest that there too slavery was not unknown: the ritual of manumission followed Greek practice, with influences from Jewish legal tradition; special types of conditional manumission such as *paramone* are also attested.[7]

Slavery at Rome took a similar form to slavery at Athens, though during the period of imperial expansion it saw unprecedented growth. As at Athens, two types of manumission existed. By the first type, the master granted his slave's freedom out of 'mere generosity'; by the second, the slave had to buy his freedom in a commercial transaction. The ability of a slave to buy his freedom presupposed the possession of a property known as the *peculium*, though it is sometimes hard to see how slaves could amass such amounts as were often required. Sometimes, perhaps, they paid part of the money required after their release. It seems that gradually manumission at Rome became a predominantly commercial transaction. The amount masters demanded from their slaves for manumission varied, but it is reasonable to assume that owners required at least the amount of money needed to buy a new slave.

One point is worth noting which has not always attracted sufficient attention. The evidence for Greek and Roman manumission shows a much larger proportion of urban than agricultural slaves manumitted, while miners were manumitted only in exceptional cases. Scholars have interpreted this fact, which rests on incontrovertible evidence – manumission lists for the years 340-320 B.C. in Attica, for example, report only 12 out of 115 males as agricultural slaves – as an indication that agricultural slaves were few in number and hence that agricultural production was not based on slave labour.[8] I do not wish to deny that, at Athens, agricultural slaves may have been fewer than domestics and miners, or that they were probably outnumbered by free peasants.[9] This, however, does not adequately explain the extremely low proportion of manumitted agricultural slaves. And what about slave miners? Their numbers were always very large, yet we know of no manumissions outside special cases. The fact is that 'agricultural slaves naturally had very much less chance of obtaining their freedom than domestics or industrial slaves'.[10] As has been noted, 'We may doubt if unskilled slaves were often manumitted at all, any more than the farm hands whom the elder Pliny describes as "men without hope"'.[11] Agricultural slaves, miners and unskilled slaves generally were much more important for production than domestics, craftsmen and artisans. Thousands of unproductive or semi-productive domestics were 'retained by men of means because it was the thing to do'.[12] Craftsmen and artisans could all have equally well been freeborn (as the greatest proportion of them probably was). But this was not the case with agricultural slaves; the large estates of Italy, for example, were heavily dependent on their labour, as was the aristocracy which owned these estates.

The same problem can be examined from a different angle. The philosophy of the Stoa, and later Christianity, has often been held responsible for the increasing numbers of manumissions during the Republic and the Principate.[13] We are not told, however, why Stoicism failed to bring about any amelioration of the undeniably horrible conditions of the miners. The answer must be that Stoics such as Seneca were concerned with the conditions of those of their slave domestics with whom they were in personal contact; as far as miners were concerned, they had little to say, and it is most unlikely that they could have brought about any change.

In the early empire, it seems that manumission at Rome was granted with unusual liberality. Augustus passed laws, never actually enforced, restricting manumissions by testamentary grant to not more than one fifth of an owners' total number of slaves and in no case more than one hundred. Manumission by testamentary grant must have been viewed by Augustus as a harmful and superstitious act which deprived the dead man's heirs of valuable property. Later, Augustus declared that no slaves under the age of thirty could be manumitted; according to Suetonius, he was much concerned 'not to let the native Roman stock be tainted with foreign or servile blood'. It is pretty obvious that what Augustus had in mind was the city of Rome and its urban slaves: no-one seems to have been prone to liberating excessive numbers of miners or rural slaves. But even in the city of Rome, to judge by the large numbers of freedmen and their descendants in the population, we must assume that the rules were often broken and that manumission was not seriously restricted by law. It has been observed, furthermore, that in other respects early Imperial legislation encouraged the advancement of freedmen.[14]

The motives for manumission are complex and to some extent unclear. We do not know how slave owners felt; we must rely on casual statements by ancient historians and our own inferences. Slaves, we are led to believe, were manumitted for a number of reasons: for attendance, as clients, on their new patrons; with a view to marriage; for attendance at the manumittor's funeral; as an act of ostentatious kindness; or out of gratitude, affection, superstition, expediency and so on. Several passages in Roman historians have been thought to provide additional explanations for the manumissions observed in the cities of Italy, and especially Rome. Suetonius writes that 'after announcing a distribution of largesse, Augustus found that the list of citizens had been swelled by a considerable number of recently freed slaves'; Dionysius of Halicarnassus relates that slaves were freed to secure shares in the wheat bounties.[15] How far mass manumissions can be explained by such arguments we cannot say. I am inclined to believe that the motives behind manumissions were as complex as any attempted explanations and that we cannot single out any one cause of the phenomenon.

Legal Forms and Consequences of Manumission

Manumissio and *libertinus/libertina* are categories of Roman law, corresponding to *apeleutheria* and *apeleutheros/apeleuthera* in Greek law. These terms suggest, at least from the legal point of view, a clear distinction between slave and freedman. But not all freedmen had the same social and legal status: some ex-slaves became citizens (this was normal when the manumittor was himself a Roman citizen), others did not. Besides unconditional manumission, according to which a slave was supposed to gain full indpendence (subject to certain restrictions), a common type of manumission was conditional liberation, the so-called *paramone*. (It is probable, however, that the practice of *paramone* in Greece differed from that in Egypt whence most of our information derives.) *Paramone* was a form of service contract, distinct from the contracts of free labourers in that 'the type of work was not delimited and the man hired became a handyman, subject to any demand of work given within the scope of the requirements customarily required of free workers' and did not always have definite limits to the length of service.[16] Roman patrons sometimes arranged manumissions in such a way that their freedmen would perform certain services after obtaining their freedom, such as working some days a week in their patron's houses or factories; this contract imposed a special oath on the slave and was called *operae*. But in any case freedmen were expected to retain certain moral obligations to their patrons which went by the names *obsequium et officium*. The former had a negative connotation and would normally prohibit a freedman from bringing a civil lawsuit against his patron; the latter implied the respect which freedmen were expected to show their patrons.[17]

Roman custom knew many formal and informal modes of manumission, each with peculiar consequences; we may refer at this point to *manumissio iusta* and *minus iusta*. Under the early empire informal manumission was legally recognized, and the difference between the two types became primarily one of custom, though each retained some of its specific legal implications. (It should be noted that the five per cent tax was levied, from an early date onwards, for both forms of liberation.) Of the formal types of manumission the most important was manumission arranged by testament; it is probably for this reason that legislators imposed restrictions on its practice. Variety in the legal forms and social consequences of manumission created a whole range of intermediary statuses, which have been called 'between slavery and freedom'.[18] But though, even from a legal point of view, the distinction between slave and freedman was not as sharp as is sometimes thought, a number of rights which accompanied most types of manumission were not without important consequence for the psychology and ideology of ex-slaves. We may single out three major rights applicable to most categories of freedmen:

i) Mobility. This privilege was not granted in cases of conditional manumission until the condition ceased to hold.
ii) Property. It is true that through the institution of *peculium* slaves were sometimes allowed to manage a certain amount of money; but the privilege did not apply to all slaves, and always remained within limits, subject to the master's good will.
iii) Family. Greek and Roman law did not recognize such a right to slaves though in practice many slave families did exist – the so-called *contubernium*. But even when these families existed *de facto* they were always under the threat of a master's or heir's right to sell one or several of the family's members.

These three major rights were of importance to freedmen as individuals; we have still to take brief account of the significance of manumission for the social system as a whole. Evidence from sepulchral inscriptions of the first two and a half centuries of imperial Rome has been interpreted as implying that nearly ninety per cent of the population of the city of Rome was of foreign extraction, and that many were of slave or ex-slave stock; further calculations have suggested that well over half the population of the imperial city of Rome consisted of freedmen or their descendants while about one fifth of the local aristocracy of Italy is thought to have been of slave descent.[19] But there are two basic problems with these calculations: first, 'the names in the epitaphs do not give us a cross-section of the population' (L.R. Taylor, one of those responsible for the above calculations, believes in fact that the names found in the epitaphs 'belong primarily to one group in the city – to the freedmen'); and secondly there are no definite criteria for classifying the bearers of these names in terms of legal status. Even if we reject the percentages as implausible, however, we must still agree that the number of ex-slaves in Rome and other Italian cities was substantial. What was the significance of the large-scale manumissions that had produced all these freedmen?

Large-scale manumissions had a double function: manumission as a social phenomenon affected both slaves and slave-owners. For slaves, the prospect of emancipation served as an incentive to work harder and to submit willingly. Not that all slaves had good chances of being emancipated: urban slaves, and among them domestics and tutors, had much better opportunities than most, and even among urban slaves those who secured their freedom were probably a minority. Nonetheless, so many ex-slaves were living and working as free citizens in the cities of the Roman empire that they must have kept others' hopes of freedom alive. To achieve their freedom slaves must often have sacrificed all their savings, which sometimes amounted to considerable sums; and they must often have struggled against rebellious predispositions. Slaves who in old age handed over to their masters all their savings, with little or no prospect of earning them afresh, serve as an example of what freedom meant; there were of course, others who by gaining their freedom found the way open to wealth and social advancement.

Let us now turn to slave-owners; in their case too we find extreme disparities. Some masters emancipated many of their slaves by will, achieving no material gain by their action; they, it seems, had purely moral or religious motives. Many masters on the other hand obtained large sums from the liberation of their slaves and sometimes services from their freedmen as well. It goes without saying that any money obtained could be used for the purchase of new slaves. It may be said, overall, that manumission served to entrench the slave system: in spite of the beneficial effects it had for individual slaves, it helped to reproduce, rather than abolish, slavery.

The Psychology and the Religious Participation of Freedmen

Freedmen did not in any sense constitute a distinctive social class. They can be seen, in the long term, as occupying an intermediary position, rooted in slavery but moving towards complete freedom. Within three, or even two, generations, traces of servile descent totally disappeared: in this sense, freedmen had a status which lasted only one generation. Depending on circumstances, freedmen were to be found in several social classes and numerous occupations; we have therefore to be cautious when discussing freedman psychology. Indeed, only a very small number of psychological features common to freedmen can be identified.

One's general impression is that, by and large, ex-slaves retained their old occupations. Obviously we have no statistics; but let us consider each case in turn. Manumission of slaves of the *Familia Caesaris* was linked to upward social mobility; it is therefore most unlikely that imperial freedmen turned to completely different occupations. Roughly speaking in fact, within the imperial household, domestics seem to have remained domestics, while members of the administration remained in this section, perhaps in higher posts.[20] Cases of conditional manumissions need not be discussed in great detail. In principle, emancipation of this sort offered few, if any, opportunities for occupational mobility.

Even when full independence was achieved – despite the attempted restrictions of Augustan legislation – freedmen were usually expected to retain some social obligations to their former masters. There are several examples of freedmen who had been employed, as slaves, in banking, commerce or their masters' firms, and who then kept their former positions; slave craftsmen and other skilled labourers had still less reason to change professions. At this point, we may recall the case of a freedwoman harlot named Hispala Faecenia. Livy, who relates her story, writes that this woman 'was worthy of a better life than the business to which she had become accustomed while a mere slave', but then goes on to report that 'even after her manumission she had supported herself by the same occupation'.[21] The occupation of Hispala might not have been typical, but if a harlot found it acceptable or necessary to support herself in the same way when emancipated, why presume differently for others? Why, in any case, would anyone voluntarily quit an occupation presumably profitable enough to have provided him with the sum required for the purchase of his liberation? It may have been different with some manumitted domestics and agricultural slaves; but the slaves who had most reason to want to alter their way of life were the miners, and they, as we have seen, were only manumitted in exceptional cases. We may conclude that as far as occupational mobility is concerned, the effects of manumission can have been felt only in the long term.

* * *

If freedmen were expected, as a rule, to retain their former occupations, the same is not necessarily the case with their religious feelings. Economically, politically, socially, slaves had been, as it were, excluded from the world; freedmen were in a sense readmitted. Many found themselves in a new position, some with families, some in substantially improved economic conditions. The world they entered was already inhabited by people who belonged to distinct orders; not all doors were open, since freedmen – especially among the upper classes – were usually considered inferior even when they had made small fortunes. It must have been in religious participation that freedmen sought shelter; or, to put it in another way, religious cults gave freedmen the sense of belonging.[22] As a slave, Hispala had been initiated with her mistress in the Bacchic cult, but when manumitted she dropped her mistress's religion and wanted to know nothing about it: though she remained a harlot, she found her former religion immoral. My suspicion is that she was actually motivated by the desire to join a new cult as a freedwoman. Freedmen served as *magistri* in several cults, while a few inscriptions of the imperial age suggest that many of the religious officials in some religious rites in Italy were of ex-slave stock.[23] It has been argued that this was so because the emperor, as *Pontifex Maximus*, appointed as temple guards members of his own *familia*. But freedmen were also priests of foreign cults like that of Isis, and Tacitus regards that four thousand adult freedmen 'tainted' with Egyptian and Jewish rites were transported to Sardinia. (Josephus, however, reports that they were all Jews.)[24] There can be no simple explanation of the phenomenon, but it seems plausible that freedmen were attracted to these cults because they were organized in the form of small communities which gave their members some prestige and a sense of new identity.

Christian Attitudes to Manumission

Given that early Christianity never questioned the institution of slavery as such, it is not surprising that no systematic approach to emancipation was developed either. Our examination of Christian attitudes to manumission therefore depends on individual cases and inference from those cases. Our general impression is that early Christians and their churches clung to the Pauline recommendation. Paul, as we have seen, did not encourage Christian slave-owners to emancipate their slaves and, more significantly, advised slaves to remain in their condition of slavery rather than seek their freedom. It is quite likely that in those early days the Pauline view was so closely interwoven with urgent eschatological expectations that its social consequences were not readily grasped. Gradually, when it became clear that the Christian communities had a long mission to fulfil upon earth before the coming of the Kingdom of God, the social implications of the Pauline attitude became visible even to the most religious. The Christian churches became consciously conservative. Our information is one-sided, coming as it does from official sources, but some reactions to this conservatism can yet be detected. It is mostly with these reactions to orthodox attitudes that the present section is concerned.

In the middle of the fourth century, not more than a few decades after the official recognition of the Christian religion, some objections to slavery are echoed in the literature. Brief consideration of these objections may serve as an introduction to the attitudes of earlier times. Canon 3 of the Council at Gangra in Paphlogonia (about A.D. 345, though the date is much disputed) enacted that

> If any one shall teach a slave, under pretext of piety, to despise his master and to run away from his service, and not to serve his own master with good-will and all honour, let him be anathema.

This canon reveals that, in spite of the official attitude, some Christians had been instructing slaves to forsake their service; in effect, some slaves may have been encouraged to escape. We are told, furthermore, that these instructions were given 'under pretext of piety' and this accounts for the church's interest in the matter. The Christians condemned belonged to the party of Eustathius, bishop of Sebaste (in Pontus), a party known for its extreme asceticism and general austerity; among other things, these ascetics seem to have condemned 'the rich also who do not alienate all their wealth'. The Synodical Letter of the Council of Gangra refers to slaves who left their masters and 'on account of their own strange apparel' acted insolently towards their masters. The meaning is somewhat hard to elucidate, but it appears that slaves did not actually run away: it is more likely that some slaves considered themselves to be ascetics and, perhaps dressed in a characteristic way, refused to obey orders that seemed to them impious.[25] In so doing, these slaves must have received encouragement from some free members of the Christian congregation, for it was with these free persons that the Council was concerned. The fact that this canon stands alone among the documents preserved suggests that the numbers and activities of these people were not significant. Some such people, however, were known to John Chrysostom too, for he refers to them in words resembling those of the Gangra Canon:

> He therefore is deserving of condemnation, who under pretence of continence separates wives from their husbands, and he who under any other pretext takes away slaves from their masters.

Chrysostom also alludes to the problem in his discussion of the Pauline statement mentioned above (p. 33). There he felt it necessary to insist that the prevailing interpretation of the Pauline passage was the correct one, although he knew of theologians who had adopted the contrary interpretation. In the fifth century, bishops like Theodoret still had to warn slaves 'not to use religion as a pretext for running away'.[26]

The combination of these pieces of information gives a picture of a conflict inside the Christian communities extending from everyday-life agitation to attempts at the theological reinterpretation of Scripture. The reformist theology gradually died away and was revived in sixteenth-century protestantism. Let us turn now to the origins of the conflict, which are out present concern.

The earliest direct information on the subject dates from the early second century. At this period, as we have seen, many Christians owned slaves; it was only to be expected, therefore, that discussions about the manumission of Christian slaves, at least, could not be avoided. Indeed,

Ignatius bishop of Antioch refers in one of his extant letters to the problem created by such discussions, and makes an explicit statement of his own position. It is worth quoting the relevant paragraph of this letter, which is addressed to another bishop, Polycarp of Smyrna, in full:

> Let not the widows be neglected. Be yourself their protector after the Lord. Let nothing be done without your approval, and do nothing yourself without God, as indeed you do nothing; stand fast. Let the meetings be more numerous. Seek all by their name. Do not be haughty to slaves, either men or women; yet do not let them be puffed up, but let them rather endure slavery to the glory of God, that they may obtain a better freedom from God. Let them not desire to be set free at the Church's expense, that they be not found the slaves of lust.[27]

Ignatius may not have been a bishop in the strong sense that the word later acquired; nor in his time, was orthodoxy firmly established. It is preferable to think of him as the leader 'of a group that is engaged in a life and death struggle against an almost overwhelming adversary'; and in Smyrna things were not very different. Reading between the lines, we detect a sort of anti-bishop challenging Polycarp[28]; Ignatius' advice to Polycarp that nothing should ever be done without his being consulted is best understood as part of the development of the monarchical episcopate. It has been plausibly suggested that the groups opposed to Ignatius and Polycarp were Gnostic.

Gnostic and semi-Gnostic sects are known to have existed then in Asia Minor and Syria. Among the documents used by the unorthodox groups of Asia Minor we should include the *Acts of Peter* (*c.* AD 180-90) and among those used by similar groups of Syria the *Acts of Thomas* (AD 200-50). Both documents exhibit an attitude to slavery which does not conform completely to the orthodox view. I shall first cite the two relevant passages and then comment on the possible implications of their divergence from orthodoxy.

In the *Acts of Peter*, the apostle is about to bring back to life the dead son of a despairing woman. At the funeral, the woman, in accordance with custom, had emancipated a number of slaves in honour of her son; fearing that by bringing the son back to life, these men might once again lose their freedom, Peter says,

> Those young men whom you set free in honour of your son, are they to do service to their master as free men, when he is alive? For I know that some will feel injured on seeing your son restored to life, because these men will become his slaves once again. But let them all keep their freedom and draw their provisions as they drew them before, for your son shall be raised up, and they must be with him.[29]

To this the woman replies that she not only agrees but will grant to the freedmen all that she meant to spend at her son's funeral.

Although Peter in this passage is doing no more than to confirm a manumission which had already taken place, his request is the strongest statement in favour of manumission that we find in any Christian text. What is even more interesting is that Peter was not motivated by the feelings of the slaves themselves, but by the objections of certain persons whom unfortunately, he does not name. What he says is that some 'bystanders' would go so far as to feel injured by the restoration to life of a dead man if his slaves are to remain in slavery. This attitude can be contrasted with that found in the *Acts of Philip* dated to the late fourth or fifth century. There, in a similar situation, the slaves themselves make signs to Philip to remember them, and are actually freed in the end.[30] It is to be noted, incidentally, that what is proposed in the *Acts of Peter* is a sort of conditional manumission, since the slaves as freedmen would have to continue drawing their provisions as before.

In the *Acts of Thomas*, the apostle Thomas reproaches the wife of a nobleman who is carried by her slaves. Looking at the slaves, Thomas says,

> You are they who bear burdens grievous to be born, you who (are driven forward) at her command. And though you are men they lay burdens on you, as on unreasoning beasts, while those who have authority over you think that you are not men such as they are. (And they know not that all men are alike before God), be they slaves or free.[31]

In spite of what some modern commentators believe, the above passage does not condemn slavery on principle.[32] What we actually have here is a humanitarian declaration such as is to be found in several other texts of the period: a passage in one of Cyprian's epistles (written in about AD 252) sounds almost like an expanded version of the quotation given above.[33] Nevertheless, the Carthaginian Fathers, Tertullian and Cyprian himself, make it clear that church funds in their own area were not used for the emancipation of slaves.[34] The idea of heavy burdens imposed upon men appears in several New Testament texts, but since it is not explicitly connected with slavery it is unlikely that it directly influenced second- and third-century authors. The common source of all such texts may have been the Stoic doctrine known to us from Seneca's letters. Seneca writes of the 'harsh and inhuman behaviour' of many masters who abuse their slaves 'as if they were beasts of burden instead of human beings', and calls on his friends to reflect 'that the person (they) call (their) slave traces his origin back to the same stock as (they them-selves), has the same good sky above him, breathes as (they) do, lives as (they) do, dies as (they) do'. But Seneca's humanism, as we have seen, did not go so far as to advocate slave-emancipation.[35]

A further piece of information is given in the *Martyrdom of Pionius*. The reported martyrdom took place in Smyrna, where, as we have seen, Polycarp had been a bishop in the early second century. According to Eusebius, the event took place in the second (or rather late second) century, but the document itself reports that Pionius was arrested during the persecution of Decius in the mid third century.[36] In the course of the story we are told that a Christian slave called Sabina was receiving sustenance from a Christian circle, which was at the same time making efforts to free her from her mistress. Before any result had been achieved, Sabina was arrested along with her protector, the presbyter Pionius, and was imprisoned in Smyrna. This incident has been taken to imply that at least some Christians were helping or encouraging slaves to run away, and that they might even have made financial contributions for the emancipation of such slaves. Closer examination shows that this is not exactly so. Sabina was not really a run-away slave, as Grant believes: she was actually 'bound and cast out on the mountains' as a punishment by her own mistress, where she 'received sustenance secretly from the brethren'. The Christians did not 'manage' to free her, but were merely making efforts to do so when the persecution broke out.[37] While being interrogated, Sabina was advised by Pionius to give a false name so that she would not 'fall into the hands' of her mistress, who would obviously have claimed her back. Once again, it is not because Sabina's mistress was tyrannical – as Cadoux felt – that the Christians were trying to protect her, but because her mistress was attempting 'to change the girl's faith': Politta, the mistress, was not tyrannical but 'immoral'.[38] Slaves were advised by Christians to accept their masters' authority 'not only when they are kind and considerate, but even when they are perverse' (1 Pet. 2:18). The *Apostolic Constitutions* instructed slaves to serve even the impious and wicked, 'but yet not to yield compliance as to (their) worship'.[39] This was the case with Sabina. She was advised to keep away from her mistress, because her mistress was interfering with her faith; and, what is more, Pionius was leading Sabina not to a free life, but to an honourable death.

The text under consideration is in many respects obscure, and little can be deduced with certainty. Religious motives, and above all the pathological eagerness for martyrdom, make a less simple matter of the statement that 'efforts were made to free (Sabina) from her bonds and from Politta'. Even so, we cannot exclude the possibility that some of the brethren were thinking of an actual manumission. The date of the martyrdom and its setting in Smyrna place the incident at the centre of the disputes to which Ignatius alluded in his correspondence with Polycarp. Pionius explicitly stated that he belonged to the Catholic church; but the boundaries separating orthodoxy from heresy were not absolute, even then. Pionius was imprisoned along with a Montanist and was joined in his execution by a Marcionite presbyter[40]: the pagan magistrates were well aware that 'the church was riddled with sects'.[41] It seems plausible, though it can in no way be proved, that the Christian group mentioned in the *Martyrdom* was also involved in the controversy over the emancipation of some slaves at the church's expense. The orthodox view, represented by Ignatius and probably Pionius too, was exclusively concerned with the religious aspects of slavery, that is, with slaves' moral conduct and interference by masters with their religious obligations. But others – the slaves known to Ignatius, the 'bystanders' mentioned in the *Acts of Peter* and some of the brethren who aided Sabina – were of a different opinion: they felt that the Christian community should go further and make its own contribution to the emancipation of at least some slaves. Even so, it must not be forgotten that all the cases mentioned above are exceptional. The Christian slaves under the supervision of a bishop and probably serving in the church themselves, the slaves manumitted in honour of a deceased person and the slave girl pressed by her mistress to return to paganism are not typical slaves. The idea of their manumission was essentially religious.

* * *

In the mid third century some Christian groups in Syria and Asia Minor may have been using church rules very like those represented in the fourth century compilation known as the *Apostolic Constitutions*. This document betrays an ascetic tendency peculiar to Eastern Christianity and an apparently clear attitude to manumission. *The Apostolic Constitutions* instruct that the brethren are to collect money and spend it for the

> redemption of the saints, the deliverance of slaves and of captives, and of prisoners, and of those that have been abused, and of those that have been condemned by tyrants to single combat and death on account of the name of Christ.[42]

This passage would be unique in Christian literature if what it meant was that church funds should be used for the emancipation of slaves in general.[43] The context, however, suggests that the beneficiaries were not ordinary slaves but illegally captured free Christians. This reading is confirmed by the general position of the *Apostolic Constitutions* on slavery: slavery is not condemned but accepted as normal.

There is an indication that, as early as the late first century, Christians looked after the welfare of captured fellow Christians, and, if we are to believe *1 Clement*, that

> many have surrendered themselves to captivity as a ransom for others, and many more have sold themselves into slavery and given the money to provide others with food.[44]

Unfortunately, *1 Clement* is highly rhetorical, and does not make clear whether it is referring to Christians or to Jews: the expression 'our own people' bears both senses in this text, and the examples which follow the statement above are drawn from the Old Testament. A letter of Dionysius, bishop of Alexandria, of the same period as the *Apostolic Constitutions* (the mid third century), reinforces the view that it was recently-captured citizens that Christians had in mind when they wrote of the 'deliverance of slaves'. In the context of the persecutions of Decius, Dionysius refers to some Christians as having been 'reduced to utter slavery by barbarian Saracens'; of these enslaved Christians, 'some were with difficulty ransomed for large sums, others have not yet been, up to this day'. Cyprian too writes of the need to rescue and redeem captured brethren from barbarian hands.[45]

But the *Apostolic Constitutions* contain a further passage which needs careful examination. In it, Christians are instructed to avoid public meetings of the heathen as well as 'those sports which are celebrated in them',

> For a believer ought not to go to any of those public meetings, unless to purchase a slave, and save a soul, and at the same time to buy such other things as suit their necessities.[46]

The context makes it clear that Christians were allowed to go to market, where pagans formed an overwhelming majority, only when they had to buy provisions. One of the things they could not find elsewhere was slaves; so slaves, obviously, would not be bought simply in order to be set free. But the qualification 'and save a soul' is still somewhat perplexing. (It may be an interpolation.) It is sometimes understood to refer to the baptism of the slave: the editor of the English translation of the text explains it as meaning that 'Slaves were bought to be baptized'.[47] This possibility cannot be excluded, but the passage seems to have a much simpler meaning: the soul of the slave would be saved by the mere fact that he was purchased by a Christian. Such a slave would belong to a

Christian household and would therefore be under the protection of God.

* * *

Our examination of early Christian attitudes to manumission ends with the edicts of Constantine. In Greece and Rome manumission was often performed in the pagan temples; in Greece it took the form of a sale to a god, while in Rome and other areas during the Roman period it was performed in the presence of priests and sealed by an oath to the gods and to the emperor. Jews too practiced manumission at their sacred places, following a ritual similar to the pagan and releasing their slaves at 'the house of Jewish prayers'. (A Jewish inscription from Panticapaeum in the Crimea, dated to AD 81, confirms the view that the Jews of this part of the Diaspora kept this custom unaltered.[48]) From AD 313, Christianity gained a new position in the Roman Empire on its official recognition as a legal religion; soon it was granted all the rights of pagan religions. In the years 316 and 321, edicts were promulgated, declaring that the Christians could emancipate their slaves in their own churches. This practice was called *manumissio in ecclesia.* It is not quite clear which model was followed in the new Christian practice: the Greek custom may have served as a precedent, but, as Barnes has noted, there was in the Christian case 'no analogue of the sale or dedication to the god or goddess'. It is probable that Constantine hereby gave recognition to a practice which had begun in an informal manner on the pattern of manumission *inter amicos.*[49] This new privilege gained by Christianity is seen by some as further confirmation of its hostility to slavery; Christianity on this view, 'gradually became one of the most potent causes of manumission'.[50] A reference to the laws of Constantine by the church historian Sozomen can be seen as giving this impression: 'Owing to the strictness of the laws and the unwillingness of masters, there were many difficulties in the way of the acquisition of this better freedom'.[51] On closer examination, however, such views must be totally rejected. First of all, if masters were unwilling, no type of manumission could increase the numbers of emancipated slaves; while Christians who had such a desire could liberate their slaves in other ways: in fourth-century Egypt, for example, slaves were manumitted by Christians in the usual way by testamentary grant.[52] There are no grounds for assuming that manumission increased after the edicts of 316 and 321; Sozomen, after all, mentioned nothing of the kind. By 'better freedom' he clearly meant freedom accompanied by Roman citizenship: 'Constantine therefore made three laws, enacting that all those individuals in the churches, whose freedom should be attested by the priests, should receive the free-dom of Rome'.[53] We learn, however, from one of these new laws that the clergy were themselves owners of slaves and that they were permitted to liberate them in church or on their death-beds.[54] The edicts of Constan-tine, then, are to be construed as Christianity's transformation into a rul-ing religion. The Christian churches took over most of the functions of the pagan temples, and among them the legal right to manumit slaves. (As we have seen in the previous section, manumission was an integral part of the slave system.) The case of Africa can be adduced as further proof that Christian practice was in conformity with social developments of the age. There, *manumissio in ecclesia* was not introduced until the early fifth century, though strong Christian communities had existed from a very early period. The same church Canons which introduced this new Christian type of manumission grouped freedmen along with slaves as forbidden to bring accusations against clerics.[55]

Christian Freedmen

There are reasons to believe that Christianity was particularly successful among freedmen. Ancient astrology is revealing testimony to the anxiety and stress induced in slaves by the hope of liberation: some astrological conditions, for example, were thought to 'produce unfortunate, hard-working slaves always oppressed by the burden of slavery', others to indicate that a slave 'will be transferred from slavery to freedom'.[56] What were the psychological consequences of such a transfer? Dodds emphasized the sense of loneliness such people must have felt; more recently Meeks has employed the sociological category 'status incon-sistency' to characterize freedmen.[57] Religious participation seems to have been a way of escaping loneliness and the stigma of servile origin; but religious participation was by no means the only way to overcome such handicaps. Several known freedmen became slave-owners them-selves and treated their slaves in the same cruel and lustful way as their own masters had treated them: we only have to glance at Trimalchio, the ex-slave featured in Petronius' *Satyricon*, to see how some freedmen were expected to behave. Aulos Kapreilios Timotheos, a first-century freedman who expressed pride in being a slave trader may not have been an unrepresentative figure of his age.[58] It would be most illuminating to possess a rough estimate of the proportion of freedmen among the early Christians, but when we look for evidence we find it to be exceedingly scarce. It must not be forgotten that to be a freedman was to be in a condition which lasted but one generation, and had almost no consequences for children born after their parents' manumission.[59] Freedmen, moreover, unlike slaves, could easily be disguised as freeborn, especially among the lower and middle classes. We can only know or suspect that someone was a freedman if we are explicitly told so or given his full name. In early Christian documents this is rarely the case: we are usually given just one name, and if the person mentioned was neither a slave nor of high rank we are not normally told about his status; nor are Christian sepulchral inscriptions much help. It thus appears that no firm conclusion can be drawn as to the numbers of Christianized freedmen.[60]

In the absence of proof we must give careful consideration to the few pieces of information bearing on this topic. Canon 80 of the Council of Elvira indicates that there had been problems with the ordination of freedmen. (It has already been mentioned that in the African church freedmen were in some respects grouped along with slaves.) Former masters, called patrons after the slave's manumission, continued to have certain rights over their freedmen. Just as slaves of heathen masters were not accepted in the Christian churches, it must have been very difficult for freedmen with heathen patrons to become clergymen. The Council of Elvira dealt with the problem of the ordination of freedmen whose patrons were still alive; for even if patrons were Christians they could still exercise their influence over their ordained freedmen. But we have no reason to believe that ex-slaves of any kind were discouraged from conversion, at least. Freedmen following their patrons to Christianity were considered as doing something quite natural, and according to Canon 19 of the same Council, freedmen were to be used as trade agents of bishops. Hermas, the famous freedman whose work *Poimen* (The Shepherd) was once regarded as Holy Scripture, had in all probability been the slave of a Christian mistress[61]; Callistus, the freedman who became bishop of Rome, also had a Christian patron (see chapter 4). In the mid second century, Christian freedmen of noble families began to take over in the Christian interest the cemeteries in which they were buried, and this can hardly have been without their patrons' consent.[62] It is more than likely, moreover, that slaves manumitted by Christian masters, in church or otherwise, were expected to remain (or become) Christians themselves. On the other hand, the entry of freedmen with pagan patrons into the Christian communities could, it is true, have led them into conflict with their patrons. Not that such converts were not welcomed; but their acceptance created problems which the Christian movement was not always willing to face. For Christianity the household was a religious unity of great value, and the respect due the head of the household was of no less importance. It was not without internal conflict and hesitancy that the breach of the household was accepted.

The strongest confirmation that the earliest Christian communities contained numerous freedmen is to be found in the New Testament epistles and Acts. About a hundred names are given; for most of them, unfortunately, no further information is added. It is interesting to observe, however, that a high percentage of these names consists of common slave names. (Some of those mentioned can be clearly identified as free persons and others can be considered in all likelihood as such, in view of their wealth, their ability to travel on their own, to have families, and so forth.) For the second and third centuries much could be learned from the names given in the *Liber Pontificalis*, the *Acta*, *Vitae* and *Passiones* of the Christian martyrs; in the meantime, I have collected from the New Testament epistles the following common slave names:

From Romans, Phoebe (as *diakonos* and *prostatis* of Paul, she could hardly have been a slave woman); Prisca and Aquila (both have been plausibly identified as freedmen of a member of the family of Acilius Glabrio); Epaenetus (claimed to be the first Christian in Asia); Rufus and his mother (Rufus' mother was Paul's benefactress or hostess); Andronicus and Junia (possibly husband and wife); those of the households of Aristobulus and Narcissus (all of them probably slaves and/or freedmen of the imperial house; Aristobulus being identified with a grandson of Herod the Great related to Claudius and Narcissus with Tiberius Claudius Narcissus, the famous freedman of Claudius); Erastus (a person of wealth and high civic status);[63] Stachys, Urban, Tryphaena, Persis, Philologus, Julia, Asyncritus, Phlegon, Olympas, Hermes, Hermas, Nereus and his sister, and Ampliatus (most of these last named are grouped according to households and some of them at least were free to make long journeys). From I Corinthians, Chloe's people (slaves and/or freedmen delegates of Chloe); Fortunatus and Achaicus (probably free persons). From Colossians and Philemon, Archippus and Epaphras. From 2 Timothy, Erastus, Trophimus, Eubulus and perhaps a few others. From Titus, Artemas and Tychicus.

All the above names, and probably a few more besides, were common slave names – but of course not exclusively so. As I have noted, there are hints that several of them were free persons; but given early Christian attitudes to slaves, I would suggest that hardly any of those mentioned were slaves. A reasonable assumption, therefore, is that most of the names mentioned belong to freedmen.[64] I will only add that in the late-first-century text known as *1 Clement*, three messengers are named; two, Valerius Vito and Claudius Ephebus, are believed to have been imperial freedmen, the third, Fortunatus, has a common slave name. (Fortunatus must have been either a freedman or slave to a Christian master, or he would hardly have been able to travel from Rome to

Corinth as a messenger. It is very unlikely, however, that a slave was ever employed as a Christian messenger.) Clement himself is believed to have been an imperial freedman. The most interesting information about Christian freedmen comes from the imperial household, the subject of the next chapter.

4

Christianity and the *Familia Caesaris*

The *Familia Caesaris*

Christianity became aware of the significance and power of the members of the imperial household at a very early stage, and Paul witnessed both negative and positive consequences. After being seized by a Jewish crowd, he was finally brought before Felix, the provincial governor of Judaea, who was an imperial freedman. Felix kept Paul imprisoned for two years, and when he left his post handed over the prisoner to his successor. Paul's relation to Felix was perhaps ambivalent – this, at least, is the impression given by Acts, our sole source of information. Acts gives contradictory explanations for Paul's prolonged imprisonment. On the one hand, Felix is said to have been impressed by Paul's theological expositions and to have discoursed with him on such matters several times; on the other (or 'at the same time', to put it in Luke's words), the provincial governor is said to have nourished hopes of a bribe from Paul – a not unusual expectation in Roman administrative practice – and to have prolonged the imprisonment with this in mind.

Most scholars have taken the second explanation more seriously than the first, but a careful reading of Acts suggests otherwise. Felix, we are told, 'happened to be well informed about the Christian movement' (24:22) and to have discoursed with Paul in the presence of his Jewish wife Drusilla. The governor appears to have had a sincere interest in Christian theology, 'But when the discourse (with Paul) turned to questions of morals, self-control, and the coming judgement, Felix became alarmed ...' (24:25). As it happens we know of this very important imperial freedman from a pagan source as well: Tacitus mentions him in his *Histories* as a man who 'played the tyrant with the spirit of a slave, plunging into all manner of cruelty and lust'[1] no wonder that the

75

topic of morals and self-control irritated him so. We would certainly like to know more about the feelings towards Christianity of Felix or his wife Drusilla (grand-daughter of Cleopatra and Antony) when they left Judaea. It is quite possible that they never had anything to do with Christianity again, but the story I have dwelt on may indicate one of the ways by which Christianity penetrated early the imperial household at Rome. Even if Felix himself remained hostile to Christianity, his wife or others of his household – or of the households of other such influential freedmen who happened to meet Paul – could have been converted. At any rate, before ever having visited Rome himself, Paul sent greetings to members of the household of Aristobulus and Narcissus (who have been identified with members of the imperial *familia*) as well-known Christians of the Roman community (Rom. 16:10-11). In an epistle written probably some years later, Paul explicitly referred to the Christians of the imperial establishment as sending greetings to the Christians of Philippi in Macedonia (Phil. 4:22).

The existence of Christian imperial slaves and/or freedmen among the earliest Roman Christian communities has hardly escaped the attention of church historians and New Testament commentators.[2] But if there had been no evidence about the existence of such Christians in later times too, there would have been little need for further investigation. However, as I show in the next section, there is evidence that the imperial household was never, at any point in our period, without its Christians. The composition of the first Christian community in the city of Rome was not a peculiarity of the earliest days which disappeared without trace; it is a phenomenon of some significance, which deserves attention. But first I shall consider the internal structure and socio-political importance of the *Familia Caesaris*; this will explain how people like Felix got to obtain such power, and how they came to be spread all over the empire.

* * *

The term *Familia Caesaris* has been used by modern scholars to designate the ensemble of the emperor's freedmen and slaves.[3] From a legal point of view there was always a clear-cut division between slaves and freedmen: a freedman's position in society, whatever its obligations or restrictions was, as a rule, far more privileged than a slave's. But the *Familia Caesaris* was united – and divided – in other respects which were of far greater significance. This is why imperial slaves and freedmen are treated by ancient historians as constituting a single social category; in fact, as we shall see, they constituted an elite group, many of the imperial slaves having better social prospects than most of the free *plebs.* All members of the imperial *familia* served a common master or patron, the emperor. Their proximity to the most important person in the empire created bonds which made other distinctions of less importance. Imperial freedmen and slaves were assigned posts vital to the running of both the imperial establishment and the administration of the empire. Most of these posts were never, during the early Principate, assigned to outsiders. Within the *familia* there was a regular system of promotion which followed the principle of seniority, and, according to custom, imperial slaves were emancipated at an age corresponding to their level of promotion. Though lacking any formal *dignitas*, imperial slaves and freedmen normally expected favourable treatment. The emperor's favourites, including his slaves, were in effect immune from the punishment normal for other servants; it was also common for a number of imperial slaves and freedmen to receive a general or specialized education, which meant that they met regularly in the relevant educational institutions. For all these reasons, the members of the imperial household developed a common sense of superiority over other social groups. It is therefore not surprising that, unlike other slaves and freedmen, the members of the *Familia Caesaris* took care that their status would be recorded in their sepulchral inscriptions.

Promotion and emancipation at more or less fixed ages, together with a sense of shared identity helped up to a point, to overcome divisions between slaves and freedmen in the imperial household. Of greater practical consequence was the distinction between those near the emperor, or under his immediate control and supervision, and those, much fewer in number, who were juridically and economically independent, connected to the emperor by name. (Some slaves had economic but not juridical autonomy and it is not always easy to decide what their exact degree of dependence was.) The *Familia Caesaris* was divided into categories according to the nature of the duties assigned: domestics were distinguished from members of the administration, while the latter were subdivided into subclerical, clerical and procuratorial grades. The fact that some imperial freedmen managed to reach the highest administrative positions is impressive, but the suggestion is plausible that the emperors employed their own freedmen in the administration in order to secure tighter control over it.[4] From the second century onwards, however, freedmen in the palace administration began to be supervised by equestrians, though procurators seem to have retained their independence. Felix is a good example of a freedman in the administration elevated to a position of great power.

As assistants to the emperor in state affairs, imperial servants succeeded the public slaves of the Republic, but advanced to much higher positions. In the late second century, when procurators replaced contractors at the customs of the Danube (and possibly elsewhere as well), the clerical staff stopped being slaves of the contractors and became imperial slaves.[5] Imperial freedmen and slaves who secured high positions (including that of procurator) were also employed by emperors to resolve differences between aristocratic officials.[6] Because of their privileged posts, many imperial freedmen and slaves managed to amass large fortunes and considerable property. Their financial position, along with the prestige of their titles, enabled some members of the group to diffuse themselves through the upper grades of Roman society all over the empire. We often meet with names in the provinces which immediately remind us of well-known imperial freedmen; it is reasonable to assume that these names belonged to descendants or freedmen of the well-known imperial freedmen. Such is the case of the Church Father of Alexandria, Clement, whose full name in Latin, Titus Flavius Clemens, is exactly the same as that of emperor Domitian's cousin, once a consul and later put to death on a charge of atheism. (It is believed by some that the ex-consul may have also been a Christian and that the Church Father was a member of the imperial *familia*.) Recent studies are also beginning to shed light on the marriage-patterns of imperial slaves in Egypt, where most evidence has survived.[7] The *Familia Caesaris*, then, has for good reason been termed as a hereditary group: imperial slaves often intermarried, and even when male slaves married freedwomen or women of free birth – which was not uncommon – their children were claimed as imperial slaves also, a practice which secured the continuity and unity of the imperial *familia*.[8]

* * *

Christian successes among members of a group from which state officials were recruited could not have been without significance. Christianized imperial freedmen, as they themselves advanced socially, would help Christianity to penetrate the upper sections of Roman society; their proximity to the emperor could influence his attitude and therefore affect Christian-state relations; Christianity, finally, could make use of the network which connected Rome to almost all parts of the empire. There are reasons to believe that all these possibilities did occur and that the significance of conversions in the imperial *familia* was much greater than most church historians have realized. Of course, not all hypotheses in this connection can be proved and much remains plausible speculation. But the existing evidence calls for a more detailed examination than has usually been provided. I have therefore first considered the evidence and then advanced some tentative claims.

The Christianization of the *Familia Caesaris*

By about AD 56, when Paul wrote his Epistle to the Romans, Rome already had a Christian community of some significance: 'all over the world,' Paul writes, 'they are telling the story of your faith' (1:8); in about AD 50, according to Suetonius, the emperor Claudius expelled from Rome the Jews because they 'caused continuous disturbances at the instigation of Christus' (almost certainly Christ).[9] What the origins of this community were we can hardly tell, but its early date and the fact that it was not established by an apostle or other important person is striking. Still more striking is that Paul was acquainted with numerous Roman Christians before ever visiting Rome. Among those Paul knew in Rome were the Christians of the households of Aristobulus and Narcissus, all of them members of the *Familia Caesaris*. A few years later, writing to the Philippians as, it is generally believed, a captive in Rome, Paul singled out as sending their greetings 'particularly those who belonged to the imperial establishment' (4:22). On Paul's authority then – and I see no reason for doubting the authenticity of the account – there were among the earliest Christians in Rome members of the imperial household, of some special significance as a group. Their existence is further attested by the second-century apocryphal *Acts of Peter* and *Acts of Paul*; both these texts, like the other apocryphal Acts, are generally unreliable as historical documents. The *Acts of Paul* reports that 'a great number of believers came to (Paul) from the house of Caesar',[10] while the *Acts of Peter* gives more details. Paul, it reports, was surrounded by Christians 'from Caesar's household'; the names of seven persons are given, one of them a presbyter called Narcissus. These documents evidently rely on the testimony of the Pauline epistles and have therefore no independent value; the presbyter Narcissus was in all probability a fiction based on the imperial freedman Narcissus, members of whose household were Christians; but we cannot exclude the possibility of a Christian Narcissus bearing his patron's name.[11] The prominent place assigned the Christians of the imperial household may be either a historical recollection or a backward projection of a contemporary situation; as we shall see, it is probably both.

At the end of the first century the Roman Christians sent a letter to the Corinthian Christians, written, according to tradition, by the Roman 'bishop' Clement. (The term 'bishop' is not strictly applicable to Rome in these early years.) The letter was entrusted to three men who had 'been irreproachable from youth to age'; these Christians must have been converted at about AD 50. The names of two of them, Claudius (Ephebus) and Valerius (Vito), also occur for imperial slaves; it has therefore been suggested that they belonged to those of 'Caesar's household' mentioned by Paul. Clement himself is thought to have been a member of the imperial household, and was perhaps a freedman of the consul and emperor's cousin, Titus Flavius Clemens, earlier mentioned. According to later traditions Clement's mother also belonged to the emperor's family.[12] (These unverified suggestions may also be extended, as we have already seen, to include Clement of Alexandria (*c.* AD 150-*c.* 214) as the descendant of a freedman of the same Clemens.

Our next evidence comes once again from Rome around the year AD 165. In the *Acts of Justin* we read that a certain Euelpistus, one of Justin's companions, was an imperial slave. (In a later and longer recension of the text Euelpistus replied that he was 'Once Caesar's slave' but now 'a slave of Christ'.) The further information given about Euelpistus is also of some interest. Euelpistus claimed to have received his faith from his parents who were at the time of the martyrdom in Cappadocia: were his parents in the service of the emperor or was he an enslaved captive? From what we have already seen, Euelpistus quite likely belonged to a Christian section of the *Familia Caesaris.*[13]

Irenaeus (AD *c.* 130-*c.* 200), a close contemporary of the Alexandrian Clement, gave two pieces of information in texts dated to about AD 180. In his work *Against Heresies* he wrote:

> And as to those believing ones who are in the royal palace, do they not derive the utensils they employ from the property which belongs to Caesar; and to those who have not, does not each one of these give according to his ability?[14]

The same idea of making provision for the poor out of goods belonging to the emperor is expressed in the *Acts of Peter*: in this work, which as a rule has scant respect for historical truth, the emperor (Nero?) said to one of his senators called Marcellus,

> 'I am keeping you out of every office, or you will plunder the provinces to benefit the Christians'; and Marcellus replied, 'All my goods are yours'; but Caesar said to him, 'They would be mine, if you kept them for me ...'[15]

This work is contemporary with Irenaeus' text and perhaps reflects the same reality, that Caesar's household had an important Christian element. At the same time, Irenaeus wrote a letter to the Roman presbyter Florinus, some fragments of which are preserved by Eusebius. Irenaeus writes that as a boy in lower Asia (in about AD 140-5) he knew Florinus, who was already a Christian, as 'a man of rank in the royal Court'. This seems to imply that Florinus, also known as an associate of the bishop of Smyrna, Polycarp, belonged to the *Familia Caesaris.*[16]

The story of Callistus (who became bishop in AD 217) is also most informative. Callistus was a slave of the Christian Carpophorus, who was a freedman of the emperor Commodus; hence Callistus belonged to the imperial *familia*. Callistus was at some time (*c*. AD 185-92) condemned to the mines of Sardinia. Through the good works of Marcia, a concubine of Commodus, Callistus and his fellow Christians in the mines were set free. The letter of liberation was taken to the governor of Sardinia by an imperial eunuch called Hyacinthus who was in all likelihood a Christian presbyter. From a single story, then, we learn that four members of the *Familia Caesaris* in Rome were Christians.[17] A few years later, in the age of the emperor Septimius Severus, as is clear from the testimony of Tertullian, there were still Christians in the imperial household, some of them of high rank.[18] From the time of the emperor Caracalla there are two inscriptions mentioning an imperial freedman and two slaves who were, in all likelihood, Christians. (Both inscriptions will be considered in some detail in the next chapter.)

For the subsequent period we have the combined testimony of Eusebius and Cyprian, the famous bishop of Carthage. According to Eusebius, when Maximin succeeded Severus Alexander as Caesar,

through ill will towards the house of Alexander, since it consisted for the most part of believers, (Maximin) raised a persecution, ordering the leaders of the Church alone to be put to death, as being responsible for the teaching of the Gospel.

During the early part of the reign of the emperor Valerian, Eusebius reports that the imperial house 'had been filled with godly persons' and thus Valerian's house was 'a church of God'.[19] Cyprian, for his part, in reporting Valerian's rescript of AD 258 says that, besides the leaders of the church and the high-ranking Romans, the Christians of Caesar's household were also severely persecuted[20]; the fact that a fairly short rescript had explicitly to refer to imperial slaves and freedmen bears witness to their significance. Eusebius also mentioned an Antiochian presbyter and imperial servant called Dorotheus who, being 'by nature a eunuch', was honoured by the emperor 'with the charge of the purple dye-works at Tyre'.[21]

Finally, as we enter the fourth century, there is increasing evidence for the existence of Christians in imperial service. Eusebius introduces his readers to the period of the 'great persecutions' with an assertion that, until then, emperors and governors had allowed members of their households (wives, children, servants) openly to practise the Christian rites. Lactantius, supported by Eusebius, reports that Diocletian in his early years considered it sufficient to forbid the practice of Christianity to officials at court and in the army. In the year 295 there were Christian soldiers in the imperial bodyguard; during the persecutions, the afore-mentioned Dorotheus fell victim at Nicomedia together with 'many others of the imperial household', of whom two are known by name: Peter and Gorgonius. Other victims of the persecutions were Philoro-mus, 'who had been entrusted with an office of no small importance in the imperial administration at Alexandria'; and Adauctus, who had passed 'blamelessly through the general administration of what they call the magistracy and ministry of finance'. The *Gesta* of the holy martyrs also reports that of the martyrs who lay in the catacombs some were servants of Caesar's household. We may also note the information given in a letter allegedly sent by the Alexandrian bishop Theonas (AD 282-300) to a Christian chief chamberlain of the emperor called Lucianus; according to this letter generally considered to be a forgery, many persons in the emperor's palace had been converted to Christianity by this chamberlain.[22]

The Significance of the Christianization of the *Familia Caesaris*

Much of the material discussed above is doubtful and unreliable; but cumulatively the pieces of information considered give a fairly clear picture of the historical situation. It is beyond question that many imperial servants throughout our period were Christians; in Rome espe-cially, a significant section of the Christian community consisted of imperial slaves and freedmen. Furthermore – and in this sense it makes little difference whether our information is historical or fictitious – the very fact that all the stories discussed above were recorded with care, and often with pride, and that they appear in documents of very differ-ent kinds, reflects an important aspect of early Christian mentality. In this section I shall discuss these two points; that is, the significance of actual conversions of imperial servants, and early Christian notions about them – notions which even led to the invention of fictitious conversions.

The importance of actual conversions among members of the *Familia Caesaris* can be grasped if we consider it within the context of this elite group's administrative functions. We have already mentioned that the imperial slaves and freedmen were in a sense the heirs of the public slaves of the Republic; in fact, they were much more than that. With the expansion of the Roman empire the former system of administration became inadequate. A new and complex administrative system developed during the Principate in which the traditional aristocracy could not, and did not, fill all positions of power as it had done until then. Some of the highest administrative positions were entrusted to imperial slaves and freedmen, and in this capacity numerous imperial servants were spread all over the empire. The choice of these people was not random. Hopkins has emphasized the element of tension, conflict or hostility between emperors and the Roman aristocracy; Ste. Croix has added qualifications to this conception.[23] At any rate, emperors, in their attempt to centralize power and strengthen their own position, especially in matters of foreign policy, found their own servants more trustworthy and amenable to control than most equestrians and senators.

Through the Christianized imperial servants, Christianity developed three important features. First, it advanced steadily, and more or less smoothly to positions of power. It is also possible that Christianity could appeal to high-ranking officials. There is evidence to support this view. Felix, the imperial freedman, gave a thoughtful and perhaps sympathetic hearing to Paul. (It is not irrelevant that Felix had a Jewish wife, but we must not forget that Jewish influence in certain imperial circles of the empire was not altogether exceptional.) Other officials were actually converted (a few cases are mentioned in chapter 6). But it was the continuous influence of Christianity in some sections of the imperial administration that carries greatest weight: by controlling such positions of power, the new religion could influence public affairs and sometimes emperors themselves.

Much has been written about the persecutions of the early Christians. From the earliest years (see The Revelation of John) until the present, an enormous literature has considered aspects of the persecutions – though much remains obscure. But the corollary is that too little attention has been devoted to the much longer periods of peace the Christian churches enjoyed; in fact, the severity of the so-called great persecutions, as viewed by contemporary witnesses, can be properly understood only when compared to the periods of almost complete tolerance which preceded them. After noting the enactments of the emperor Diocletian against Christians, Eusebius in his *Church History* gives some details of the persecutions. At one point he writes the following account:

> But among all those whose praises have ever yet been sung as worthy of admiration and famed for courage, whether by Greeks or barbarians, this occasion produced those divine and outstanding martyrs Dorotheus and the imperial servants that were with him. These persons had been deemed worthy of the highest honour by their masters, who loved them no less than their own children.[24]

As I have said, much has been written about the motives and the consequences of these persecutions, but passages such as the above (and there are many others) call for further consideration as well. How can it be that all those imperial servants were so honoured and loved by their masters while obviously Christians? Lactantius, in describing the same events, writes that the 'exceedingly superstitious' mother of the emperor Galerius was disturbed because 'the Christians of her family would not partake of (idolatrous) entertainments'; when the persecutions broke out, it was believed at first that it would be enough 'to exclude persons of that religion from the court and the army'.[25] Before those persecutions, in other words, Christians were allowed to practise their religion at court and the army! The significance of statements such as this has not been sufficiently emphasized; in the present context, I can do no more than to suggest that, during the relatively long periods of religious peace when Christianity advanced and prospered, Christians at the imperial court enjoyed influence and power.

The second feature I should like to discuss relates to the geographical extent of the imperial administration. In dealing with the mysteries of Mithra, Cumont made the following observation:

> In all the provinces, the lowly employees of the imperial service played a considerable part in the diffusion of foreign religions. Just as these officers of the central power were representatives of the political unity of the empire in contrast with its regional particularism, so also they were the apostles of the universal religions as opposed to the local cults.[26]

From what we have seen, this is equally true of Christianity. We have met imperial servants in several cities of Asia Minor and Egypt – the two major Christian strongholds. On promotion members of the administration often changed their place of residence; it is among such people that we may suspect the existence of the most efficient Christian missionaries. But I should also like to draw attention to another consequence of Christianity's diffusion in this manner: imperial servants employed in the administration were to be found all over the empire, but the centre of the administration in our period was always Rome. It was from the imperial capital that the network of civil servants was controlled, and this fact gave the church of Rome an advantage over most of the other Christian churches. Although much has been written about the origins of Rome's primacy in the Christian world, little attention has been paid to the contribution made by the Christian element in the imperial administration. The comment of Irenaeus mentioned above, repeated in the *Acts of Peter*, suggests that the early Christians themselves were aware of the financial superiority enjoyed by their brethren in the imperial household at Rome. Financial and administrative power were the basic advantages of the church at Rome; theologically and numerically other Christian churches were, of course, far ahead.

The above observations can be seen as still more significant if we consider a third point. Officials of the Christian churches all over the empire were not infrequently associated with the imperial *familia*. Bishop Clement and several other leading members of the Roman Christian community seem to have been members of the *Familia Caesaris*; a close associate and fellow martyr of Justin, leader of a Christian school in Rome, was an imperial slave; a Roman presbyter and close associate of Polycarp of Smyrna was an imperial servant; Clement, the head of the Alexandrian catechetical school, may have been the descendant of an imperial freedman; the bishop Callistus was a former slave and a member of the emperor's household, while a contemporary presbyter was an imperial eunuch; an Antiochian presbyter was also an imperial eunuch; and so on. Cumulatively, these bits of information have weight. It is quite clear that the Christians associated with the emperor's household did not lose the privileged position they had in the days of Paul: on the contrary, they increased in numbers, and from their ranks leading members of the Christian communities were constantly being drawn. I believe that the 'presbyter Narcissus from Caesar's household' mentioned in the *Acts of Peter* reflects, in fictional form, a reality well known to contemporary Christians.

To sum up, we have the following picture. For some reason Paul's fellow Christians managed at an early date to convert a number of imperial slaves and freedmen. We have no idea what happened to them during the persecution of Nero's reign, but somehow, some at least managed to survive. They played an important role in the reorganization of the Christian community in the city of Rome and went on to extend their influence to other communities, such as Corinth and Alexandria. (The Carthaginian church was also linked to Rome, but little is known about its early years.) The Christians' success was guaranteed by their superior organization; by their considerable wealth, used to support those in need at Rome and elsewhere; and by their connections throughout the empire. It is possible that the Christian community in Rome managed so soon to become the strongest Christian community partly because it included some of the powerful imperial slaves and freedmen; but we have gone far enough with our hypothesis, and we had better stop here pending further evidence.

* * *

We have still to give some explanation for the fact that the Christianization of the *Familia Caesaris* was so dutifully recorded, and for the existence of so many myths about converted imperial slaves and freedmen. I can think of two reasons which would account for this attitude in early Christian sources. In the first place, Christians realized early that the decisive factor in their struggle would be the conversion of the emperor; and who could influence an emperor more easily than his domestics and ministers? The hopes and desires of the early Christians inspired the fictional conversion of an eastern king and a Roman emperor many decades before Constantine became a Christian in reality (more about this in chapter 6). The same hopes and desires do much to explain myths about Christian imperial slaves and freedmen but most of the recorded cases of Christian imperial slaves and freedmen are not wishful thinking but fact. The second reason I posit for the myths, accordingly, is that the early Christians actually worked towards their aim and succeeded in converting imperial slaves and freedmen. The question is, how did they succeed? We do not have the information to answer this question with certainty, but the phenomenon of status inconsistency, which, as Meeks has argued, contributed to religious conversions, has greatest application to members of the *Familia Caesaris*. For as Weaver has demonstrated, 'As a group the *Familia Caesaris* constitutes one of the most notably "unstable" elements in Imperial society'.[27]

PART II

Christianity in Cities and Countryside

5

From the Palestinian Countryside to the Cities of the Roman Empire and Back to the Countryside

Few questions about early Christianity have caused greater disagreement than the question of its social standing. Practising Christians, historians and theologians have always been divided as to whether early Christianity was a revolutionary or a conservative movement. Today, much more easily than in the past, it is coming to be accepted that Christianity was both revolutionary and conservative. To accept this, however, is to reject the traditional view that there ever existed such a thing as a single early Christian Movement or Church.

The theory of a continually existent Orthodox and Catholic Christianity is theological, not historical. Unity and conformity were always highly valued but remained always unattainable. It is an irony of history that, while for Christian theology unity was a *sine qua non*, it was precisely on theological issues that the greatest divergences arose. Internal conflicts, mutual accusations of heresy, schismatic communities, have existed ever since the Apostolic age; and they have continued to derange Christianity over the centuries. From a theological point of view, it has always been maintained that instances of internal strife have constantly served to separate Orthodoxy from a variety of heresies; historical research, however, has shown that Orthodoxy was actually a constantly evolving product of history.[1] It is possible to say in retrospect which was the orthodox and which the heretical position; at the time such a distinction was not self-evident. It must not be forgotten that as Christianity developed and advanced, it had constantly to face new situations and problems: the third century, for example, witnessed major conflicts and schisms over the treatment of those who had lapsed during the persecutions. It is easy to say which position was preferable for the growth of Christianity, but it is very difficult to say which position was more orthodox. First-and second-century Christianity had never faced

this problem on a large scale and had therefore never provided an orthodox solution. Another issue which divided the Christian churches for
centuries was the date of the celebration of Easter. It is as clear today as
ever that Christians in Asia Minor had preserved the oldest custom, that
of celebrating Easter at the same time as the Jewish Passover; yet it was
the later custom always to celebrate Easter on a Sunday that prevailed as
orthodox. As Henry Chadwick has elegantly put it, the Asians 'had
become heretics simply by being behind the times'.[2] Although most
disputes were over theological issues, or practical issues theologically
conceived, social implications though not clear social motives or
programmes, are often to be detected. This much is amply attested by
our sources. When, however, we attempt to draw more general conclusions, we realize that the complexity of the circumstances which gave
rise to internal divisions resists simple explanation. Nevertheless, the
difficulties of the problem have not discouraged scholars from expanding a number of theoretical positions with a view to a better understanding of the internal tensions of the early Christian churches. As I said
earlier, what is of interest at this point is the social standing of early
Christianity, its attitude to society and the state, and its implicit attitude
to social reform.

So far as mainstream Christianity is concerned, we could say with
Frend that 'Reform of society, even as a sign of preparation for the
Coming, proved to be beyond the imagination of the time'.[3] This is a
nice way of putting it, but it admits of exceptions. Voices are known to
have existed within Christianity which, if not calling for the rejection of
the existing social order, at least warned against its unconditional
acceptance. The early Marxist tradition seems to have favoured a theory
of stages in the evolution of Christianity: the primitive Christian
community, represented according to Engels by the Revelation of John,
was, on this view, a more or less revolutionary group exhibiting clear
signs of class hatred and vengeful anti-Roman and anti-oppressive class
ideology. But since for the most part this community did not consist of
slaves and other members of oppressed classes involved in production,
Kautsky concluded, it was soon transformed into a new form of aristocracy; and instead of abolishing classes, it added a new form of
domination to society.[4] This theory of stages has many weaknesses;
above all, it does not fit the agreed fact that the subversive voices did not
cease to exist at any given point. On the contrary, reformist tendencies
in the first three centuries of Christian history are constantly represented
by heretical and semi-heretical groups.

Examining Christianity in a comparative perspective, Max Weber
came up with a different conclusion. As with Judaism and other oriental
religions, internal strife in Christianity was the product of a tension

between prophetic and priestly elements. According to Weber, 'Prophets and priests are the twin bearers of the systematization and rationalization of religious ethics'. But prophets and priests, he continued, belong to different stages in the development of religions; more than that, they belong to conflicting and mutually exclusive institutions. Prophets produce new moral codes and doctrines; they usually speak in a spontaneous and unpredictable way; they are primarily uncompromised teachers of ethics; and they derive their power from personal qualities, as bearers of charisma. Priests, on the other hand, are responsible for the codification and preservation of pre-existing doctrines and moral commandments; they specialize in commentaries of Holy Texts; they are concerned primarily with the pastoral care of the community; and they depend upon the power of their office and the hierarchy to which they belong. More often than not, Weber observed, prophets are rebellious and subversive; priests are compromising and cooperative with secular powers.[5] There is much that is attractive in this theory, and Harnack has, by and large, substantiated it, for the first two centuries of Christianity in particular.[6] The major problem with this theory, as with much of Weber's work, is that it is descriptive rather than analytical; it constructs a typology rather than explaining the origins of the differentiation. It is true that, guided by his observations on ancient Israelite religious history, Weber was led to consider the possible connections between the prophetic elements in religion and the influence of agrarian social reform movements; but he soon concluded that in the case of early Christianity no such connection could be made: early Christianity was an urban religion.[7]

The urban character of early Christianity has been assumed as a matter of course by most scholars. Writing in the late nineteenth century, W.M. Ramsay drew attention to the fact that the apostle Paul had been deliberately selective in choosing the cities of his mission.

> The towns which he visited for the sake of preaching were, as a rule, the centres of civilisation and government in their respective districts – Ephesus, Athens, Corinth, Thessalonica, Philippi. He must have passed through several uncivilised Pisidian towns, such as Adada and Misthia and Vasada; but nothing is recorded about them. He preached, so far as we are informed, only in the centres of commerce and of Roman life ...[8]

In the next century or so the spread of Christianity continued after the same pattern: the most significant communities were city-based; the early missionaries travelled, as a rule, from town to town, only occasionally visiting the suburban districts and almost never the villages in the countryside. The great bishops and church leaders who controlled the

Christian movement both spiritually and administratively were always residents of provincial capitals. This much is clear from Acts, the New Testament epistles, the letters of the Church Fathers, early Christian histories and other related documents. This simple fact, that early Christianity was an urban religion, can not have been without social significance. Ramsay was one of the first to draw appropriate conclusions at a time when the oppressed-class theory was prevailing:

> Now, the classes where education and work go hand in hand were the first to come under the influence of the new religion. On the one hand the uneducated and grossly superstitious rustics were unaffected by it. On the other hand, there were 'not many wise, not many mighty, not many noble' in the Churches of the first century, *i.e.* not many professional teachers of wisdom and philosophy, not many of the official and governing class, not many of the hereditary privileged class. But the working and thinking classes, with the students, if not the Professors, at the Universities, were attracted to the new teaching ...[9]

But if Paul and his followers seem to have avoided the empire's villages and countryside, Jesus himself seems to have avoided the towns. As has been clearly demonstrated, 'the Synoptic Gospels are unanimous and consistent in locating the mission of Jesus entirely in the countryside, not within the *poleis* proper, and therefore outside the real limits of Hellenistic civilisation'.[10]

When we next meet the followers of Jesus in the New Testament, after the Crucifixion, they are already gathered in Jerusalem. In the first chapter of Acts, the disciples are told that they will receive power and that they will bear witness for Jesus 'in Jerusalem, and all over Judaea and Samaria, and away to the ends of the earth' (1:8); elsewhere they are told 'Do not take the road to gentile lands, and do not enter any Samaritan town; but go rather to the lost sheep of the house of Israel' (Mt. 10:5-6). But instead of the Palestinian countryside, Acts actually follow the mission in the cities of the Graeco-Roman world and end up with Paul a prisoner at Rome. The Palestinian countryside where Jesus had travelled and taught in fact disappears completely from all New Testament sources. Acts has thus, for good reason, been described as 'a story of movement'. 'First, the Christians move from Palestine to the Mediterranean Diaspora, and thus, second, from the Jewish world to the gentile one. That is, from being a Jewish sect, they become a Graeco-Roman cult. But third, this is also, and most importantly, a theological movement, since the author ('Luke') is chiefly concerned to explain and justify Christianity's departure from Judaism and its transformation into a gentile region.'[11] The transformation of Christianity from a Jewish sect into a gentile religion has not failed to attract the attention of many scholars as a process with important social implications, but what needs to be stressed above all is the background to this transformation. Between the Aramaic-speaking peasant society of Jesus and the Greek- (and Latin-) speaking urban society of the Pauline mission there existed economic and cultural differences of such dimensions that they left a decisive mark on the origins of Christianity.[12] It is unfortunate that so little is known about this process of transformation: our sole source of information is the New Testament. On the one hand we have the Synoptic Gospels with their rural environment; on the other we have most of the epistles which are communications between urban communities; in between we have Acts, which, as mentioned above, describes the movement from the Palestinian countryside to the Graeco-Roman cities. But it must be understood that the whole of the New Testament as we now have it (and, more or less, as most Christian communities had it from as early as the second century, in spite of differences in the works contained) was written or edited after the transition had been completed; in fact, after the Palestinian Christian congregations had suffered a decisive blow. The New Testament as a whole is, therefore, in the nature of a compromise: linguistically, it is often translating Aramaisms, which either become incomprehensible or acquire a new meaning[13]; culturally, it allegorizes paradigms drawn from rural life to make them meaningful to urban readers; socially, it adds qualifications minimizing the implications of a peasant society's subversive and reformist sentiments; theologically, it attempts to justify the gentile mission and the departure from Palestine.[14]

In the early second century, when Christianity emerges again into history after New Testament times, it was already an urban religion. Culturally, socially, theologically, Christianity became adapted to needs and systems of thought of the cities. From that time onward we can, in spite of insufficient documentation, steadily follow the gradual spread of the new religion to the villages and countryside of the Roman empire. The earliest evidence concerns Asia Minor, Syria, Egypt and North Africa, but it is possible that elsewhere in the West similar developments were in progress. This second phase of expansion was more or less under the general direction and guidance of the leaders of the major urban Christian congregations. Throughout our period the Christianized countryside remained under the jurisdiction of the bishops of the provincial capitals. It would therefore seem reasonable to conclude that when Christianity reached the countryside of the Roman world in its new form, it was socially, culturally and theologically marked by urban predispositions. We find, however, that this was not so. As soon as Christianity came into contact with the world of peasants and villagers, much of its original nature was revived. We have no idea in what way and to what extent this happened, but there are reasons to believe that the original message developed in the countryside of Palestine, and though allegorized by church leaders was once again understood by people living under similar conditions of material existence and exploitation by city dwellers. More about this subject will be said in chapter 7, but it is worth while to note here a couple of examples.

One of the greatest heretical movements which divided Christianity for almost two centuries was Montanism. This heresy originated in a village on the borders of Mysia and Phrygia; it gradually spread all over Asia Minor, and later in North Africa as well, but its strongholds and principal centres of influence were always in isolated regions and small villages. Montanism was known for its ascetic tendencies, its advocacy of celibacy and its inclination to martyrdom. Little, if anything, in its doctrines could clearly be condemned as heretical and its conflict with mainstream urban Christianity centred on its prophetic and ecstatic character. The first leaders of the Montanist movement were considered prophets, and its adherents called opponents 'murderers of the prophets' ('*prophetophontas*').[15]

My second example derives from the early years of the life of the hermit Antony, who grew up in the Egyptian hinterland. The information is given by the great bishop of Alexandria, Athanasius:

> Six months had not passed since the death of his parents when, going to the Lord's house as usual and gathering his thoughts, he considered while he walked how the apostles, forsaking everything, followed the Savior, and how in Acts some sold what they possessed and took the proceeds and placed them at the feet of the apostles for distribution among those in need, and what great hope is stored up for such people in heaven. He went into church pondering these things, and just then it happened that the Gospel was being read, and he heard the Lord saying to the rich man, *If you would be perfect, go, sell what you possess and give to the poor, and you will have treasure in heaven ...* Immediately Antony went out from the Lord's house and gave to the townspeople the possessions he had from his forebears (three hundred fertile and very beautiful *arourae*), so that they would not disturb him or his sister in the least.[16]

Athanasius, of course, had no way of knowing these details, which must have taken place more than twenty years before his birth. But what he, as a typical city dweller and church leader, must have known well was that the mentality described above represented the way of thinking of numerous Christians in the Egyptian countryside. It must be noted that we are already at the end of the third century; which means that the Church Fathers of Alexandria had been allegorizing the New Testament passages mentioned above for more than a hundred years.

The conflict between Montanism and orthodoxy can be seen at various levels. Montanism represented a rural type of Christianity, uneasy with existing social relations; orthodoxy the typical urban development of Christianity, with its spiritual rather than social concerns. Montanism took the form of an enthusiastic movement led by prophets and ecstatics, and spread through the missionary activity of itinerant preachers; orthodoxy, already organized under the leadership of priests and bishops, reacted by calling local synods and by trying to silence the spirit that spoke through the Montanist prophets. The Alexandrian congregation of Athanasius and the ascetics in the Egyptian countryside who followed Antony were not in open conflict (though, as we shall see, tensions and schisms did occur at an earlier period). But they represent two different types of early Christianity. Athanasius was a priest in more than a technical sense; he well fits the sociological category developed by Weber. In Christian terminology, Antony was a hermit-ascetic; in some respects he was much closer to Old Testament prophets than to Christian priests of his own age. The Weberian distinction between prophets and priests can now, thanks to historical work currently being undertaken,[17] be placed against a much more clearly drawn background of city–country relations and conflicts. It must be stressed, however, that although urban and rural Christianity represent two different types of the new religion – the former more conservative and tending to compromise with secular power, the latter more subversive and with social reformist tendencies – their conflict but rarely came out into the open. As a rule, Christianity in the countryside was dominated by the bishops of the urban communities; the orthodox bishops like Athanasius preferred to embrace the ascetic movement rather than confront it. The major issues which divided Christianity and which led to open and sometimes bloody strife among sects go beyond the limits of city–country relations, and indeed the scope of the present work. In chapters 6 and 7 I shall consider some aspects of the Christianization of the city of Alexandria and the Egyptian countryside. Once more I shall focus on social groups and classes.

6

Christianity and the Cities

And at the same time in the reign of Commodus our treatment was changed to a milder one, and by the grace of God peace came on the churches throughout the whole world. The word of salvation began to lead every soul of every race of men to the pious worship of the God of the universe, so that now many of those who at Rome were famous for wealth and family turned to their own salvation with all their house and with all their kin.

Eusebius, HE, 5.21.1.

The Christianization of the Upper Classes

In the earliest Christian community at Corinth, Paul wrote, there were 'not many wise men after the flesh, not many mighty, not many noble' (1 Cor. 1:26). Many scholars have taken these words to imply that the earliest Christian communities were predominantly poor and insignificant; others have held that *all* the Christian communities before Constantine were poor and insignificant. A few, at least, have noticed that Paul said 'not many' and that, therefore, a few wise, mighty or noble people may have existed.[1] It seems to me that we cannot take the Pauline statement literally, not just because it is rhetorical, but because we do not know Paul's social standards; from what we know it seems that they were high.[2] In this chapter I shall argue that, no matter how we interpret the statement about the Christian Corinthians at the time of Paul, by the second half of the second century large numbers, at any rate, of the Christians in the great cities such as Alexandria were of some education and wealth.

By the end of the fourth century in the eastern Roman empire and the beginning of the fifth century in the western empire, the Christianization of a great part of the aristocracy has been more or less taken for

97

granted. Modern scholars no less than ancient have often tried to explain the conversion of aristocratic families principally in terms of the influence of Christian emperors. This, however, is not completely convincing. In Constantinople, as Jones has argued, the traditional governing classes were replaced by new men, whose dependency on the emperor led to their speedy conversion. But Constantinople was not typical of the whole empire. In the West pressures exercised by Christian emperors may not have been so successful; and in Rome itself, as Peter Brown has argued, imperial intervention seems to have had the opposite effect, forcing pagan leaders such as Symmachus, Flavianus and Volusianus 'to bring their religious grievances into the open'.[3] More recently, a detailed study by Raban von Haehling has demonstrated that it was not until the reign of Gratian that high officials were predominantly Christian. Under Constantine and his immediate successors most high officials were still pagans.[4]

Careful consideration of the evidence suggests that over all the Christianization of the upper classes followed its own independent course. Traces of conversion can be detected even at the new religion's earliest stages. What I propose to show is, first, that the upper classes were not immune to Christianity in the pre-Constantinian period, and, secondly, that the upper classes were in the main won over by peaceful means rather than by radical confrontation. The manner of the Christianization of the upper classes in the first three centuries does something to explain later developments. The change in the official religion of the empire, then, did not take the form of an out-and-out rejection of the cultural and religious past, 'but of a transformation in which much of the Roman secular tradition was preserved'.[5]

The steady advance of Christianity, however, among the upper classes must not obscure the fact that, compared with the urban middle classes, the aristocracy of the Graeco-Roman world was more reluctant by far to embrace the new religion. This is a problem, which calls for some preliminary clarification. Actually, the obvious question to ask is why people abandoned old religions and systems of belief in order to embrace new, not why they persisted in their traditional way of thinking. This is no mere quibble: when we consider the evidence, we see that numerous new converts to Christianity felt the urge to explain their motives and to call others to follow their example, whereas only occasionally did pagans consider it necessary to explain why they did not become Christians. It is most regrettable that most pagan works on Christianity have been destroyed and that those few which survive exist only in miserable Christian epitomes. Judging from what little exists, it is possible to make plausible assumptions.

In the ancient world religious conversions were not religious alone.

'In the cities of the ancient world, religion was inextricably intertwined with social and political life'.[6] The aristocracy had the leadership of this social and political life, which at first was not found compatible with Christian precepts. Next, as has been argued earlier in this book, and as will be argued in greater detail in the present chapter, conversions to Christianity were linked to feelings connected with matters of social mobility and instability. Members of the Graeco-Roman aristocracy, so long as they remained secure in their social ranks, lacked the motivation to seek a new way of looking at the world, religious or other. But perhaps one of the most important features of Christianity which made it unattractive to the upper classes was its lack, in its early stages, of the philosophical rigour to which they were accustomed. Christianity is presented in the New Testament in a form that was unacceptable, even incomprehensible, to people of education, such as most aristocrats. It is no coincidence that the three major attacks on Christianity of which we learn (those by Celsus, Porphyry and the emperor Julian) are of philosophical construction. Early Christians were not unaware of the problem. One of the dearest concerns of the second-century apologists from Justin Martyr to Tertullian and of third- and fourth-century Christian thinkers from Clement and Origen to Basil and the two Gregories was, as it were, the translation of Christianity into a language that could be understood and accepted by the upper classes.

It is possible perhaps to go a little further. The notion of class consciousness, as used in the analysis of contemporary societies, is of little application to the ancient world. The vast majority of the population, free peasants and slaves, were for different reasons never able to develop an ideology of common identity and interests. But if there ever was a social group in the Graeco-Roman world to which the notion class consciousness may be applied, it was the Roman aristocracy. Strictly speaking, the aristocratic elite was the members of the senate – which means a few hundred people, together with their families – but we may loosely extend this social group to include a large number of equestrians and some leading members of the provincial capitals as well.

All these people, those who lived in Rome in particular, had a clear notion not only of their administrative, political and social importance, but also of their cultural significance. Many were men of letters, and major philosophers came from among their ranks. Above all, the Roman aristocracy had a sense of history – of Roman history and of its own history; Tacitus was a senator, and Suetonius an equestrian. Along with a sense of history went a sense of destiny. Not that all these ideas were elements of 'pagan religion' – but they were certainly elements of a general culture to which what we call paganism itself belonged. When facing the possibility, or rather the challenge, of conversion to Christianity, members of the Roman aristocracy had not only to forsake their gods and cults, they also had to abandon their cultural and historical consciousness: Christians had a totally different view of history and destiny, derived from the Old Testament. The extensive literature on the subject demonstrates that we are discussing no minor issue: we need only recall Eusebius' two lengthy treatises *Preparation for the Gospel* and *Demonstration of the Gospel*, which discuss Hebrew and Greek world views. I do not mean to say by all this that the purely religious problems were of less significance; I simply wish to stress that the aristocracy faced an additional cultural obstacle to conversion. When, under the influence of the great fourth-century Fathers much of the secular tradition found its way into Christian culture, the aristocracy found conversion to Christianity much easier. After the Gothic invasions in the West, it realized that only through Christianity could it preserve anything of Roman culture; in the East, as the case of Synesius illustrates, pressure on the aristocracy came both from imperial circles and from their fellow countrymen. Synesius' major objections to becoming a Christian and a bishop were his pagan views on issues fundamental to all Christians; there is no reason to believe that he abandoned his pagan beliefs on being consecrated bishop.[7]

The Aristocracy

By aristocracy or aristocratic elite, then, I mean the Roman senators, and in a loose sense many equestrians as well. The term 'upper classes' I use in a much wider sense as including town councillors, as well as others qualified to become councillors.[8] Owing to the imprecise nature of the evidence, the term will here be used rather loosely to indicate the possession of wealth or of the higher education, which as a rule presupposes wealth. Discussion of the Christianization of the upper classes, I shall argue, is of great significance for the profile of the Christian communities. Once more, no statistical conclusions may be reached; I shall begin with a brief presentation of the evidence for the conversion of the aristocracy.

Christian tradition, as fixed by the late second century, claimed that equestrians and even senators had been converted as early as the reign of Nero. Clement of Alexandria writes that Peter had preached the Gospel at Rome before some of Caesar's *equites*, while the epistle of James implies that some people of equestrian status were present at the early congregations. In the *Acts of Peter* we are given the names of two Christian senators, Demetrius and Marcellus, and of two equestrians from Asia, Dionysius and Balbus.[9] How far these early traditions are to be trusted we cannot say; some scholars hold them to depart 'from historical truth by way rather of exaggeration than sheer invention',[10] but the possibility that they are a pious invention cannot be excluded.

From the age of Commodus on the picture becomes clearer and the evidence more trustworthy; as a guiding source historians use the quotation of Eusebius cited at the beginning of the chapter. Eusebius goes on to report the story of the martyr Apollonius, 'a man famous among the Christians of that time for his education and philosophy'.[11] Judging from the alleged presence at his trial of 'a crowd of senators, councillors and prominent philosophers', it seems that the case was of some significance; but Jerome is probably wrong in believing that Apollonius was a Roman senator.[12] To the same period belongs the famous statement of Tertullian, 'We are but of yesterday, and we have filled everything you have – cities, islands, forts, towns, exchanges, yes! and camps, tribes, decuries, palace, senate, forum.'[13] This exclamation may appear highly rhetorical, but a rescript against the Christians, issued by the emperor Valerian in AD 258, seems to confirm it. The rescript makes explicit mention of senators, equestrians and men of rank: if found to be Christians, such men are to lose their dignitas and property; and if they persist, their lives as well.[14] In the reign of Gallienus a certain Astyrius is mentioned by Eusebius as being a 'Christian senator', 'a favourite of emperors, and well known to all both for birth and wealth'.[15] We may accept the qualifications but probably not the fact that Astyrius was a senator. In the period before the so-called great persecutions, Christians, according to Eusebius, were granted favours and honours; they were 'even entrusted the government of the provinces' and what is more, they were freed 'from agony of mind as regards sacrificing, because of the great friendliness that they used to entertain for their doctrine', (we may take this to mean 'in spite of their doctrine').[16] Eusebius is exaggerating but he is referring to the years of his childhood – he may, therefore, be not far from the truth, although no Christian provincial governors are known. As early as in the early third century Christians felt uneasy about the participation of army officers and local magistrates in their congregations: according to the *Apostolic Tradition*, such people were to withdraw from public office or be rejected by Christians.[17] It is possible that some of these Christians were imperial freedmen: Eusebius clearly made the connection in his account. In the early fourth century, the *Apostolic Tradition*'s prohibition was repeated by the Council of Elvira (Canon 56), which forbade city magistrates (*duumviri*) from entering the church so long as they were held in office.

All the relevant evidence concerning the Christianization of the aristocracy has been discussed by modern scholars.[18] The list provided above is not complete, but most of the additional cases are highly conjectural and add little to the general picture. Even if twice as many cases were known, they would still not alter our impression that conversions among the aristocracy were exceptional. The aristocracy remained a more or less closed group with a strong attachment to traditional values. It is really after Constantine's conversion that it was grasped how elements of Roman tradition could be preserved through Christianity. But the aristocracy as a whole was a small and quite exceptional group; it is much more interesting and revealing to consider conversions among the upper classes. It was success among sections of these classes which gave Christianity its principal features on the eve of Constantine's conversion.

The Christian Community of Alexandria: Clement's Evidence

'Neither, then, should we be idle altogether, nor completely fatigued.'
Clement of Alexandria, *Paed*. 3.10.

The spread of Christianity among the upper classes outside the aristocracy is confirmed and documented by so many sources that it is impracticable to go over them all in detail. Apart from the wealthy Christian community in the city of Rome, we know from Eusebius that in Syria, Palestine and Egypt many of the martyrs were 'distinguished for wealth, birth and reputation, as also for learning and philosophy'. This was not rhetorical exaggeration, because Eusebius gives convincing biographical details which may be supplemented by the Acts of the Martyrs.[19] Since it is not possible to go through all the known cases, what I should like to do here is to examine just one city of great importance for the history of early Christianity, which has been far less discussed than Rome: Alexandria.

Alexandria was the prime centre of Christianity in the East. By the late second century, its Christian community had established enduring links with the Egyptian countryside and all the major cities, East and West. Prominent figures of other Christian communities gathered there to teach or to study in its catechetical school, which by the time of Origen had numerous distinguished students. The Christian community of Alexandria recruited its members from all social strata, all professions and occupations and all classes, from the poorest to the richest. Many Christian communities saw their own future in what Christianity was during the third century in Alexandria. The Christian community of Alexandria is fairly well documented; but even for Alexandria, of course, no statisitcs exist. A key source is the work of the Alexandrian Fathers. Modern scholars often regret that Clement gives so little information about the history of the Alexandrian church: in his massive extant work he even fails to give the name of the contemporary bishop in Alexandria. This failure is all the more striking when we recall that bishop Demetrius, of whom Clement wrote not a word, had kept his see for more than thirteen years when Clement left Alexandria in around AD 202. During this time Demetrius organized the urban community, appointed bishops in the country and communicated with Rome on important ecclesiastical issues, holding his see between about AD 189 and 232. Nevertheless, Clement gives one valuable piece of information which, so far as I know, has been inadequately explored. This information lies not in Clement's work itself, but in its possible audience. Scholars usually avoid such considerations; after all, what conclusion can be drawn even if we do detect the existence of learned, rather than uneducated, readers? A small number of educated people could have read these works, and then could have expanded and popularized their ideas for a larger and possibly uneducated congregation; our picture of the congregation would still remain dim.

It so happens that one of Clement's works is a fairly detailed exposition of 'rules for the regulation of the Christian, in all the relations, circumstances, and actions of life'. This work, called *Paedagogus* (The Instructor), 'is addressed', as its editor observes, 'to those who have been rescued from the darkness and pollutions of heathenism, and is an exhibition of Christian morals and manners – a guide for the formation and development of Christian character, and for living a Christian life'.[20] Rules about morals cannot possibly fail to give information about the social standing of those to whom they are addressed since they have much to say about everyday habits, actions and passions, as Clement writes in the opening sentence of his work. Their significance has been noted by several scholars, but most have not, I believe, drawn the appropriate conclusions. Martin Hengel, for example, thought that Clement 'was seeking a hearing among educated and well-to-do groups'[21]; in similar vein, F.C. Burkitt asserted that 'Writing for a society more or less leisured and educated, Clement warns his readers at length and in detail against the perils of licence, luxury, and extravagance'.[22] What these, and many other, scholars failed to notice was that the *Paedagogus* was not addressed to the Alexandrian community at large but to people in Alexandria who were already Christians. Harnack realized this but paid the question little attention, writing in a brief footnote that 'The *Paedagogus* also proves that the church, for which its instructions were designed, embraced a large number of cultured people'.[23] Some of them, it is true, may have been cultured, but, as we shall see, the major characteristic of these people was not their culture. One of the few scholars to have noticed that this work 'was certainly written for the well-to-do' was Dodds who, however, made this observation in a footnote as a qualification to the general statement that 'In the second century and even in the third the Christian Church was still largely (though with many exceptions) an army of the disinherited'.[24] Only Marrou seems clearly to have noticed that the *Paedagogus* was addressed to already-converted Christians and that Christianity in Alexandria had penetrated the upper classes.[25] In fact, more than half of the subjects treated in the *Paedagogus* reveal immediately the social status of its addresses: they include the correct use of costly vessels, ointments and crowns, jewels and gold, as well as other matters which though apparently of interest to the common people too – this category includes eating and drinking – leave no doubt, on closer examination, that wealthy people alone came in for consideration. It is of course impossible to go through all the rules, but a couple of examples will illustrate the argument. The first may be taken from the section on eating, which occupies a large part of the work.

Clement makes it quite clear that so far as he was concerned his instructions are meant to apply to the Christian community as a whole, not simply to one regional or social section of it. He reiterates this in passages scattered right through the work, as, for example, in the first sentence of the section under consideration: 'Keeping, then, to our aim', he writes, 'and selecting the Scriptures which bear on the usefulness of training for life, we must now compendiously describe what the man who is called a Christian ought to be during the whole of his life' (2.1, 237).[26] Clement then proceeds to give a vivid description of Alexandrian upper-class food customs:

> For my part, I am sorry for this disease, while they are not ashamed to sing the praises of their delicacies, giving themselves great trouble to get lampreys in the Straits of Sicily, the eels of the Maeander, and the kids found in Melos, and the mullets in Sciathus, and the mussels of Pelorus, the oysters of Abydos, not omitting the sprats found in Lipara, and Mantinican turnip; and furthermore, the beetroot that grows among the Ascraeans: they seek out the cockles of Methymna, the turbots of Attica, and the thrushes of Daphnis, and the reddish-brown dried figs, on account of which the ill-starred Persian marched into Greece with five hundred thousand men ... (2.1, 237)

So as not to leave any doubt on whether or not he is referring in this paragraph to Christians in particular, Clement goes on to reproach those who 'dare to apply the name *agape* to pitiful suppers, redolent of savour and sauces' (2.1, 238). It is perfectly clear (for parallels of such descriptions may be found in pagan authors also) that Clement is exaggerating. But it is also clear that these endless descriptions, page after page, can not be addressed to 'an army of the disinherited'. Lower-class people would not have been able to follow the arguments: they themselves had just about enough to survive – if that. (Even to middle-class people this kind of instruction would sound strange.) We are in late-second-century Alexandria, the home of great wealth and extreme poverty; the vast majority of the population in between consisted of day-labourers, owners of small properties who were neither starving nor extravagant. And yet, Clement gives his instructions the following form:

> For it is the mark of a silly mind to be amazed and stupified at what is presented at vulgar banquets, after the rich fare which is in the Word; and much sillier to make one's eyes the slaves of the delicacies, so that one's greed is, so to speak, carried round by servants. And how foolish for people to raise themselves on the couches, all but pitching their faces into the dishes, stretching out from the couch as from a nest, according to the common saying, "that they may catch the wandering steam by breathing it in!" ... For you may see such people, more like swine or dogs for gluttony than men, in such a hurry to feed themselves full, that both jaws are stuffed out at once, the veins about the face raised, and besides, the perspiration running all over, as they are tightened with their insatiable greed, and panting with their excess; the food pushed with unsocial eagerness into their stomach, as if they were stowing away their victuals for provisions for a journey, not for digestion (2.1, 240).

Again, when Clement writes of 'excessive fondness for jewels and gold ornaments' or of 'magnificence of bed-clothes, gold-embroidered carpets, and smooth carpets worked with gold, and long fine robes of purple', it is obvious what sort of people he had in mind. Once again Clement is not merely being rhetorical but explicitly referring to members of his Christian congregation he probably knew. There were Christian women who objected to a simple life: 'Why may I not use what God hath exhibited?' they asked; and 'I have it by me, why may I not enjoy it?'; or 'For whom were these things made, then, if not for us?'. Clement replies that such questions betray total ignorance of the will of God. Wealth was meant for charity, for 'it is monstrous for one to live in luxury, while many are in want' (2.13, 167 f.).

There is no need to go into any further details. The picture which emerges is clear enough. We must not, however, get the idea that the Alexandrian Christian community consisted in the main of rich families or individuals. On a number of occasions Clement advises his fellow Christians to spend some of their money on alms-giving. We have no reason to doubt that the poor mentioned by Clement were also members of the Christian community. (With all their good feelings and almsgiving sentiments, Christians were reluctant to feed the pagan poor; those occasions on which people in need outside the church were fed or helped are reported explicitly.) Nor should we think that the wealthy were predominant in the Alexandrian community: texts like the *Paedagogus*, with all their claims to present the Christian way of life, could be and were biased, reflecting the author's interests or social environment.[27] In Clement's case, however, the bias cannot amount to sheer distortion for his leading position in the catechetical school did bring him into contact with the whole community. We may thus draw the following conclusions:

i) The Christian communities of Alexandria in the reigns of Commodus and Septimius Severus consisted of wealthy families and individuals to such an extent that a work of instruction could refer to them as if they represented the most significant section of these communities.

ii) The personal interests of the leading instructor of Christians in Alexandria were directed towards the wealthy and socially most respectable among their number.

If we take Clement seriously in this respect we are left then with a very different impression of early Christianity in the major cities of the empire.[28] Of course, there are many scholars who hold that Clement's work cannot be read in this way, preferring to consider it from a clearly philosophical and theological point of view. However, even if, notwithstanding Clement's specific references to everyday life, his work is seen solely as a philosophical contribution to Christianity, it can still be held to presuppose an audience capable of following his arguments and his frequent references to classical authors. This is what lay behind Harnack's conclusion that the church 'embraced a large number of cultured people'. Clement himself, however, was of a different opinion; and this time there is no excuse for not taking him seriously, for his testimony corresponds with what is otherwise known about literacy in the Graeco-Roman world.

Before ending his *Paedagogus* Clement observes that some, perhaps many, of his fellow Christians may object that 'we do not all philosophize', others that they 'have not learned letters'; further on, he writes of his congregation as if it consists of merchants and of people who frequent the marketplace and the shops. If it was the case that the Alexandrian Christian communities included numerous rich merchants, shopkeepers or artisans, it may be expected that literacy could not be assumed, as it could among the aristocracy. On the other hand, Clement does not find it contradictory that people who do not know how to read can be possessors of great wealth: 'If thou hast not learned to read,' he writes, 'thou canst not excuse thyself in the case of hearing, for it is not taught'. This suggests that, beside himself, there would have been other instructors teaching and preaching in church or in the homes of Christians. In fact, Clement is one of the first authors to refer to the church as a place of worship. What he has to say in his *Paedagogus* concerns life outside the church, but just before concluding his instructions, he adds a few words on behaviour inside: 'Woman and man are to go to church decently attired, with natural step, embracing silence, possessing unfeigned love, pure in body, pure in heart, fit to pray to God'. But it was mainly behaviour outside church which troubled Clement. Because he knew from experience that 'after having paid reverence to the discourse about God, they leave within (the church) what they have heard. And outside they foolishly amuse themselves with impious playing, and amatory quavering, occupied with flute-playing, and dancing, and intoxication, and all kinds of trash' (3.12, 290).

* * *

A tendency to asceticism expressed in Clement's work has sometimes been understood as an exhortation to the rich to renounce their riches and lead a life of poverty: all members of the church, then, would become practically equal in poverty. But this is a very superficial reading. Clement never asked his fellow Christians to renounce their wealth; the opposite is true, for he even wrote a short treatise in reply to those who still took the Dominical saying on the rich man seriously. This treatise, *The Rich Man's Salvation*, has caused a problem for those who hold the traditional view about the social structure of the early Christian communities. The work's English translator who believed that 'the Church had spread among poor people and had always been chiefly composed of them', wrote in his introduction that 'The rich man who was well-disposed towards the new religion had to consider many things which, as Clement in this treatise admits, often drove him to the conclusion that the Church had no place for him'. On this view, rich people, approaching Christianity on their own account, found that their wealth created personal problems. But if the rich were so exceptional among second-century Christians, Clement's concern with wealth would be difficult to explain; therefore, the English translator concluded, Clement was 'personally interested in the question' of wealth.[29] It is, of course, most unlikely that a figure of Clement's status and significance would have written the works mentioned purely because of a personal interest in the matter; it must have been the established social conditions of Christian Alexandria which led him to treat of the correct use of wealth. Furthermore, the reconciliation of wealth with faith was not a personal problem: it was a general problem faced by the Christian movement. The party represented by Clement was replying to attacks by other groups, not necessarily heretical, which, as we shall see in chapter 7, represented in the main the poorer countryside. I should like to reiterate, finally, that just as in the *Paedagogus*, Clement, in *The Rich Man's*

Salvation, is not 'seeking a hearing among educated and well-to-do groups' but is addressing himself to rich people who were already Christians: he directly attacks those who 'behave with insolent rudeness towards the rich members of the church'.[30] Clement's view on the subject of wealth is clearly expressed in the following passage:

> For what wrong does a man do, if by careful thought and frugality he has before his conversion gathered enough to live on; or, what is still less open to censure, if from the very first he was placed by God, the distributor of fortune, in a household of such men, in a family abounding in riches and powerful in wealth? ... Why need wealth ever have arisen at all out of earth, if it is the provider and agent of death?[31]

These words brought Clement very close to those women who asked, 'For whom were these things made, then, if not for us?'; except that Clement did not leave it at that: as we have seen, the whole *Paedagogus* was meant as a guide to the *correct* use of wealth.

There still remains one point which should not be left without a brief discussion. Clement, in a number of cases, advised fellow Christians to give alms to the poor. Although these cases occupy only a few lines out of his work, they can be used to support the view that Clement's communities consisted equally of poor and rich members. But to realize how erroneous this assumption is, we have only to compare the treatment of the same subject in Clement of Rome and in Clement of Alexandria. In the work of the former, we get a glimpse of the views predominant in late-first-century Rome, in the work of the latter a glimpse of the views predominant in late-second-century Alexandria. Clement of Rome writes that 'The strong are not to ignore the weak, and the weak are to respect the strong. Rich men should provide for the poor and the poor should thank God for giving them somebody to supply their wants'.[32] Clement of Alexandria exclaims: 'How uch wiser to spend money on human beings, than on jewels and gold! How much more useful to acquire decorous friends, than lifeless ornaments!'[33] In Clement of Rome rich and poor are addressed alike; in Clement of Alexandria the poor are still present and the rich still advised to give alms, but the centre of gravity has shifted: Clement of Alexandria does not feel that he has to address himself to the poor. The social composition of the Christian communities and the significance of each social group within the communities had changed in the course of one century. As for the theology of poverty of which so much has been written, we have only to turn to *The Rich Man's Salvation* to see the way it had developed:

For when a man lacks the necessities of life, he cannot possibly fail to be broken in spirit and to neglect the higher things, as he strives to procure these necessities by any means and from any source.

And how much more useful is the opposite condition, when by possessing a sufficiency a man is himself in no distress about money-making and also helps those he ought?[34]

The shift in social composition had led to a shift in theology.

Linguistic and Archaeological Considerations

'We have often said already', Clement warned his readers, 'that we have neither practised nor do we study the expressing ourselves in pure Greek; for this suits those who seduce the multitude from the truth.'[35] There is an element of truth in this statement: compared to that of some contemporary pagans, Clement's language was inferior in both style and purity. And yet, compared to the spoken idiom, Clement's language was in line with the archaizing purist movement of the times. This observation is useful for the present considerations since, as Robert Browning has argued, 'a society sharply divided into classes needs status symbols ... So in the ancient world the living developing speech of the common people, who had no literary education, was despised by those wealthy enough to have had a literary education and who found in the distinction between their purist speech and that of the masses just the kind of symbol they sought.'[36] Written Greek tends to preserve the idiom of the most educated classes. In the first place, it was the educated, in the main, who had the ability and the time to write and such people obviously preferred the literary style to the vulgar speech of the masses; after all, that was what rhetorical studies were all about. Moreover, when the common people did write, they tended to imitate the mode of expression of the learned and write in an idiom other than the one they spoke. This tendency is to be found in private letters, and still more in official certificates, which were written, almost exclusively, in a uniform style, a technical language, which had little to do with everyday speech. Numerous documents and personal letters of the illiterate, written for them by professionals, have survived: the numerous mistakes betray a gap between spoken and written language. It is even possible that many illiterates could not even understand the language of the documents they signed.

In the last few centuries BC when the Greek language had been diffused in the East and adopted by numerous foreigners as a *lingua franca*, a new idiom gradually emerged known as the *koine* ('the common dialect'). One of the best-known specimens of the *koine* is the Septuagint, the most popular Greek translation of the Old Testament.

(The Septuagint and other texts of the period tend to bridge the gap between spoken and written language.) Primitive Christianity developed in a Hellenistic milieu in which the *koine* was dominant; the New Testament was written in a language which may not have departed far from the common spoken language of the period, and which was followed more or less by the post-apostolic epistles and Christian documents. Meanwhile, educated pagans were working hard to replace the *koine* by the Attic dialect of the classical ages. The tendency, known as the Second Sophistic, had begun in the years before Christ, but reached its peak as a strong literary movement by the mid second century.[37] In the Hellenistic age the *koine* had not left unaffected even the most educated classes, and had found its way into literature and philosophy; the Atticist or purist movement was an attempt to push the Greek language back a few centuries into the Golden Age. (Similar, though less striking, developments were taking place in the case of Latin as well.) The educated classes were attempting to restore the linguistic status-symbols which for a few centuries had lost much of their power.

The first Christian documents were written in an age when the Second Sophistic had not yet reached its peak. But it soon became evident that the language of the New Testament was an obstacle to the spread of Christianity among the upper classes, which by now had moved on to the purer forms of Attic dialect: 'Men who had been through the grammatical and rhetorical mill found the Greek and Latin translations of the Scriptures intolerable.'[38] Had Christianity remained a religion of the underprivileged and the poor, this problem would not have occurred. The apocryphal Acts of the apostles, written after the second century and read mostly by the lower classes, continued to use the vulgar *koine*. But the Church Fathers quickly started to replace, and finally succeeded in completely eliminating, the *koine* in their own writings and official documents. As Browning has remarked, this process started quite early and may even be detected within the New Testament itself: 'Luke often corrects what he finds in Mark', while 'the Pauline epistles are more literary than the Gospels'. Of the texts which followed, 'The *Shepherd* of Hermas is a monument of spoken *koine* as is also the *Didache*; Clement of Rome has occasional literary pretensions.'[39] The second-century Christian apologists, such as Justin, a converted Greek philosopher, attuned their language and style to the Atticizing Greek of their pagan contemporaries; in Clement of Alexandria such a development is patent. Although the New Testament *koine* was still the spoken language, all of Clement's works were written in a more or less scholarly language, which owed much to Atticism. This provides us with an indication of the social status of Clement and the other second-century Fathers; it is, moreover, an indication of the priorities of the Christian movement. The recipients of the Christian message were now to be found among people who despised the language of the New Testament. The fourth-century Fathers wrote and preached in the best archaizing literary style, even though it could not be understood by many of the common people. (Similar developments took place in the West as well: just as the Cappadocian Fathers modelled their Greek on Plato, Jerome modelled his Latin on Cicero.)

* * *

The archaeological material which might add to understanding of the spread of Christianity among the upper classes is scanty. The discovery of a catacomb on the Via Latina on the outskirts of Rome is of rare importance. From its frescoes, which depict pagan along with Christian scenes, Peter Brown has drawn the conclusion that this 'frank syncretism' was a peculiarity of the Christianization of the Roman aristocracy.[40] The peaceful way in which Christianity penetrated the senatorial elite assisted preservation of several pagan symbols. The conversion of the Roman aristocracy occurred after the chronological limits of the present work, but another piece of archaeological evidence points to the early conversion of the rich in Egypt. Many mummies and mummy-portraits may be classified as Christian from the early second century onwards.[41] Since mummification and mummy-portraits were too expensive even for those of moderate wealth, it may be inferred that in early-second-century Egypt several members of the upper classes were converted to Christianity, bringing to their new religion practices which originally belonged to Egyptian paganism. Once again we cannot say how numerous these upper-class Christians were, but we at least have evidence of their existence independent of our literary sources. Finally, though extremely few in number, Christian papyri from Egypt have also corroborated the view that members of the upper classes in the metropolitan cities were early converted to Christianity: the earliest papyrus referring to the affairs of wealthy Christians, found in the Great Oasis, dates from the early third century. This is a very early date for Christianity outside Alexandria and the fact that well-to-do people are mentioned makes it all the more interesting.[42] Unfortunately, no papyrus documents survive from Alexandria.

Social Developments in the Cities

The reign of Commodus, as we saw earlier, inaugurated an era of unprecedented Christian success in the conversion of members of the upper classes. Besides the scattered information about individuals all over the empire, we have the testimony of Eusebius, which seems to be based on much more detailed knowledge of the situation. Relying on the independent authority of Clement, we have seen that in Alexandria in particular the Christian community embraced large numbers of the wealthy. Archaeological evidence suggests that outside Alexandria too, in the nome-capitals, people of wealth had turned to Christianity. It is appropriate, therefore, to ask what was so special about the age of Commodus that injected Christianity with this new vigour. It would be interesting to know, furthermore, whether it was members of the traditional upper classes who were converted or Christians of lower birth who pushed Christianity upwards as they themselves advanced socially. Some of the new converts were philosophers of fairly high attainments and a small number of others belonged to the aristocracy, but we should concern ourselves most with the social origins of those Christians wealthy enough to qualify for the urban magistracies, for it was they who above all indicate the social advance of Christianity. In the next section I shall turn to this problem; here I shall try to examine more carefully the evidence about the Alexandrian Christian community in relation to more general social developments of the age of Commodus.

Clement's *Paedagogus* seems to have been written shortly before or shortly after the death of Commodus;[43] as we have seen, it was addressed to wealthy Christians in Alexandria. How long had these people been members of the church? It is fairly clear that most of them were not newly baptized; they had participated in the life of the community and had a voice in it for some time. On the other hand, they could not long have been Christians: arguments from silence are always dubious, but had a large section of upper-class people long been participating in the life of the Christian churches in Alexandria, it would, surely, somehow have made its presence felt. Yet before the last decades of the second century almost nothing is known about Christianity in Alexandria. Bishop Demetrius took over in about AD 189 and it is only from that date onward that Alexandrian Christianity emerges into the light of history. The silence of our sources has been interpreted as a sign of predominant Gnostic influence in the area.[44] But, orthodox or heterodox, the Christian communities in Alexandria cannot have been either very significant or very prosperous before Demetrius. The presence at about the same time in Alexandria of an obscure Christian philosopher called Pantaenus may be a first sign of Christian success with the educated; Pantaenus, in turn, was succeeded by Clement. We are left with the plausible hypothesis that wealthy Christians started joining the church in numbers during the reign of Commodus.

Clement's world, as we discern it in his works, was real enough. As we should expect, it was marked by sharp social inequalities: some lived in luxury, others in want (2.13, 268). Poor women and orphans are mentioned (3.4-5, 279), as well as women of high rank (3.11, 288). Workers in wool, spinners and weavers (numerous in Alexandria as we know) make a brief appearance (3.4, 278), but Clement was not interested in them. Almost all Clement's instructions concern people with luxurious houses, slaves to look after their needs, and plenty of free time to spend in barber-shops and taverns (3.11, 289). In this context slaves and domestics are constantly mentioned: cooks, table-layers, carvers; custodians of clothes, gold, horses; cup-bearers, eunuchs and servant girls (3.4, 278). Of those none appears to have been a Christian – or if he was, Clement had no advice for him.

And yet Clement's Christians do not seem to have belonged to the traditional aristocracy: the ideal was that one should be neither altogether idle nor completely fatigued (3.10, 284); and several among them, though wealthy, were illiterate (3.11, 290). Very little is said about their occupations, but we are given at least some hints. First, it appears that the need for frequent journeys was common; sometimes men were accompanied by their wives (2.12, 267). Such journeys may point to absentee landlords who once in a while had to visit their estates, especially since it is said that they were 'discharging other avocations in the country' (3.11, 285). Secondly, some frequented market-places and shops. Clement advises them to be honest in buying and selling (3.11, 290). They may, therefore, have been shopkeepers or merchants themselves. Thirdly, some were evidently engaged in public business; what kind of business we are not told, but those engaged had often to be away from home (3.11, 285). Finally, there were those who had to walk when going off to the country or coming back to town; for them walking was sufficient 'exercise', but if they also handled the hoe 'this stroke of economy in agricultural labour would not be ungentlemanlike' (3.10, 283). Such people were obviously landlords, living on their farms not far from town not normally tilling the soil with their own hands. The wives of all these categories of people, we imagine, had plenty of time to hang around. According to Clement they were, of course, to spend most of their time at home, 'to exercise themselves in spinning, and weaving, and superintending the cooking if necessary'; nor was it a 'disgrace for them to apply themselves to the mill' (3.10, 283).

From the information given it becomes clear that the kind of people Clement had in mind belonged to certain sections of the upper classes. They may have been involved in commerce, they owned land, which they either leased or cultivated under their own supervision; and they were sometimes engaged in public business, liturgies perhaps.[45] Traditionally such people, though they did not belong to the hereditary aristocracy, were on good terms with local authorities and, through them, with the imperial government. They participated in local cults and made public sacrifices in honour of the emperor. But now some among them, without abandoning their way of life, were converted to a new religion. Participation in pagan cults and public sacrifices was out of the question; if they were to follow Clement's directions they also had to part with their pagan fellow countrymen; amusement and public spectacles were to be avoided. Instead, new company awaited them: They were to meet frequently in church and exchange visits with other believers. This alteration in behaviour points to some kind of unrest, especially as the new life embarked upon was accompanied by numerous dangers. We are to ask, then, whether the age of Commodus was known for any such kind of unrest among members of the upper classes in provincial cities and capitals such as Alexandria.

The traditional approach of historians who in this respect follow our ancient sources tends to attribute to the personal characteristics of the emperors much of what went on in the Roman empire: Gibbon had more to say about Commodus' personality than about social and economic developments of his time. Even a social historian such as Rostovtzeff was tempted into the following way of talking:

> We need not be surprised that under the pressure of these circumstances Commodus, the son of M. Aurelius, who inherited his father's power but not his energy, resolution, sense of duty, and influence over the soldiers, decided ... to abandon the military operations against the Germans ... The answer of Commodus was a new Terror, and the developments of Domitian's reign were repeated.[46]

And yet Rostovtzeff was highly sensitive to the rise in the importance of the Roman army. By the age of Marcus Aurelius, the Marcomanni and other tribes on the Danube started to press dangerously on the Northern frontiers.[47] This military problem, which led to a gradual build-up of the army, brought with it financial difficulties. There were no institutions lending money, and the Roman government never borrowed any; it had either to increase taxation or to debase the currency. Rostovtzeff's description of the second alternative is vivid:

> To crown all these calamities, the emperors in their need for money issued a vast quantity of coin. Not possessing enough of the precious metals for these issues, they alloyed the gold with silver, the silver with copper, and the copper with lead, thus debasing the coinage and ruining in the end men who had once been rich. This measure cut at the root of trade and industry.

But Rostovtzeff, unfortunately, did not develop the argument further, for it was not exactly clear how inflation affected life in the provinces, where tension and unrest were clearly to be seen. Like many who followed him, Rostovtzeff preferred to insist on the problem of taxation: 'The only means of getting money was to increase taxation', he argued, in the course of attempting to explain the general discontent of town councils (who were responsible to the central government).[48] However, while there is plenty of evidence for debasement of the currency, claims that there was an increase in taxation during the principate are very difficult to substantiate: on the contrary, it seems that taxation continued unchanged.[49] As has been plausibly suggested 'any attempt to increase taxes threatened the privileges of the prosperous intermediaries upon whom the central government relied'[50]; it was not until a century later that taxes were finally raised. During the Principate the Roman government did its best not to threaten its alliance with the local privileged classes: by keeping taxes at a low level the government enabled local landlords to maintain their income, primarily from rents, at a high level; by the debasement of the currency the privileges of the provincial upper classes were not immediately threatened. During the reign of Marcus Aurelius the silver denarius was devalued by 25 per cent of its first-century level, by the reign of Septimius Severus by 50 per cent. After a period of economic stability lasting more than a century, the money supply rose steeply. From the age of Commodus, inflation increased to unprecedented heights. (The bankruptcy of the Christian slave banker Callistus, later bishop of Rome, may have been caused by such financial problems.)[51]

Today we are in a position to know that the monetary economy of the period in question was integrated, and that the money supply followed similar patterns throughout the empire until the reign of Septimius Severus.[52] With no increase in taxation, the financial difficulties of the central government reached the provinces: 'Towards the end of the second century and even more in the third, the system of local government began to break down. The cities had very slender financial resources, and it was decurions and especially the magistrates who were expected to foot the bill.'[53] Local notables became reluctant, even unwilling, to stand for office in provincial cities, and were thus often forced to become decurions and magistrates under ever severer legal compulsion. Decurions and magistrates were normally expected to finance local festivals, games and the erection of new public buildings; the immense rise in prices made the burden heavy even for the wealthy, especially if they were landlords letting land or houses. The third century saw a notable decrease in the erection of public buildings; in the field of literature and art little of importance was produced.

Duly qualified citizens, our evidence suggests, were not standing for office, obliging provincial governors to turn to legal compulsion: the

alliance of the Roman imperial government with the local upper classes
was shaken. It is probably in this context that we are to see the emperor
Severus's grant to Alexandria and other Egyptian cities of constitutions
of the municipal type – a privilege rejected ever since the age of Augustus. Mounting difficulties now made this concession preferable,
especially since responsibility for financial administration would now fall
upon wealthy citizens. But not all sections of the provincial upper classes
suffered to the same extent. As has been argued, 'the Antonine age was
a period of prosperity for the *primores viri* and ruin for the *inferiores*
within the councils'.[54] The *primores viri* had no reason to complain and
they must have maintained their traditional good relations with the
Roman government and its culture, and hence the imperial cult. But the
inferiores – members of traditional noble families or newcomers pressed
into the councils because they owned the minimum required wealth –
had good reasons for resisting: in fact, they were 'found among the
recruits to unrest and rebellion'.[55] If under financial burdens some
decurions and other members of the provincial elite lost their places
among the privileged groups, they had to be replaced by newcomers;
from the second century onwards, social mobility seems to have
increased among these lower sections of the upper classes.[56]

Social mobility, social tensions, unrest, lack of interest in public
affairs – all provoked rearrangements in belief-systems and religious
sentiments. Mithraism and other eastern cults witnessed success among
the educated and the upper classes, especially from the reign of
Commodus; the same is true, as we have seen, of Christianity. The
feature common to Clement's Christians is that, although they had
money to spend, they had no interest in public affairs. Instead of bene-
fiting their city, as their predecessors had done, they were turning to
personal salvation and almsgiving, a poor substitute for public expendi-
ture. Christianity had much to offer these people in this respect; all it
asked in return was a simpler, less extravagant way of life.

Obviously, there is no way of proving these suggestions. It is only
speculatively that we may attempt to relate social tensions and religious
conversions. It is, however, interesting to notice that documentation may
offer some support: from the very small number of third-century papyri
deriving in all likelihood from Christians, quite a few people of social
standing or of good Greek education emerge. The fact that upper- rather
than lower-class people tend to be represented in this kind of evidence is
not surprising: poor farmers and uneducated people had no pressing
reason to produce such documents, including personal letters. Still,
though nothing can be said about the proportions of rich and poor
members, it is at any rate attested that some Christians belonged to what
we may call the municipal elite. Among these few Christians represented

in the papyri we meet a few of magisterial status: one is 'threatened with appointment to the gymniarchy', another is 'an emissary of the *boule*' (council), yet another is under arrest at Alexandria 'on charges relating to financial matters'. Two minor officials of the tax administration also make their appearance, while a chief metropolitan magistrate belongs to a family of Christian landlords. It is most interesting to note that all these people belong to the social groups with which we were concerned in the present section.[57]

Patterns of the Christianization of the Upper Classes

From the late second century onwards, the poor and insignificant Christian communities belonged to the past – if the primitive communities outside Palestine were ever as poor and insignificant as has so often been assumed. Converted aristocrats and high administrative officials may have been very few in number before the late third century, but upper-class people in large cities were quite numerous and influential among the early Christians. Prevailing social and economic conditions throughout the empire increasingly created a restless, unstable society. Within the traditional upper classes important changes and divisions were in progress. Roman society already socially mobile became still more flexible, as some members of the provincial elite lost not only some of their old privileges but also their faith in imperial government. What I should like to do now is to trace some of the major routes by which Christianity spread among the wealthy layers of Roman society. I shall examine, first, the evidence for the view that Christianity benefited by the upward mobility of some of its adherents; next, the conversions of upper-class people through marriage or through the conversion of the head of a family; and, finally, the alleged conversions of kings and emperors.

A. Christians and Upward Mobility

Christianity – as the case of a few philosophers, a few aristocrats and a few people in high administrative posts demonstrates – sometimes had appeal for people at the very top of Roman society; it probably appealed directly to upper-class people in general. Although there is little prosopographic material on which to rely, it is hard to believe that large numbers of wealthy second-century Christians had been less wealthy before their conversion. According to Clement's testimony, it was common place for brethren, 'by careful thought and frugality', to have gathered enough to live on before their conversion; or, even more commonly, to have originated 'from the very first ... in a family abounding in riches and powerful in wealth'.[58] What needs more careful exploration, however, is the potential for upward social mobility among members of the Christian churches. From a sociological point of view, the subject is of some interest for the study of early Christianity. It would be of still greater interest if it could be shown that being a member of the church itself provided prospects of social advancement. Once again, a hint is given by Clement: some Christians, we are told, cringed before the rich members of the church 'through personal love of gain'.[59] There is little doubt that this practice became common after the conversion of Constantine,[60] but, as we shall see, it can be substantiated for an earlier period as well.

At first, with the expectation of the 'Day of the Lord' close at hand, Christians in the primitive communities had no interest in personal gain – though the story of Ananias and Sapphira in Acts suggests that even at an early date the love of money was not unknown (5:1 ff.). On the contrary, so strong was belief in the approaching End that some Christians of the first generation were 'idling their time away, minding everybody's business but their own'. In such extreme cases reaction was sharp: 'the man who will not work shall not eat' (2 Thess. 3:10 f.). With Second Thessalonians we see, perhaps, the start of a move towards the realization that the present world had still some while to continue its course before its destruction. The principle was no longer sharing but working quietly for one's living (2. Thess. 3:12). By the late first century, the Christian community in Rome included both rich and poor. This did not seem to cause major problems: most converts were still primarily concerned with the eschatological expectation. The letter of the Roman Clement to the Corinthians was preoccupied with weaknesses of the flesh, but there are no signs that Christians in this period had been neglecting their spiritual duties in order to concentrate on business or the accumulation of wealth; if some had been rich before their conversion, that was all right, so long as they cared for the poor.

Before long, however, as is attested in *The Shepherd* of Hermas, the Christian communities in Rome were in a quite different condition. By the early second century the eschatological hope, or at least the hope of its immediate realization, was fading away. (It was, as we have seen in chapter 2 of this book, occasionally revived among isolated groups.) Hermas reproached those 'who were faithful, but became rich and in honour among the heathen'. This new development created problems; not because some Christians were rich, but because they had become rich as Christians. The pursuit of wealth required business relations inimical to a pious way of life; contacts with pagans, even on a social level, could not be avoided; and consequently Christian businessmen, put on great haughtiness and became high-minded, and abandoned the truth, and did not cleave to the righteous, but lived together with the heathen, and this way pleased them better. But they were not apostates from God, but remained in the faith, without doing the works of the faith.[61]

The *Didache*, which belongs to the same period but originated in some eastern province (Syria or Egypt), instructed Christians to appoint bishops and deacons of the Lord, 'meek men, and not lovers of money'. A bishop's or deacon's office, it seems, was already tempting and perhaps profitable.[62] In Philippi a Christian presbyter was known to have been guilty of avarice during this period. Bishop Polycarp of Smyrna (*c*. AD 69-*c*. 155) warned his fellow Christians that 'IF any man does not abstain from avarice he will be defiled by idolatry, and shall be judged as if he were among the Gentiles'.[63] This means that either, as we have seen in *The Shepherd*, seeking wealth required contacts with pagans, or, as we have seen in *Didache*, church officials were susceptible to money making. We are thus beginning to catch a glimpse of a new development. Some Christians in the early second century were participating in business; some were guilty of avarice; some were taking advantage of their position in the Christian community. The spiritual leaders of the churches, especially those like Hermas who still entertained strong eschatological expectations, were facing new problems. It is important to notice, however, that even to Hermas, these Christians were not 'apostates'; Polycarp, too, advised Philippians to be moderate in this matter and to call back the guilty 'as fallible and straying members'. Wealth was not in itself an obstacle to faith; after all, Hermas himself was prospering from his own business,[64] while Tatian (*c*. AD 120–*c*. 174) declared that 'Not only do the rich among us pursue our philosophy, but the poor enjoy instruction gratuitously.'[65]

After more than a century had passed without clear signs of the approaching End, more and more Christians started taking care for the present life also. During the long periods of peace, numerous Christians concentrated on business and profit. Irenaeus confirms the general impression given by his contemporary Clement: writing before the end of the second century, the bishop of Lyons argues that

in some cases there follows us a small, and in others a large amount of property, which we have acquired from the mammon of unrighteousness. For from what source do we derive the houses in which we dwell, the garments in which we are clothed ... unless it be from our heathen parents, relations, or friends who unrighteously obtained them?

To have obtained wealth prior to conversion was common and quite blameless. But the most interesting part of Irenaeus' argument comes next. In the early second century care for one's trade or business, it seems, was exceptional; now it has become the rule. The passage goes on as follows

> – not to mention that even now we acquire such things when we are in the faith. For who is there that sells, and does not wish to make a profit from him who buys? Or who purchases anything, and does not wish to obtain good value from the seller? Or who is there that carried on a trade, and does not do so that he may obtain a livelihood thereby?[66]

But the periods of peace did not last forever. They were interrupted by outbursts of persecution, which the leaders of the churches, in the best tradition of the Jewish prophets, interpreted as signs from heaven. Eschatological fears and hopes were revived. In the mid third century, after more than a generation had passed peacefully, Cyprian, the famous bishop of Carthage (AD 200-58), writes:

> It has pleased the Lord to prove His family; and as a long period of peace had corrupted the discipline which had come down to us from Him, the divine judgement awakened our faith from a declining ... state ...
> Individuals were applying themselves to the increase of wealth; and forgetting both what was the conduct of believers under the Apostles, and what ought to be their conduct in every age, they with insatiable eagerness for gain devoted themselves to the multiplying of possessions. The bishops were wanting in religious devotedness, the ministers in entireness of faith; there was no mercy in works, no discipline in manners.[67]

It is interesting that whenever accusations of this kind are made by Christians against other Christians, bishops and church officials almost always make their appearance as well. Under the monarchical episcopate too much power was concentrated in the hands of just one man and his associates; control over all financial matters in which a church was involved made a bishop's post tempting. Much could be said about abuses recorded in the sources of this period, but the most striking case is that of Paul, bishop of Antioch (known as Paul of Samosata). Paul became bishop at about AD 260 and shortly after was condemned as a heretic. After several attempts he was finally ejected from Antioch in AD 272. According to Eusebius 'an exceedingly large number of bishops was assembled' to discuss Paul's case before his final ejection. Since he was found guilty of heresy, the synod did not consider it necessary to go into matters of his personal conduct, but made only a few remarks, from which we learn that

> though he was formerly poor and penniless, neither having received a liveli-

hood from his fathers nor having got it from a trade or any occupation, he has now come to possess abundant wealth, as a result of lawless deeds and sacrilegious plunderings and extortions exacted from the brethren by threats.

Paul was also accused of having enriched even the presbyters and deacons in his company. The orthodox bishops found this behaviour extravagant, but it was doctrine and morals in which they were most interested. As we shall see later on, bishops were very often wealthy without provoking the sentiments of the community; what was objectionable (but not unknown) was to consider 'godliness as a way of gain'.[68] But leaving bishops aside for the present, let us consider first the cases of ordinary Christians.

Artisans

Paul the apostle and his associates Aquila and Prisca may have been tentmakers (Acts 18:3; 20:34).[69] Lydia, an early wealthy convert of Paul, was 'a dealer in purple fabric from the city of Thyatira' (Acts 16:14). Through an analysis of Paul's language, Meeks has arrived at the conclusion that it 'bespeaks the economy of small people, not destitute, but not commanding capital either. This, too, would fit the picture of fairly well-off artisans and tradespeople as the typical Christians'.[70] Reporting on the early Christians, the Slavonic version of Josephus' *Jewish War* remarks that they 'were working men, some only shoemakers, others cobblers, others labourers'[71]; according to another report on the early Christians by Justin Martyr, 'not only philosophers and scholars believed, but also artisans and people entirely uneducated, despising both glory, and fear, and death'.[72] The Christian philosopher Athenagoras, writing in about AD 180, mentions that in his own days 'common men, artisans and old women' could be found in the ranks of Christians[73]; the church order called *Didache* declared that if a newcomer was only passing through he should be helped as much as possible, but if, being a craftsman, he wished to settle for more than two days he was to work for his bread.[74] In a passage recorded by Origen, the pagan Celsus writes of Christians that they were found in private houses among 'wool-workers, cobblers, laundry-workers, and the most illiterate and bucolic yokels'[75]; the context leaves little doubt that the 'illiterate and bucolic yokels' were also employed in similar occupations (it is known that in Egypt numerous peasants fled to Alexandria to work as linen-weavers). The early third-century *Apostolic Tradition* of Hippolytus states that among the accepted occupations for Christians were those of painter or other craftsman – provided they did not make idols.[76] The above testimonies are part of the evidence to suggest that artisans and craftsmen were to be found among Christians from the earliest days. It seems quite probable that in primitive Christianity artisans made up a sizeable part of the communities, while later on numerous persons of other professions were won over as well. It is of interest, therefore, to ask whether artisans in general, and Christain artisans in particular, had any prospects of social advancement in the Graeco-Roman world.

To begin with, urban craftsmen, in spite of the widely held view to the contrary, were not hereditarily tied to their occupations until much later – and even then with little success. This sort of compulsion was first enforced in the fourth century, and even then it only applied to the guilds of the western empire.[77] Thus, although it cannot be claimed as certain that artisans were occupationally or socially mobile, it is at least clear that no law restricted such mobility. From a study, detailed and unique of its kind, of Egyptian artisans I.F. Fikhman produced the information that follows.[78] Artisans did not work only in cities; many were to be found in villages, often occupied in jobs not immediately related to agriculture. (It may here be recalled that in the Apocryphal *Acts of Thomas* the apostle appeared as a carpenter. Asked what craftsmanship he knew in wood and what in stone, he gave the following reply, which was clearly meant to impress: 'In wood, ploughs, yokes, balances, pulleys, and ships and oars and masts; and in stone, pillars, temples and royal palaces.'[79]) For the Roman period 110 different artisan occupations are recorded, their number increasing to 180 in Byzantine times; this points to a great degree of specialization, though some craftsmen would generally be expected to command more than one skill. In spite of ambiguities and controversies, it also seems justifiable to assert that among artisans free workers were predominant. Among Egyptian artisans, especially those working in the production of textiles, many were women, usually worse paid than men. In Egypt artisans were generally poor: it appears that many had no house of their own; even more had debts. Attention must also be paid to the internal organization of artisanal clubs. (The most obvious word to use would be guilds if it did not recall so strongly the idea of medieval corporations.) During the Roman period such clubs had in Egypt a more or less democratic character which gradually faded away: juridical power, for example, exercised by club presidents in a later period, originally belonged to the general assembly. It is also attested that during the Roman period clubs fought for the rights of their members sometimes even resorting to what in good reason might be called strikes. Artisanal corporations originally had a social character as well, which also faded away by the late Roman period: their members used to meet at festivals, marriages and other important social events, but after the conversion of the empire it fell to the Christian churches to organize such meetings.

On the basis of what is known about artisans in Egypt, a number of plausible propositions may be formulated, applicable perhaps to other Eastern provinces. Artisans were not tied by law to the jobs of their parents. As they worked both in cities and villages, Christians among them could help spread their religion in the countryside. The textile manufacture seems to have been a privileged branch for conversions to Christianity; this may be related to the fact that women predominated both in textile manufacture and Christianity. Most artisans seem to have been rather poor; a small number, however, were wealthy enough to become creditors or guarantors and in this capacity, attested by papyri documents, some were pressed into the curial order during the period of general strain.[80] Thus, though in practice prospects for social advancement were closed to most artisans, exceptions were not unknown. Comparisons with other societies (compare the cases of, say, the Quakers, the Mormons, the Ismailis) suggest that, by belonging to a minority group, early Christian artisans, to whom other avenues were closed, might have been more likely to find themselves exceptions than their pagan colleagues.[81] This is, of course, no more than hypothesis which would need prosopographic evidence to be substantiated; unfortunately such evidence is lacking. Artisanal occupations carried no dignitas in the Roman world and were therefore normally not recorded; actually very little is known about the professions of early Christians unless they were philosophers, aristocrats, members of local councils and so on. It is thus all the more interesting to note that in the late second century an excommunicated cobbler of the Roman church became the leader of an important schismatic group. This group was joined by a banker and several other influential and highly educated personalities, appointed its own bishop and was one of the very first to pay its bishop a fixed salary.[82] The collaboration of a cobbler with a banker in religious matters seems to have been followed also by financial collaboration to secure the group's funds. Eusebius records these details only with reference to a particular heretical and schismatic group, but there is no reason to believe that such collaboration was unknown among orthodox Christians. Further evidence for individual artisans with prominent positions in the early communities is, so far as I know, unavailable, but the evidence for bankers is much more concrete.

Bankers

Some Christians, as we have seen, were wealthy before joining the church. After the late second century, to the astonishment of the most rigorous church leaders, an increasing number of Christians grasped the chance to be rich whenever it was provided and acquired riches even after their conversion. The case of Paul of Samosata suggests that it was also possible for some Christians to take advantage of their power within the church and improve their financial position. Referring to a heretical group, the Montanists, Eusebius records an accusation that through 'avarice' and 'robbery' their leaders made 'gain not only from the rich but from the poor and from orphans and widows'. 'Avarice', 'robbery' – these are strong words to claim that these leaders had 'taken gifts' or 'lent money'; such practices were common in orthodox churches as well.[83] I shall have more to say about church leaders later on; for now I shall examine the evidence for banking business in the early churches. We may use the term 'banker' here to include money-changers, usurers, savings bankers and other financiers who needed a small capital and a good reputation to enter the credit business. (It is to be noted that all interest exacted upon loans of money was considered by Christians as usury.)

The language employed in Christian documents suggests that transactions involving money were common from an early date. A saying attributed to Jesus (but not found in the Gospels) demanded of early Christians to be 'competent money-changers'; though uncanonical, this saying was frequently repeated by the Church Fathers, and as late as the third century it was used in a metaphorical sense by bishop Dionysius of Alexandria.[84] According to Pliny, Christians in the early second century bound themselves by oath 'to commit no breach of trust and not to deny a deposit when called upon to restore it'.[85] The accusation against the Montanists that they were lending money belongs to the second half of the second century. Lucian, in his work *The Death of Peregrinus* (*c*. AD 170), gives a graphic account of his hero's Christian years. Lucian was not well disposed towards Christianity, or to any other 'superstition', but the details of the story he gives – though written in jest – have their parallel in the story told about the Montanists, and represent an authentic Christian milieu of the period. Peregrinus Proteus, we are told, leaves his homeland in the Hellespont as a fugitive and goes to Palestine, where he becomes a Christian. Passing through all the hierarchical grades, he finally becomes bishop; as a Christian leader he is arrested and imprisoned. What happens then is interesting:

> from the very break of day aged widows and orphan children could be seen waiting near the prison ...
>
> Indeed, people came even from the cities in Asia, sent by the Christians at their common expense, to succour and defend and encourage the hero ... much money came to him from them by reason of his imprisonment, and he produced not a little revenue from it ... So if any charlatan and trickster, able to profit by occasions, came among them (the Christians) he quickly acquires sudden wealth by imposing upon simple folk.[86]

Proteus' interest in money is confirmed by Tatian[87], but what is of greater interest than this amazing personality is the fact that through voluntary contributions of 'widows and orphans', the common members of the communities, church leaders could become rich.

About fifteen years later, another Christian, the imperial freedman Carpophorus, started a banking business in Rome through his slave, the later bishop Callistus. (Slaves and freedmen were often employed by their masters and patrons as bankers.) Hippolytus, a declared enemy of Callistus, tells the following revealing story:

> To Callistus, as being of the faith, Carpophorus committed no inconsiderable amount of money, and directed him to bring in profit from banking. He took the money and started business in what is called Fish Market Ward. As time passed not a few deposits were entrusted to him by widows and brethren thanks to the reputation of Carpophorus.

It will be noticed, of course, that widows are always present in these accounts. All three stories, about the Montanists, about Peregrinus Proteus, about Callistus, were recorded by enemies who had reason to stress that poor and unprotected people were being exploited. There is no reason to doubt, however, that in all these cases money was given by the brethren as a gift to a leader or as a deposit. After Callistus' bankruptcy, many Christians went to Carpophorus telling him 'with tears that it was because of *his* reputation that they had entrusted their deposits to Callistus'.[88] The reason why Carpophorus had a good reputation might be related to the fact that he belonged to the *Familia Caesaris*, which, as we have seen, included numbers of Christians. There is a parallel to this in Mithraism: in Mithraic texts from the frontier provinces, where 'the financial agents of the Caesars must have been numerous', Cumont was able to identify cashiers, tax-gatherers and revenue collectors.[89] A further most interesting, but unfortunately hazy, case relating the Christian section of the *Familia Caesaris* to a banking business on a much larger scale dates from the late third century. The Alexandrian bishop Maximus (AD 264-82), through his assistant (and successor) Theonas, seems to have acted as a banker or depository for Christian traders in Egypt.[90] This Theonas, of whom extremely little is known, appears also as the addressor of a letter sent to a Christian chief imperial chamberlain. On Harnack's authority, the letter is a forgery, but even so it may preserve an element of truth. Theonas is reported to have given detailed advice on how the emperor's private moneys should be kept in order by his Christian servants.[91]

The banking business required two things: accumulated money for capital and a good name. Their position in the communities gave bishops and other clerics the reputation they needed (Origen admits that 'some became leaders of the Christian teaching for the sake of a little prestige'); the money they either got from their patrons or collected little by little from believers in the form of gifts. According to Justin Martyr, the contributions of wealthy Christians were deposited with the presidents of the churches (the bishops) who succoured orphans, widows and those in need.[92] Of course, it was always much more respectable and perhaps more secure to invest money in land, and many church leaders must certainly have invested in land. But banking and trade opened up opportunities for faster accumulation, especially to those with a ready circle of friends and believers. In the light of the prosopographic evidence discussed above, we discern that some further pieces of information acquire a clearer meaning. Thus, bishop Cyprian, thinking of the situation in Africa in the period of peace before the Decian persecutions, writes that

> Numerous bishops ... despising their sacred ministry, engaged themselves in secular vocations, relinquished their Chair, deserted their people, strayed among foreign provinces, hunted the markets for mercantile profits; tried to amass large sums of money, while they had brethren starving within the church, took possession of estates by fraudulent proceedings, and multiplied their gains by accumulated usuries.[93]

Information of this kind is always presented as an exception, but the frequency of such reports suggests that the practice was rather common: Cyprian speaks of 'numerous bishops', and half a century later a Council had to make special arrangements. Canon 20 of the Council of Elvira declared that 'If any cleric be found taking usury, he shall be deposed and excommunicated'; but then, on consideration of the numbers of ordinary Christian usurers, it added: 'If, moreover, a layman be proved to have taken usury, and promise, on being reproved for it, to cease to do so and not exact it further he shall be pardoned.' As for the clergy, the Council of Elvira felt that it should be permitted to engage in profit-making in more decent ways. Canon 19 declared:

> Bishops, presbyters and deacons are not to leave their places in order to engage in trade; nor are they to go the round of the provinces in search of profitable markets. To gain their living, let them send a son, a freedman, an agent, a friend or some other person; and, if they want to trade, let them trade within the province.[94]

Freedmen

On the basis of more than one thousand sepulchral inscriptions, M.L.

Gordon has argued that 'It would be a cautious estimate to conclude that about one fifth of the local aristocracy of Italy was descended from slaves'.[95] This conclusion has not met with general approval. It is not always easy to decide who was and who was not a freedman's son; and what is more, there is no way of telling whether these inscriptions were representative of the population as a whole. We may, however, agree with Finley that even if the percentage were reduced by half, it 'would not invalidate the conclusion that a significant number of freedmen had succeeded through their sons in attaining high social and political status'.[96] The great majority of freedmen must have been former slaves who either managed to collect large amounts of money to buy their freedom or impressed their masters with their knowledge and skills. By gaining their freedom they gained three major rights: the option of mobility, the right to possess property, and the right to have a family. Up to a point, the way was then open to social advancement and if most of these freedmen were already successful as slaves there is no reason to believe that they would not do their best to improve their social status. On the other hand, the legislation of Augustus restricted participation of freedmen in local government positions; Claudius excluded them from the Alexandrian ephebate (through which all those qualified for the urban magistracies had to pass); while Marcus Aurelius excluded them from high posts such as the Athenian Areopagus. Other emperors too restricted the privileges of freedmen by various decrees.[97] Thus frustrated, prosperous freedmen reacted by trying to get their sons elevated to positions of honour. (As a rule, restrictions did not apply to freedmen's sons.) The urge for social advancement, which must have been much greater among freedmen than among other people, therefore involved the whole family: by achieving social recognition the sons or grandsons of freedmen more or less eliminated traces of servile origin.

Up to the middle of the first century, according to Gordon's calculations, very few decurions appear to have been of servile origin. The position started to change in the second and third centuries, the centuries when Christianity made advances among those of wealth and rank; from then on numerous datable inscriptions point to a golden age for freedmen. It must not be forgotten that members of the traditional provincial upper classes were now being pressed into the city councils: prosperous freedmen, who would be the next to be called to contribute to city expenses, had their reasons for accepting this burden, and among them there must have been many Christians. Jones' impression that Christianity rose in the social scale and gradually conquered the curial order as prosperous freedmen began entering the city councils cannot be far from the truth.[98]

In the apostolic age a certain Erastus mentioned by Paul in his Epistle to the Romans seems to have been a freedman of wealth who reached high civic status[99], but for the second and third century prosopographic evidence is again lacking. We should certainly like to know more about the social origins of those Christians who, according to a document preserved by Eusebius, were among the 'eminent persons' of their city when the persecution of Decius broke out at Alexandria. These people, we are told, came forward to sacrifice immediately through fear; some because they held public positions and were compelled to do so by their business, others because they were 'dragged' by those around them.[100] In all likelihood, they will have included in their number *nouveaux riches* freedmen and descendants of freedmen.

The *Familia Caesaris*

What has been said about freedmen's prospects of upward social mobility applies to a still greater extent to the special case of the slaves and freedmen of the emperors. The privileged position of this group, obvious from the time of Augustus, became of great importance to the administration of the empire from the reigns of Claudius and Nero on; among the best known and most frequently discussed cases of imperial freedmen who became rich and powerful are those of Narcissus, Pallas and Nymphidius. But, leaving on one side these exceptional figures almost all members of the *familia* had better social prospects than most of the free *plebs*. Imperial domestics were often so well off that they were able to pay large sums of money to obtain higher posts or to influence the emperor in favour of friends: Suetonius reports cases in which ten thousand gold pieces were paid for a stewardship.[101] Starting with subclerical grades, imperial slaves and freedmen were employed in almost all administrative posts, including some senior grades (*a rationibus, ab epistulis*) and even that of procurator. The duties assigned them either brought high social status immediately or opened the way to it. A few imperial freedmen were awarded honorary titles by the senate, which probably meant in this way to please the emperors: Narcissus was awarded an honorary questorship and Pallas an honorary praetorship along with fifteen million sesterces. Pallas was content with the title; he had enough money to be able to decline the financial offer: according to Tacitus, Pallas was at that time worth three hundred million sesterces.[102] Instructive conclusions may also be drawn from the marriage patterns of imperial slaves and freedmen. Up to the middle of the first century these patterns did not differ much from those of common freedmen. But from then till the mid third century large numbers of known imperial slaves and freedmen are found to have married free-born women (*ingen-*

uae).[103] Through marriage imperial servants increased their prospects of upward social mobility.

The evidence bearing on the emperor's Christian slaves and freedmen has been examined in some detail in chapter 4. It was observed there that, during the reigns of Claudius and Nero, the Christian community within the imperial household was of some size and importance. From the mid second century on, we are repeatedly reminded at intervals never greater than twenty years, that there were Christians in the imperial household. To the evidence of Paul, Clement of Rome, Justin, Irenaeus, Hippolytus, Tertullian, Cyprian, Eusebius and Lactantius, must be added two sepulchral inscriptions. The better known of the two is that of the imperial freedman Marcus Aurelius Prosenes who had risen to the status of imperial butler, steward, treasurer and chamberlain. On his epitaph (dated by de Rossi to AD 217) the phrase *reseptus ad Deum* was engraved. Because of this phrase and the lack of any pagan symbols, de Rossi classified the inscription as Christian; other commentators have drawn attention to the fact that the inscription was written by Prosenes' slave or freedman and that it may not reflect the religious sentiments of the deceased.[104] But it would be rather absurd for a Christian servant to add this phrase to the sepulchre of a pagan master or patron! If this phrase was indeed Christian, Prosenes would have been an excellent example of an imperial slave or freedman, promoted to a number of important posts, who at some point joined the Christian church. Unfortunately, the classification of inscriptions and private letters as Christian is considered now to be a much more complex problem than was once thought: Wipszycka, among others, has argued that, particularly after the third century, monotheism and monotheistic expressions cannot be taken as designating Christians exclusively.[105] The case of Prosenes must therefore remain of doubtful evidential value.

A second inscription, to which G.W. Clarke has drawn attention, appears more reliable. The text reads as follows

> Alexander, slave of Augustus, erected in his own lifetime this tomb to Marcus, his very dear son, a pupil of *Ad Caput Africae*, who was a keeper of the wardrobe and who lived 18 years, 9 months, and 5 days. I beg of you kind brethren, by the one god, to prevent anyone molesting this tombstone after my death.

The key phrase is obviously 'I beg of you kind brethren, by the one god'. Here we not only have the word god in the singular, we also have a categorical remark that there is only one god. The expression 'kind brethren', moreover, would have no meaning unless addressed to brothers in God, a clearly Christian idea.[106] Marcus, we learn, had been a pupil of *Ad Caput Africae.* According to Weaver, slaves who were to serve in the top administrative posts were selected at a relatively early age; *Ad Caput Africae* was one of the senior training establishments for the young slaves of the *Familia Caesaris,* situated on the Caelian in Rome.[107] Marcus was thus already a member of a special group and had good reason to expect a high post. It is reasonable to expect that he would probably have married an *ingenua* and that he might one day have entered high circles with *de facto* power, if not with a high rank; high rank would have been a further, though not certain, development. Through the career of a man like Marcus, Christianity too would have risen to a position of power.

B. Family Politics

Upward mobility among Christians was not the only way the new religion penetrated the upper classes of Roman society. Mixed marriages (marriages, that is, between Christians and pagans) and conversions of heads of families along with their whole household also had positive effects on the social advancement of Christianity. In the early Republic, family ties in upper-class Roman society seem to have been too strong for outsiders and foreign cults to penetrate; but gradually marriage became a means of political alliance and lost much of its former closed and indissoluble character.[108] Christianity was able to take advantage of this situation; I shall attempt to trace here the policy of church leaders in this respect.[109]

The general instruction given to Christians in Second Corinthians that they should not unite with unbelievers ('Do not unite yourselves with unbelievers; they are no fit mates for you.' 6:14) never lost its significance; in Second John this commandment seems to have been extended to forbid even social intercourse with non-Christians ('If anyone comes to you who does not bring this doctrine, do not welcome him into your house or give him a greeting.' 10). But in the course of time less and less emphasis came to be placed on this Judaic inheritance. Indeed, Christians were always instructed to preserve, if possible, marriages already entered into before conversion, even when – perhaps especially when – the partner was a pagan. Paul gives his motives for the instruction in the following words:

> If a Christian has a heathen wife and she is willing to live with him, he must
> not divorce her; and a woman who has a heathen husband willing to live with
> her must not divorce her husband. For the heathen husband now belongs to
> God through his Christian wife, and the heathen wife through her Christian
> husband. Otherwise your children would not belong to God, whereas in fact

they do. If on the other hand the heathen partner wishes for a separation, let him have it (2 Cor. 7:12-5).

It is clear that in Paul's mind such mixed marriages could lead to the conversion of pagan partners; even if pagan partners could not be converted, it would still be possible to give children a Christian upbringing. Family unity was not of prime importance: if there could be no gain from a mixed marriage, divorce was accepted as the best solution.

In First Peter, which is of a later date, the same idea is repeated, only this time instructions apply primarily to women (3:1 ff.); in early Christianity women seem to have been the first to be converted to the new faith. The conversion of women in early Christianity raises a number of interesting questions. New Testament texts, Acts especially, refer persistently to women converts, as do several later documents. Two passages in Acts, for example, report that Paul had converted at Thessalonica 'a good many influential women' (17:4) and at Beroea 'women of standing as well as men' (17:12); such references imply both Jewish and pagan women. It is not exactly clear whether there was anything special about these women; their numbers seem to have matched and even exceeded those of men. The perplexity of the early New Testament copyists, evident from the numerous variants of these passages – the text reads 'a good many influential women', as well as 'a good many wives of leading men' – suggests that there might have been something odd about them. Had Christianity something to offer women which other cults did not? Were women of wealth and rank more easily attracted than others? Were women more sensitive, religiously speaking, than men? These questions need further consideration; at a general level the problem as a whole has been placed in an appropriate social perspective by Averil Cameron. Female activity, she has argued, found its major outlet in religion. Male dominance in public posts and positions of power must have been particularly frustrating to women of status or wealth; this circle of competent and cultivated women, excluded from social participation, created a pool of available converts, from which Christianity, as well as rival creeds, benefited.[110] Coming back to the original question, we must now assess how conversions of women to Christianity affected their pagan or Jewish families.

The official Christian attitude to mixed marriages never changed after Paul's regulations. But the fact that prohibitions had constantly to be reiterated bears witness to increasingly frequent violations. Clement of Rome refers to the problem in passing; Tertullian and Cyprian persistently and at length.[111] When converted to Christianity after marriage, women often faced major problems. Indicative of the situation is the story, reported by Justin, of the troubles a woman aristocrat had with her pagan husband; and also perhaps that of a certain Pomponia Graecina, wife of Aulus Plautius – though she was finally acquitted after being tried by her husband.[112]

Among the main issues of controversy in the Roman church was the Christian attitude to marriage. The dispute, which finally led to a schism, broke out as the Roman bishop Callistus adopted a line on marriage which was not in conformity with law. To understand the issue we should bear in mind the legal restrictions imposed on marriage. Slaves, as has already been mentioned, lacked the capacity to marry legally. A *de facto* relationship between slaves, the so-called *contubernium*, had no legal status and could be dissolved by masters at any time: by the sale of one of the partners, especially, slave families were often broken up. Christianity, following Roman law, recognized slave unions only when they were permitted by masters, and preserved the right of these masters to forbid such unions even when the slaves happened to be Christians themselves.[113] Even free persons otherwise capable of civil marriage might not be allowed, under certain circumstances, to intermarry. From the late second century freedmen and freedwomen were forbidden on pain of severe punishment (such as condemnation to the mines) to marry their patron, their patron's widow or his female descendants; the *Lex Julia* (18 BC) prevented freed people from marrying men or women of senatorial rank or their male descendants up to and including the third degree.[114]

By the early third century, these restrictions had already created significant problems among Christians. Christian women and, what is more important for the present argument, Christian women of rank, outnumbered Christian men, and especially Christian men of rank. At the age of marriage Christian girls of property or rank often had to choose between marrying a pagan of their own social status and a Christian poor or of low rank. (A third option, favoured by the churches, remained an exception: virginity.) Mixed marriages were rejected by Christian morals; marriages between women of rank and men of low birth flew in the face of public opinion, and were contrary to law when these men were ex-slaves. But there is no doubt that such unions existed. Women of rank, including Christian women, were often in contact with imperial freedmen and slaves; such relations sometimes led to unions, though not to legal marriages. This situation led to divisions among the churches. The rigorist side – represented so far as we know, by Hippolytus – demanded of these women to renounce their rank and marry legally. This position had weaknesses: slaves, imperial or not, could in no way marry Christian women of free birth, while marriages between freedmen and women of rank could be performed at the expense of rank. The other side was more far-sighted; its major advocate was bishop Callistus. In the account given by Hippolytus, Callistus

> even permitted women, if they were unwedded, and burned with unworthy
> passion, or if they were not disposed to overturn their own rank through a
> legal marriage, to have whomsoever they would choose as a bedfellow,
> whether slave or free, and that a woman, though not legally married, might
> consider such a one as a husband.[115]

The polemical character of Hippolytus' distorts Callistus' actual position
for it appears that Callistus in fact allowed a concubinate to be treated
by the church *as if* it were a proper marriage – in effect a departure from
Roman law.

Christianity was also concerned with concubinage. A Christian
concubine who was a pagan's slave was accepted in to the church if she
confined herself to her master alone; if, on the other hand, a Christian
man had a concubine he was called either to marry her, if she was a free
woman, or to leave her and marry legally, if she was a slave.[116] This
attitude appears at first somewhat contradictory: a concubine was
accepted if she was a slave to a pagan master, otherwise rejected. There
can only be one explanation consistent with Christian marriage policy. A
Christian slave to an unbeliever was accepted by the church because in
this way she could influence and perhaps convert her master; when the
master or patron was already a believer there was no benefit in permit-
ting concubinage. (By Roman custom it was mostly men of high social
status who kept concubines before their legal marriage.)

Christian women continued to outnumber men in the fourth century,
and the Councils of Elvira and Arles specifically pronounced on the
problem: Christian women were not to marry pagans, and in no circumstances were they to marry pagan priests. But it is interesting to note
that, if Christian maidens did in fact get married to pagans, the church
Councils declared that they should be kept from communion 'for some
time', while for other minor offences they were not received into
communion 'even at the last'.[117]

* * *

The religious unity of households was considered desirable and natural
in the Graeco-Roman world. A household would normally include the
whole family living under the same roof, along with its slaves and
perhaps some dependent freedmen. According to Acts and the Pauline
epistles, conversions were made of whole families at an early date:
Peter's preaching, for example brings salvation to a certain person and
all his household (Acts 11:14). In Philippi, Lydia (though a woman, she

seems to have been head of the family) hears Paul and is baptized along with her household (Acts 16:15); in the same town Paul advises the jailer to put his trust in the Lord Jesus and he and his household will be saved: the jailer and his whole family are baptized (Acts 16:30 ff.). In Corinth, Crispus, who holds office in the synagogue, becomes a believer in the Lord with his entire household (Acts 18:8), and Paul also baptizes the household of Stephanas (1 Cor. 1:16, 16:15). In such cases the religious unity of families was preserved as the conversion of heads of families was followed by collective baptism.[118]

To judge from later authors, conversions of whole households never lost their importance in the spread of Christianity: Clement of Alexandria writes that Christianity 'was diffused over the whole world, over every nation, and village, and town, bringing already over to the truth whole houses ...', Eusebius that 'many of those who at Rome were famous for wealth and family turned to their own salvation with all their house and with all their kin'.[119] Overall, the religious unity of families, though not an invention of Christianity, was carefully observed by its missionaries. Christian preachers were interested in mass conversions, so they took care to preserve the unity of families which provided the first congregational units. Meeting-places for prayers and religious instructions were at first the family-houses themselves; it was only gradually that house units were united into a single community in each city. Even then households did not lose their importance in religious practices: in *The Shepherd* of Hermas, for example, the head of the family is expected to oversee the religious observances of his house.[120] There is no need to stress how much Christianity benefited by the conversion of whole households.

Wives, children and servants seem to have followed their husbands, fathers or masters when they became Christians; very seldom do we hear of children in Christian families returning to paganism or Judaism. Christian parents were instructed to take good care that their children would learn the Word of the Lord; they were even to 'Bring them under with cutting stripes, and make them subject from their infancy, teaching them the Holy Scriptures, which are Christian and divine, and delivering to them every sacred writing'.[121] But this conception of the unity of families did not apply when children or wives alone were converted to Christianity, without the consent of fathers or husbands. The case of Perpetua and her father's efforts to change her mind are well illustrated in *The Martyrdom of Perpetua and Felicitas*; again, a certain Christian called Appianus found on returning to his house after his conversion that he could not go on living with his family and relatives because they had different customs.[122] There were many others like Perpetua and Appianus (both of whom belonged to the upper classes) who were never encouraged by the Christian churches to make peace with their families. Instead, the Dominical sayings which called Christians to leave their homes and to hate fathers, mothers and children (Mt. 10.29; Lk. 14.26) were often put into practice. Once again it was Clement of Alexandria who undertook to explain the precise meaning of Jesus' words.

> If, for instance, a man had a godless father or a son or brother, who became a hindrance to his faith and an obstacle to the life above, let him not live in fellowship or agreement with him, but let him dissolve the fleshly relationship on account of the spiritual antagonism.[123]

In the same vein the *Apostolic Constitutions*, after advising parents how to raise their children in fear of God, called for the dissolution of families when this was best for the faith:

> Let us therefore renounce our parents, and kinsmen, and friends, and wife, and children, and possessions, and all the enjoyments of life, when any of these things become an impediment to piety.[124]

It is obvious, then, that family unity was not an end in itself: if families became an obstacle to faith, they were of little value. (It should be recalled, however, that slaves who wished to become Christians were not allowed to leave their pagan masters.) It can be said that Christian family politics had it both ways: when the head of the family was converted, the whole household was expected to follow; but when children or wives alone were converted, they were expected to abandon their families.

C. Alleged Conversions of Kings and Emperors

Constantine's conversion was of decisive importance for religious developments in the empire: one of its most significant consequences was the gradual Christianization of the governing classes, especially those living in the new capital. Not a few members of the traditional aristocracy were converted by realizing that it was in their own interest to please the emperor. But it was principally among the 'new men' promoted by Constantine to high rank and office that the new religion proved most successful; these new men were not prepared to go against the religious inclinations of their patron. As emperor, Constantine had the financial and administrative power to give effective assistance to Christianity. The Christian emperor proclaimed himself bishop of those outside the church, explicitly acknowledging his missionary intentions. A number of important works have discussed the significance of

Constantine's conversion.[125] What does not seem to have attracted much attention is the recorded detail that Constantine turned to Christianity, not through instructions by human agents, but by direct communication with the Divinity. (This, at least, is what he himself and his biographers wanted others to believe.) The idea of a supernatural conversion has been neglected as insignificant for the religious history of the period, but, as I argue presently, it was an essential feature of Christian mentality – indeed, it can be traced back to the earliest years of Christianity. The story of Constantine's conversion followed a pattern which was well known among early Christians and was meant to serve a higher purpose.

The full version of Constantine's miraculous conversion before the battle with Maxentius is reported twenty-five years after the event by Eusebius in his *Life of Constantine*. Eusebius claims that he has been told the story by the emperor himself, when esteemed worthy of the emperor's acquaintance and familiarity. There is no reason to reject the possibility that the matter was indeed discussed between the emperor and his biographer, but I do not think that we can agree with Jones that 'The vagueness of the setting in which the incident is placed bears the stamp of truth'; nor does it seem reasonable to attribute the delayed publicity given to the story to Constantine's reluctance to communicate his experience.[126] The essential details of the emperor's conversion were made known almost immediately after the event. A few years earlier, Constantine was reported to have come into some sort of communion with the Divinity which deigned to reveal itself to him alone. The night before the decisive battle of the Milvian Bridge Constantine was, according to Lactantius, instructed to mark the heavenly sign of God on the shields of his soldiers.[127] Eusebius, who wrote Constantine's posthumous biography, claims that before the decisive battle the whole of Constantine's army had seen the vision of a cross of light in the heavens, above the sun and that the same night Jesus had appeared in the emperor's dream and given him directions which would lead to victory.[128]

In its developed form, the conversion story is closely parallel to the miraculous conversion of Paul as reported in Acts. Paul is on his way to Damascus when, in broad daylight, he sees a light from the sky, above the sun, shining around him and his fellow-travellers; all of them fell to the ground, but only Paul hears the voice saying that it is Jesus who has appeared in order to appoint Paul to his service. The miraculous conversion is reported for the first time, a few years after the event, in First Corinthians, though with none of the details. Paul had good reasons for claiming that he had seen the risen Christ in person. There were many who did not accept his apostlehood and who were to be reminded: 'Am I not a free man? Am I not an apostle? Did I not see Jesus our Lord?' (1 Cor. 9:1). If Paul had been converted by a human agent – say, Peter – in serious disputes (and there were many) he would have to submit to him. It was already common knowledge that only those who had not learned the truth from mortal men were really favoured (Mt. 16:17). Just as with Constantine's conversion story, the brief account given by Paul was subsequently further developed into a full-scale miracle (Acts 9:3 ff.; 22:5 ff.; 26:11 ff.).

According to tradition, Constantine was not the first king miraculously converted to Christianity. King Abgar V Ukkama of Edessa was believed to have written to Jesus asking to be cured of a sickness. In a letter known to Eusebius Abgar wrote that he had heard of Jesus' healings and that he came to the conclusion that Jesus was either God or the son of God; Jesus replied that Abgar was blessed because he had believed without having seen. A few years later, after the Ascension of Jesus, the apostle Thaddaeus was sent to Edessa to preach and heal; Having asked to see Thaddaeus, Abgar witnessed a miracle of the Pauline type. As Thaddaeus entered, a great vision appeared to Abgar 'and all who stood around were amazed; for they had not seen the vision, which appeared to Abgar alone'. The story's end explains why it was that the king had believed in Jesus without having seen and why the vision had appeared to him alone: 'Then Abgar commanded that on the (following) morning his citizens should assemble to hear the preaching of Thaddaeus.' It is almost as if Abgar was commanding his citizens to become Christians. Royal power Abgar already had; what he had lacked was unrestricted religious authority; that he found in his miraculous conversion.[129]

Christians in Syria and elsewhere in the early third century, and possibly earlier, were telling the story of yet another miraculous conversion, that of the oriental king Gundaphorus. The apocryphal *Acts of Thomas* reports the apostle's mission to India. Thomas is said to have been using royal money for alms instead of building the palace the king had asked for. The apostle was cast into prison for his actions. Meanwhile, the king's brother died and discovered in heaven a royal palace built in the king's name. On being brought back to life again, he asked the king if he could buy that heavenly palace; but the king asked in amazement, 'Whence should I have a palace in heaven?' Then, the king, considering the matter, understood where his money had really gone, and both he and his brother became Christians. It is interesting to note that, though the apostle had already met the king on his arrival in India, he made no attempt to convert him. The king was convinced by his own considerations: truth was, in a sense, revealed to him, not taught. 'Being now well disposed to the apostle', the story concludes, the king and his brother followed Thomas, 'departing from him not at all and themselves supplying those who were in need, giving to all and refreshing all'.[130]

* * *

Although King Abgar V and King Gundaphorus were both historical personalities whose reigns fall within the first century AD, it cannot be accepted that there is any element of truth in these stories. Christian dreams, it was also said, had almost converted Tiberius, and had made pious Christians out of the emperors Alexander Severus and Philip Arab.[131] We know little of the stories told about the alleged Christianity of these Roman emperors, but it seems likely that similar types of conversion would have been reported. What we do know, including the tale of Constantine's vision, is sufficient, I believe, to suggest the existence of a common pattern of ruler-conversions dominant in Christian thought. The explanation I offer is a simple one.

After two or three generations had passed with no sign of the approaching end of the world, Christian missionary activity, stimulated by the exclusiveness of Christianity, produced the unavoidable idea of a universal conversion; of this idea. Origen is only one of the best known exponents.[132] After almost two centuries of intense missionary activity, the spread of Christianity had met with notable success. There were, however, still some sections of the population which had not only remained largely unaffected by Christianity but had totally rejected it. Despite notable exceptions, the empire's aristocratic elite was the most important of these sections. The Christianization of aristocrats seemed to Christians to be as vital as it was difficult. If only the emperor became a Christian he would have the power to convince the leading men of the empire; but that power had to be not only secular but religious. Paul had once been reproached for not having been one of Jesus's disciples; he retorted that he had seen Jesus in person and been instructed by him. The Christian mentality invested pious rulers with similar powers, as Constantine and his successors understood – and exploited to the full. The Christian emperors helped Christianity to become universal and to win over the aristocratic elite in the East as well as other resistant groups of the population. In return, they secured for themselves the upper hand in ecclesiastical affairs.

After the conversion of the empire, neighbouring tribes and kingdoms too began to turn to Christianity. The general pattern is well known: first the king became Christian, then he called his subjects to follow him. The church historian Sozomen gives early versions of the conversion of the Iberians (in Asia) and the Armenians. In both cases the kings were led to Christianity on their own accord after miraculous divine signs and revelations; invested with religious power, these kings issued commands to their subjects to adopt the new religion.[133]

Power and Leadership in the Urban Christian Communities

The early urban Christian communities were of complex social structure. It seems that in most almost all social classes were represented. There do not seem to have been many slaves or many aristocrats, but middle- and upper-class people of various occupations are clearly attested, among them artisans, merchants, farmers living in the cities and day-workers. But our sources tend to ignore such people: as a rule, it was felt, there was nothing noteworthy to report about common people and their occupations. Research on the social structure of the Christian communities, then, has to rely on passing remarks and inferences from accumulated details; in the circumstances any prosopographic evidence that exists is warmly to be welcomed. In the present work, prosopographic material has been used as much as possible to illustrate the general impression given by other sources. The fact must be stressed, however, that this material, though certainly of great value, is not representative of the Christian communities as a whole. Prosopographic information is usually provided for exceptional cases: to quote Origen, 'Among men noble birth, honourable and distinguished parents, an upbringing at the hands of wealthy people who are able to spend money on the education of their son, and a great and famous native country, are things which help to make a man famous and distinguished and get his name well known'.[134] It is therefore for good reason that prosopographic information is generally treated by scholars with some scepticism. On the other hand, it is to be noted that most individuals appearing in the early Christian sources are church leaders, whether clerics or teachers, and considered from this point of view the prosopographic evidence is revealing. For though it is quite clear that very little information can be derived about common Christians, the profile of church leaders which emerges is a consistent one. By the late second century several urban Christian communities were disciplined and well organized. While a number of teachers continued to direct the moral and social conduct of Christians, a rigorous ecclesiastical hierarchy with bishops, presbyters and deacons was in control of church affairs. What information exists suggests that church leadership corresponded in some degree to high social status. During the same period there seems to have been a struggle for power between teachers and clerics; the outcome of this conflict in turn affected the social composition of the Christian communities. In the present section I shall deal with these questions, focusing once more on Alexandria, from where most of our information derives.

As the reign of Commodus was approaching its end, Demetrius became bishop of Alexandria and Clement took charge of a school of instruction or catechism in the same city. Demetrius and Clement represent two poles of power and probably two different types of orthodox Christianity, though no clear boundaries separated their adherents and almost nothing is known about any theological differences. Clement, being a highly educated teacher, can be seen as the heir of the charismatic and inspired prophets and Apostolic Fathers of the primitive churches. Of his predecessor Pantaenus very little is known: Pantaenus belongs to Weber's 'transitional phase' linking prophets to teachers of ethics.[135] It is reported that though Pantaenus 'had charge of the life of the faithful in Alexandria', 'he was appointed as a herald for the Gospel of Christ to the heathen in the East, and was sent as far as India', thus being one of the last long-distant missionaries of the early churches.[136] On the other hand, Pantaenus can be seen as being already half way through the 'transitional phase' in that, according to tradition, he expounded the divine doctrines both orally and in writing. (Written commentaries are a clear sign of the demise of the age of the prophets.) Having achieved some reputation as an interpreter of scripture, Clement became Pantaenus' successor by consent. Like his predecessor, Clement seems to have had little to do with the bishop of the time, of whom he says not a word; in his oral teaching and his written work Clement was one of the first to develop Christian theology in a systematic way.

Clement was at the head of an independent institution, a catechetical school or a school of Christian learning – it is not exactly clear. There are parallels to such schools in several other cities, including Rome. The chief aim of such a school was to educate Christians and to prepare catechumens for baptism. In this sense Clement's institution was close to Gnostic and other heretical sects. Unlike the Gnostics, however, Clement was convinced of the importance of church organization and hierarchy. As has been argued by Pagels, orthodox monotheism, as opposed to Gnostic radical dualism, offered theological justification for obedience to episcopal authorities.[137] In Clement's words 'the grades here in the Church, of bishops, presbyters, deacons, are imitations of the angelic glory'.[138] And yet, in the eyes of the Alexandrian Father clerics were not as sharply distinguished from laymen as the monarchical episcopate claimed. What mattered most was moral conduct, not institutions and offices:

Those ... who have exercised themselves in the Lord's commandments ... may be enrolled in the chosen body of the apostles. Such a one is in reality a presbyter of the Church, and a true minister (deacon) of the will of God, if he do and teach what is the Lord's; not as being ordained by men, nor regarded righteous because a presbyter, but enrolled in the presbyterate because righteous.[139]

In essence Clement remained a Greek philosopher, valuing knowledge and truth above all else. On the theological level he stood half way between the Gnostics and the orthodox bishops, denouncing Valentinian and Basilidian gnosis, but advocating true gnosis. 'As philosophy has been brought into evil repute by pride and self-conceit', he argues, 'so also gnosis by false gnosis called by the same name'.[140] Consistent with this belief, Clement, though aware of the distinction between canonical and apocryphal literature, quotes from both without any hesitation.

At the other pole there was Demetrius, said to have succeeded Julian as bishop of Alexandria. (Of Julian and the no doubt somewhat fictitious list of previous bishops nothing is known.) The monarchical episcopate in Alexandria seems to have been established during Demetrius' office: Demetrius himself was not appointed by other bishops (there were hardly any in the whole of Egypt) but by his fellow presbyters in Alexandria.[141] As the episcopate developed, it gradually came to integrate all a city's household congregations into a single community or church. In Eusebius' report, which draws on older sources, the Alexandrian congregation appears until the time of Demetrius to have consisted of several churches or communities; subsequently the plural forms tend to disappear and are replaced for the most part by the common singular forms.[142] This may be taken as a sign of the unification by Demetrius of the Alexandrian congregation. Preoccupied with matters of organization, Demetrius wrote nothing in the way of theology: his concern was to bring the entire community under the bishop's control. (As we shall see in the next chapter, he is said to have been the first to appoint bishops outside Alexandria. Christianity was already reaching rural Egypt and Demetrius was taking care to extend his control there as well.) He remained bishop for more than forty years and by his death could claim to be, in the full sense, the head of Christianity in the whole of Egypt.

Clement and Demetrius represent two distinct institutions, the school and the monarchical episcopate. The first was, or rather tended to become, in a manner of speaking secular. Like its pagan philosophical counterparts, it divided Christianity into sects using intellectual criteria; it had no hierarchy in the strict sense and was in need of no special funds: a member became teacher because of his learning. The prime aim of all the school's devotees was to learn; hence the prime importance of gnosis (in both its Gnostic and its more orthodox sense): gnosis of God and moral conduct. The monarchical episcopate, by contrast, can be termed more religious. It struggled to integrate all local communities into one church, it had a rigid hierarchy which depended on fixed salaries and organized charity – hence the prime importance of finance; its members were promoted to successive grades through internal mechanisms inaccessible to outsiders.

The conflict between these two institutions was normally resolved by the dissolution of the school and the acquisition of absolute power by the episcopate. Unfortunately almost all our information on this subject derives from the orthodox account by Eusebius. Even so, the general picture is quite clear. A few schools were strong enough to resist for a while. Some (like Lucian's in Antioch) were thrust out of the churches until finally, they disappeared, while others left the churches of their own volition and became schismatic communities (like that of Theodotus in Rome). In this last case, they had, in order to survive, to organize themselves just like the established communities, with bishops, salaries, and so on. (Note in this connection the schismatic Roman bishop Natalius.) But even in this way they were unable to escape the fate of their final dissolution: their battle was on their opponent's ground.

Demetrius must have thought of dealing with the Alexandrian school in some similar manner; only his position was still too weak and the catechetical school too strong. He had to wait. The opportunity to intervene came with the local persecutions in the reign of Septimius Severus. Unlike later persecutions, these fell only upon new converts, catechumens and laymen; bishops and other church officials were not sought out.[143] In Alexandria, those who suffered were students of the catechetical school, lately baptized, and others who were not yet baptized: neither Demetrius nor Clement are reported to have been troubled; and Origen, who was soon to succeed Clement, was present at the martyrdom of his pupils to the very end. (Origen, though almost put to death by the crowd as 'clearly responsible' for the death of his pupils, was not arrested by the authorities.)[144] At about that time Clement left Alexandria. Whether this was due to the persecutions or to increasing difficulties with Demetrius is not known, but Clement's alleged ordination as a presbyter in Palestine before his death and the fact that church leaders were not persecuted suggest that the latter is more probable. (Chadwick is right to interpret the ordination in the light of a desire on the part of the bishop to bring lay teachers under ecclesiastical control; but it must have been the bishop, not of Alexandria, but of Palestine.)[145]

At the time of Clement's departure from Alexandria, Demetrius had already been bishop for more than thirteen years and his position was by then much more secure. He agreed – not necessarily wholeheartedly – to the appointment of Origen as head of the school under popular pressure, but he imposed his own terms: no one could assist Origen without the bishop's approval. Several attempts to have the school reorganized were rejected; finally, Heraclas was chosen to assist Origen. Heraclas may have been Origen's pupil, but later events show that he was Demetrius' man: when Origen was condemned and obliged by Demetrius to leave Alexandria for being uncanonically ordained in Palestine as well as (some sources claim) for doctrinal matters (though Origen was much less 'unorthodox' than Clement), Heraclas was appointed as his successor. Later Heraclas succeeded Demetrius as bishop of Alexandria and the same pattern was followed by his own successor Dionysius (first head of the school, then bishop). The conflict between school and episcopate was thus resolved in Alexandria with the gradual fusion of the two institutions under the control of the episcopate.

In spite of the differences between school and episcopate, the two institutions had a common feature: the teachers of the school had to be men of great learning, the bishops be men of influence and authority; in the social structure of antiquity, both sets of qualifications could be found only among members of the upper classes. The existing prosopographic information, as I shall argue, confirms this view.

Clement was born around AD 150-160 and had an Athenian training, if he was not himself an Athenian. He remained head of the Alexandrian school for thirteen years (*c.* AD 190-203). His full name Titus Flavius Clemens, as has already been mentioned, strongly reminds us of the imperial Flavian family and in particular of Titus Flavius Clemens, the nephew of Vespasian and consul in AD 95. Clement had the wide learning only a wealthy family could provide. Origen was probably born in Alexandria around AD 185-6; he too had a Greek education, which indicates a wealthy family. He was head of the school for about thirty years (*c.* AD 204-232). Origen's father, who died as a martyr in Alexandria, had himself been a learned man, for he had been taking personal charge of his son's educational progress. How great their property was, is not known, but it was confiscated for the imperial treasury; Origen was subsequently taken care of by 'a certain lady, very rich in this world's goods'.[146] Of Clement and Origen's successors Heraclas, Dionysius, Theognostus, Pierius and Achillas little is known (Achillas was possibly succeeded by the later bishop Peter). Apart from the fact that they were all very learned, we are told that Dionysius had well-to-do pagan parents, and that it was his extensive reading that led him to Christianity; Pierius had elegance of language and was devoted to voluntary poverty; and that Achillas 'displayed a wealth of philosophy most rare and inferior to none'. Except for Theognostus, all the rest were clergymen and the first two, indeed, became bishops of Alexandria.[147]

Interesting information has survived concerning a certain Alexandrian, Anatolius, who in later life became bishop of Laodicea. Eusebius reports that 'for his learning, secular education and philosophy (he) had attained the first place among our most illustrious contemporaries'; it is also recorded that 'he had reached the pinnacle' in arithmetic, geometry, astronomy, logic, physics and in the arts of rhetoric. For this reason he was asked to become head of the Aristotelian school in Alexandria. But the most important information about Anatolius' activities comes from the time (AD 262) when the Greek quarter at Alexandria was fighting against the Romans, the rest of the population in alliance with them. Anatolius assembled a council of the anti-Roman Alexandrians and, failing to convince them to turn to the Roman side, he persuaded many to desert to the enemy: 'He took care that first of all those belonging to the Church, and then the rest remaining in the city' should escape.[148] (It is not known what position Anatolius held in the Christian community of Alexandria, but it is certain that he combined a degree of secular and ecclesiastical authority.) Of bishop Demetrius' social background, however, nothing is known; while of his successors Heraclas, Dionysius, Maximus, Theonas and Peter all we know is that they were very learned and that they enjoyed great authority within the Alexandrian Christian community. The cases of other cities, when information is available, suggest that bishops were often men of secular consequence. In Carthage, for example – we note that Tertullian, the most important Christian teacher in Carthage, was the son of a centurion — bishop Cyprian (*c.* 200-258) was reported to have been wealthy, with considerable landed property and a beautiful house and gardens; Cyprian was a converted rhetorician who never lost the friendship of high-ranking pagans. At Neocaesaria in Pontus, bishop Gregory Thaumaturgus (*c.* 213-270) came from a noble family; and at Rome it seems that it was usually distinguished men who were considered as candidates for bishops. By the fourth century most bishops came from the upper classes.[149]

The above evidence is admittedly meagre, but it indicates that Christian leaders were often members of the upper classes. Not surprisingly, this holds true above all for teachers, whose learning would otherwise have been hard to obtain. At a later period, and in particular after the fourth century, it is clear that major bishops were also members of the upper classes. In the age of the Councils bishops had to be competent theologians as well, but in the late second and the third century the bishop's authority did not necessarily depend on his learning. The office itself created authority by giving bishops control over church affairs and funds.[150] Thus, whether or not they belonged to the upper classes by birth, bishops, once elevated to the top of the ecclesiastical hierarchy, exercised power far greater than that possessed by middle-class, and many upper-class, people. I would therefore venture the proposition that the early Christian congregations were, as a rule, organized under the direction and leadership of people who commonly belonged to the upper classes, or else who had entered the upper classes by virtue of their office. This observation, if valid, is of some importance since it was in large measure the social status of church leaders which appealed to the outside world. Furthermore, Christian doctrine and theology, reflecting the views of teachers and bishops, incorporated much upper-class pagan culture not because the upper classes were predominant in the Christian congregations but because their leaders were of the upper classes.[151]

The outcome of the conflict between teachers and bishops had important social consequences. If the school had prevailed, the Christian communities would have assumed an intellectual character, with little place for the uneducated. The circles of Clement and Origen, as they appear from their writings and the scanty prosopographic evidence given by Eusebius, consisted of people who already had Greek learning and who were sometimes students of philosophical schools. The monarchical episcopate, on the other hand, was much more effective in bringing together members from all social classes, learned or illiterate, and uniting them under the authority of a strict hierarchy. The episcopate asked not for wisdom or education but for discipline. The subordination of the school to the bishop, as at Alexandria, preserved much of the intellectual character of the Christian communities and hence favoured the participation of educated and wealthy people – without, however, excluding the poor and underprivileged.

7

Christianity and the Countryside

The Spread of Christianity in the Countryside

Early Christianity was, by and large, a religion of the cities. The sources of the period, from the New Testament epistles and the canonical and apocryphal Acts to the works of Eusebius, leave little doubt about the new religious movement's urban character.[1] Most of the countryside remained pagan till the fourth century, and peasants often reacted violently to attempts at their conversion. But this was not universally the case. In the third century parts of rural Asia Minor, Syria, Egypt and North Africa were beginning to be Christianized. As early as the early second century Pliny reports that 'It is not only the towns (of Bithynia), but villages and rural districts too which are infected through contact with this wretched cult'; in the mid second century, while living in Rome, Justin writes that there are Christian assemblies in city and country alike.[2] But these were exceptions. Peasant religious conservatism is something usually taken for granted. In agrarian societies, Weber argued, peasants fell into a pattern of traditionalism and turned against the ethical rationalization of the cities, fearing proletarianization.[3]

The most widely accepted framework for the belated Christianization of the rural part of the empire is built around an opposition of city and country. (The same framework has been employed for investigations of fourth-century schismatic movements, some of which are thought to have been country-based.) It has been argued that peasants at first opposed Christianity because it was a religion of the cities and that, when converted, they were inclined to heresies rather than to urban orthodoxy.[4] This model is not without value, but it stands in need of further considerations and qualifications. For it is not only of interest why Christianity spread in cities faster than it did in the countryside, but also why some rural districts were more resistant than others; and since peasant societies in the countryside of the Roman empire were highly stratified, it should be inquired, furthermore, which sections were converted first. The richest or the poorest? Those in contact with Greek and Roman culture or those more or less isolated? So far as I know, the conversion of peasants has not been the subject of a special inquiry; at any rate not for the first three centuries AD. The present chapter touches on the problems mentioned above, but has strict limitations. Because of the significant regional variations, I have restricted my remarks to rural Egypt. This choice has been made because much more is known about social and economic life in Roman Egypt than about any other province; and besides, I have dealt with Egypt's capital Alexandria in some detail in chapter 6. From what is known of Egypt it is clear that no direct comparison can be made to other Roman provinces; the results of the present investigation, therefore, do not necessarily have more general application. What I try to do is to trace the earliest spread of Christianity in the Egyptian countryside and establish the stages of its expansion. I put forward a number of hypotheses which relate religious conversion to aspects of social change: the development of land owner-ship; the penetration of Greek culture and the revival of the old Egyptian language with a new alphabet; the Jewish rebellion and the integration of Egypt into a world system.

City-Country Relations

City and country in ancient societies were in a state of more or less constant confrontation.[5] This view, expressed in various ways, is shared by many scholars and has often been used as a key in analyses of social developments. Before examining the case of Egypt in particular, it is worth making some general remarks about relations between city and country in the Roman world.

A glance at a map which shows the location of cities in the late Roman empire gives the impression of an uneven distribution. North Africa, Northern Syria, Asia Minor, a small area in central Greece, Egypt – all had a dense distribution of cities and a more or less greater density of total population; in the rest of the provinces cities were sporadic. This observation gives an idea of the proportions between urban and rural populations which is particularly interesting as the areas with the most dense urban population are those in which Christianity spread faster to the hinterland. (Unfortunately it is not exactly clear what is meant by 'city' in the ancient world: In Egypt and North Africa, for example, it is often very difficult to distinguish between large villages and cities. But since we are dealing only with general tendencies, the vagueness of these terms does not affect the argument.) Generally speaking, most peasants had to some degree been influenced by urban culture, as they were engaged in constant economic transactions with the cities; but some remote villages may have remained culturally and economically isolated. In North Africa many villages were converted into cities in the second century AD, with the aim of securing the population from attacks by native tribes; these cities were inhabited to a large extent by peasants who went out daily for work to the fields. The hinterland of these converted cities must significantly have been affected by the dominant urban culture, for the peasants who worked there were in close contact with the Romanized population.

In the Egypt of the Ptolemaic period most of the population lived in villages. Some of these were called *metropoleis*, although they were not cities in any significant meaning of the term. In the second century AD what we could call urbanization was taking place, although the new cities did not much differ from the Ptolemaic *metropoleis* except in administrative and economic functions. The foundation of Antinoopolis in AD 130 was an expression of the urbanizing policy of Roman emperors. These developments are well attested. But when we look for explanations, we usually get Rostovtzeff's influential exposition:

> No doubt these rich Greeks desired to live, not the miserable life of the Egyptian natives, but the comfortable life of their fellow countrymen in Asia Minor, Syria, and Greece. They needed a city life and they created it. The government did not interfere; on the contrary, it promoted the movement from the time of Augustus onwards, for reasons which will presently appear.

Rostovtzeff went on to recount the administrative advantages of the movement which remodelled life in Egypt, 'on the pattern of the other provinces'. But, so the argument goes, 'In Egypt more than in any other land the cities were a superstructure', for they did not affect the life of peasants.[6] These quite commonly held arguments, obsessed with cultural and administrative aetiology, are no longer satisfactory; nor does H.I. Bell's explanation that 'Hadrian, with his philhellenic tendencies and his urbanizing policy, was a great founder of cities' take us any further.[7] Recent investigations discount such arguments and relate the growth of cities to taxation and trade. Being required to pay taxes in money, peasants had to sell their surplus in the local markets to raise the money; in their turn consumers of agricultural products in the provincial towns raised money to pay peasants by expanding artisan production. (Artisan production thus assumes much greater importance than it was once thought to possess.) 'Thus taxation increased productivity, threw extra produce onto the market and helped the growth of towns, as this

produce was transformed by urban artisans into goods exported in order
to buy money to pay their taxes with.'[8] This, I believe, is the secret of the
'urbanizing policy' of the Roman emperors. When taxes started being
raised in kind again the cities declined, or at least stopped developing,
some sections of the upper classes, as we have seen in chapter 6, being
worse hit than others. 'It is the fragmentation of the upper classes', Peter
Brown has argued, 'not necessarily any increased resistance or pressure
on the part of the villages, which marks the cultural and social history of
late Roman Syria'[9]; Egypt and Syria, in this respect, had much in
common.

As administrative and economic centres, cities, large or small,
exercised a constant influence upon the countryside. But if, from an
economic point of view, country was always exploited by city, from a
cultural point of view relations seem to have been much more ambivalent. Urban culture was at times the object of admiration, and attempts
were sometimes made to have it introduced even in small villages: Latin
and Greek names appeared in areas which can hardly have spoken anything but their native tongues. At the time provincial cities started
stagnating or declining, however, local cultures and native tongues
underwent a revival in the countryside: assimilation gave way to differentiation. These developments are far too complex to be treated here in
any detail, but they must be kept in mind through any discussion of
religious interactions between town and countryside.

The Case of Egypt

Thmuis was a town of Lower Egypt which later became of considerable
consequence and enjoyed a separate government of its own. In about
AD 303, just before the great persecutions, Thmius had a new Christian
bishop, Phileas; not long after his consecration, he died a martyr's death
in Alexandria – in AD 307 at the latest. In more than one way Phileas
was a typical Christian leader of his time: he was rigorous in matters of
ecclesiastical order, siding with the orthodox party against the Melitian
heretics; he took care to guide his flock, especially in persecutions, when
he stood firm and gave encouragement to those under arrest, pressure or
torture; when his turn came, he met his death with faith in God,
Christian dignity and a willing heart. What makes him an exemplary
paradigm of particular interest to sociological investigation, however, is
the outstanding secular position he held alongside his ecclesiastical
status. By cross-checking biographical information about Phileas from
several documents, we reach the following conclusions:[10]

1. Phileas was considered by his own flock and pagan officials to be

the undisputed ruler of the Christian community of Thmuis and an authority in Egyptian Christianity as a whole. Together with three other Egyptian bishops he took the initiative in confronting the later schismatic leader Melitius. He was reproached by the prefect for having brought about the deaths of many by refusing to sacrifice, his conduct being an example to the others. Even while a prisoner he was at the head of twenty clergymen, representing them all in the interrogations. Requested by the prefect to spare himself and all his people, he replied that it was in sparing himself and all those who 'belonged' to him that he refused to sacrifice.

2. Phileas, we are told, 'was distinguished for the service he rendered to his country in public positions and also for his skill in philosophy'. Elsewhere, he is admired for his secular learning and is said to have been 'ruler of Alexandria',[11] which probably implies that he had served there as a magistrate or perhaps as a curial.

3. In an attempt to persuade Phileas, the prefect said: 'Bear in mind that I have respected you. I could have subjected you to outrage in your own city, but I wished to respect you, and so I did not.' Explaining his motives the prefect continued:

> If I thought you were in need and had thus got into this folly, I would not spare you. But you possess great wealth: you can support not only yourself but almost the entire district. Hence I wish to spare you and to persuade you to offer sacrifice.[12]

Phileas seems, therefore, to have been a sort of a patron in his district, supporting the peasants of the area in times of need. Since his consecration had taken place only a few years earlier, Phileas must have come from a wealthy family; as a mere presbyter it seems improbable that he could have amassed the riches mentioned.

Combining these three elements – preeminence in the Christian communities, secular reputation and wealth – we arrive at an interesting picture of Egyptian Christianity. Christians at Thmuis and all over rural Egypt – numbering among them peasants and poor people, but also men of consequence – were, as I shall argue presently, led by church leaders who usually possessed social standing, secular learning and wealth. What made these church leaders effective in the practice of their duties was their own fixity of purpose, especially in times of trial, and their power to give financial relief to those in need. (Whether their financial power derived from their control over church funds or from their personal property is of little importance, but they seem most often to have been members of wealthy families.) For their part, rural church leaders were under the direct supervision and control of the bishop of Alexandria, as Phileas was under the control of the Alexandrian bishop Peter. To understand the scale and the significance of the phenomenon we must first give a brief account of the origins of Egyptian Christianity.

The Origins of Egyptian Christianity: Judaeo-Christianity

The history of the origins of Egyptian Christianity is the history of the gradual emergence of orthodoxy out of a Jewish and a more or less Gnostic milieu. In the saying attributed to one of the Gnostic sects that they were no longer Jews but not yet Christians we are to read three stages of development in Egyptian Christianity.[13] I shall attempt to trace these stages and their social significance. Our knowledge of the early spread of Christianity in Egypt, however, is fragmentary and dubious: it would be next to nothing if we had to rely exclusively on Eusebius' history and the works of the other early Christian authors, including the Alexandrian Fathers. Fortunately, papyrological and archaeological evidence has provided the basis for a number of plausible hypotheses. From papyri we can in fact trace the Christianization of Egypt from the earliest years of the second century[14]; as we shall see, the silence of early authorities is not unconnected with the nature of the origins of Egyptian Christianity.

The period under our consideration can be divided into two phases, the first extending from the earliest days until the Jewish rebellion under Trajan, the second from Trajan's reign up to the last decades of the second century, when the history proper of the Egyptian churches begins. During the first phase, Christianity in Egypt was in many ways dependent on the existence of strong Jewish communities in Alexandria and in the countryside. The first question to be answered is how Christianity reached Egypt in the first place.

The day of Pentecost symbolically marks the origin of the apostolic mission. Jerusalem at this period should be envisaged as the centre of a large area of commerce and of an even larger area of pilgrimage: it was a meeting place for Jews and proselytes from all over the empire. Among such gatherings, Peter and the other apostles are supposed to have started their preaching. According to Acts 2:10 inhabitants of Egypt were also present. Jews in Egypt were numerous and special territories had been set apart for their settlements, including part of Alexandria. The Jewish element in Alexandria was so significant and so notably Hellenized that under Ptolemy Soter their sacred scriptures were translated into Greek. Alexandria is also known as the city of the philosopher Philo (c. 30 BC-AD 45), a leader of the Jewish community and probably the principal mediator between Hellenistic philosophy and Christianity. Dispersed around Alexandria, on the shores of Mareotis Lake, there was a large Jewish sect, the *Therapeutae*, whom Eusebius, judging by their ascetic way of life, identified with the earliest Egyptian Christians (an idea now totally rejected). In a passage of Acts Stephen is reported to have been arguing for the Christian cause in the Synagogue of Freedmen with Cyrenians and Alexandrians, while 'The word of God ... spread more and more widely' (6:9); a second passage, as phrased in a western reading of Acts, refers to the Jew Apollos, the associate of Paul, as having been converted to Christianity in his native Alexandria in the mid first century. Two apocryphal Gospels associated with Egypt, the *Gospel of the Egyptians* and the *Gospel of the Hebrews*, seem to have had clear Judaeo-Christian characteristics. Pantaenus, the first historical Christian teacher in Alexandria to be connected with the orthodox party, may, to judge from the knowledge of Hebrew and Judaeo-Christian tradition he transmitted to Clement, have been a Judaeo-Christian himself. The structure of the hierarchy of the Christian communities in Egypt links them to Palestine rather than to Asia Minor and the Pauline mission, while recent papyrological investigations have confirmed the close relations between Jews and Christians in Egypt in the earliest years.[15] In view of the above we can infer with fair certainty that Christianity in Alexandria and Egypt had originally had a Jewish character.

After the Jewish revolt, the picture of Christian Egypt undergoes a sudden and profound change: a distinct Christian community first appears. The earliest discovered Christian papyri (with the possible exception of an even earlier fragment of a Christian copy of the Septuagint) date from the reign of Trajan: it is interesting to note that Christian papyri appear as the traces of Jewish papyri disappear. That Jewish traces disappear is not strange. The revolt ended with the destruction – some say extermination – of the Egyptian Jews. While for the first 150 years of Roman rule nearly 300 documents containing references to Jews exist, from the Jewish revolt in AD 117 up to AD 337 there are only 44.[16] After Philo, no Jewish personality of significance is known at Alexandria, and Hellenistic Judaism almost died out. It is therefore plausible to conjecture that the defeat of the Jews led to the emergence of Christianity as a distinct movement. By the late second century, the two communities were so far apart that Clement of Alexandria could write that he was making use of a few Scriptures 'if perchance the Jew also may listen and be able quietly to turn from what he has believed to Him in whom he has not believed'.[17]

The emergence of Egyptian Christianity from a Jewish background is further illustrated by the use of the so-called *nomina sacra* in Biblical manuscripts and the adoption of the papyrus codex instead of rolls for New and Old Testament texts. The *nomina sacra* were certain words of Christian significance contracted by the omission of certain vowels and sometimes of consonants also. The best known of these words were

Theos, Kyrios, Iesous and *Christos* (God, Lord, Jesus and Christ); the contraction was indicated by a line above the remaining letters. Similar devices are found in Hebrew and Greek texts, but of such a different character that they cannot be considered as the direct source of the Christian *nomina sacra*. In classical antiquity all manuscripts wre in the form of rolls; from the second century AD on, rolls started to be replaced by codices which had more or less the shape of modern books. In the second century the proportion of codices to rolls – to judge from what has been preserved – was just above 2% for non-Christian documents; while in the fourth century more than 70% of the manuscripts were in the form of codices. When we turn to the Biblical texts of the second and third centuries, we see that they are all, without exception, codices – though non-Biblical Christian manuscripts made use of both forms.[18]

Several attempts have been made to explain the reasons for these two innovations, ascribing them, as a rule, to practical considerations: the *nomina sacra* were a sort of abbreviation, while the adoption of codices made the search for Biblical quotations much easier. But it is not quite clear why these innovations first appeared in Christian Biblical literature. The best insight up to now must be credited to T.C. Skeat:

> The significant fact is that the introduction of the *nomina sacra* seems to parallel very closely the adoption of the papyrus codex: and it is remarkable that this development should have taken place at almost the same time as the great outburst of critical activity among Jewish scholars which led to the standardization of the text of the Hebrew Bible.[19]

The coincidence is even more interesting given that the standardization of the Hebrew Bible was in all probability a reaction to Christian success. We thus arrive at the tentative conclusion of a reciprocal reaction between Judaism and Christianity, centred in Egypt (neither the *nomina sacra* nor the codex were used regularly outside Egypt before the fourth century). As far as is known, what followed for the next sixty years was a more or less Gnostic type of Christianity with no clear signs of orthodoxy[20]; this may seem a strong assertion, but most modern scholars would agree that no distinct boundaries separate orthodoxy from heterodoxy during this period in Egypt.

Gnosticism and Orthodoxy

The anti-heretical Fathers and above all Irenaeus give the impression that Egyptian Christianity was originally under strong Gnostic influence. Judging from comments made by Clement of Alexandria, it looks as if 'almost every deviant Christian sect was represented in Egypt during the second century'.[21] All the outstanding Christian representatives in Egypt until Pantaenus (including Carpocrates and his son Epiphanes, Basilides and his son Isidore, Valentinus and his followers Ptolemaeus and Heracleon) were leading figures of the Gnostic schools or sects. A number of recent papyrological discoveries, translations of mid second century originals, all belong to Gnostic schools.

At this point mention must be made of the strong objections put forward by C.H. Roberts against the theory of the predominance of Gnosticism in Egypt. Roberts noted that most of the Gnostic papyrological fragments from Egypt were written in the fourth and fifth centuries, 'when orthodoxy was at the height of its power'. Only one out of the fourteen documents dated definitely before AD 200 (a fragment of the *Gospel of Thomas*) 'may be reasonably regarded as gnostic'.[22] This, I believe, is the strongest of the arguments Roberts brings against the theories which argue that Christianity in Egypt was originally of a Gnostic type. In my opinion, however, the manuscript evidence is interesting but misused: what is not taken into consideration is the relative importance attributed to written texts. The orthodox party (in this respect influenced by Marcion) was keen to put its tradition into writing at a much earlier point than the Gnostics. The Gnostic Basilides is said to have composed twenty-four books on the Gospel of which not even a fragment has survived. The reason is that his followers made very few copies of their documents, and even those they kept carefully out of sight. 'It is not at all fitting to speak openly of (the) mysteries', they thought, 'but right to keep them secret by preserving silence'.[23] Sects which depend on oral teaching cannot be expected to have left behind written documents; it was only much later that the Gnostics felt compelled to expand their literary activities, and even so, most of the Gnostic texts which have come to light belong to a single library, that of Nag Hammadi.

That Gnosticism emerged from a Judaeo-Christian milieu seems obvious enough from what has already been said. The Nag Hammadi library alone includes, suggestively, three Apocalypses of James, the leader of the Christian church in Jerusalem and the principal representative of the Judaeo-Christian trend. Apart from Jewish theology, Gnosticism made use of a great variety of sources, including Greek, Babylonian, Egyptian and Iranian systems of thought, though none of the above in its orthodox form.[24] The relative importance of each for Gnosticism is a matter of great dispute; however, it seems reasonable to assert that what motivated the Gnostic movement was the failure of Jewish apocalyptic hopes after the disastrous revolution in the early second century. This accounts for the ambivalent attitudes of Gnostics towards Judaism, from whole-hearted acceptance of Jewish myths to a radical rejection of the Hebrew Bible. One last point to be made about the character of second-century Egyptian Christianity is its adoption of an extreme 'syncretism'. This attitude is clear from an alleged letter of Hadrian to the consul Servianus and the archaeological evidence pointing to an 'extraordinary jumbling of Christianity and paganism'.[25] According to Irenaeus, Basilides attached no importance to meats offered to idols, and partook of them without any hesitation; he allegedly also considered the practices of other religious rites and of every kind of lust a matter of perfect indifference.[26] 'Syncretism' saved the Gnostics from the persecutions, but it deprived them of orthodoxy's exclusivist rigour and strength.

The first signs of an organized orthodoxy in Alexandria appear with the bishop Demetrius and the teacher Clement, both of whom assumed their posts in the last decade of the second century. The gradual shift of Egyptian Christianity towards orthodoxy went hand in hand with an increasing band of association between the Alexandrian and the Roman churches. From Eusebius, as I have already mentioned, we learn next to nothing about Christianity in Egypt before AD 180; the list of Alexandrian bishops which he gave up to Demetrius is a fiction, so is the story relating how Mark, the associate of Peter, was 'the first to be sent to preach in Egypt the Gospel which he had also put into writing, and was the first to establish churches in Alexandria itself'.[27] Another legend, also of the fourth century, attributes the first preaching in Alexandria to Paul's associate Barnabas.[28] There is no historical value in either account: with just one exception, no papyrus of Mark's Gospel dating before the fourth century has been found in Egypt, and Clement of Alexandria was unaware of either Mark's or Barnabas's mission. It is interesting to note, however, that Mark was supposed to have travelled to Egypt from Rome, while Barnabas was said later to have been joined by the Roman Clement, who also arrived at Alexandria from Rome. What these stories probably reflect at a mythological level is the original spread of Christianity to Egypt from Palestine (Barnabas) and the subsequent mission undertaken by the Roman church which introduced or strengthened orthodoxy in Egypt (Mark, Clement). It is probably to the late appearance of orthodoxy in Egypt that we must attribute Eusebius' reluctance to give information about Christianity's first stages there — though we cannot rule out the possibility that our sources' silence is to be explained by the fact that Egypt did not enter into Paul's sphere of activity, with which they are mostly concerned.[29]

The evidence for early relations between the Roman and the Alexandrian churches is scanty, but increases rapidly as we enter the third century. It has been noted, first of all, that the church of Alexandria was organized in parishes approximately in the same way as in Rome.[30]

Moreover, a second-century fragment of the *Shepherd* of Hermas, specially marked for reading aloud, has been found near Arsinoe: the existence in Egypt of a fragment of this document, written in Rome not long before, points to Roman influence in theological matters. A fragment of Irenaeus' antiheretical treatise has been found in Oxyrhynchus; this too dates a few years after the composition of the original in the late second century. (Irenaeus was not living in Rome but was a direct associate of the Roman bishops; the presence of his work in Egypt is an indication of anti-heretical campaign.) At the end of the second century, finally, Demetrius started corresponding with Rome on the Easter controversy, and some years later Origen, who had in the meantime succeeded Clement, travelled to Rome in person and remained there for a while 'Desiring to see the most ancient church of the Romans'.[31]

So far as the motives for Rome's interest in Alexandrian Christianity are concerned, nothing can be said with certainty. It seems likely, however, that Rome was responding to an ever-increasing Gnostic influence in its own territory. Valentinus himself had lived and preached in Rome at least until *c.* AD 165; his disciples gave his system a new vigour and leading figures of the late second-century Christian movement, as far away as Mesopotamia (such as Bardesanes of Edessa) had not been immune to Valentinianism; Marcellina, one of the Carpocratians, had also gone to Rome in the same period as Valentinus and achieved notable success.[32] Roman church leaders may have felt that a lasting blow against Gnosticism could only be dealt in its very homeland, Egypt. The later history of Egyptian Christianity shows that Gnosticism faded away, but how far this was due to internal factors and how far to Rome's intervention we cannot say.

Social Differences Between Gnosticism and Orthodoxy

Archaeological and other evidence suggests that Gnosticism was more successful among the less Hellenized natives of the Nile valley, while orthodoxy first conquered the city of Alexandria with its more educated, Greek-speaking population. Plotinus reproached the Gnostics for having taken much from Plato's doctrines, supplementing them with new ideas 'outside the truth', and added that 'what is said by the ancients about the intelligible world is far better, and is put in a way appropriate to *educated* men'.[33] This could be so, for Gnosticism, in spite of its Greek philosophical background, was open to syncretism, and Egyptian country people, closely attached to their traditional religion, could adapt themselves to it more easily. Orthodoxy, on the other hand, had assimilated theological and philosophical elements of Greek thought and was tending towards a rationalism alien to mysticism and magic.

However, there is evidence to the contrary. The Gnostic leaders were all Greek speakers with a philosophical education; their system was far too complicated for the uneducated peasant. On these grounds, it has been suggested that Gnosticism had powerful attractions 'for Christians of moderate or mediocre education who were troubled by the more sub-Christian parts of the Old Testament and repelled by the crudity of uninstructed believers'. Orthodoxy, for its part, had not emancipated itself completely from vestiges of old Egyptian religion. It may also be that 'reaction to Gnosticism led simple believers to make strident denials that baptismal faith required any supplementation and correction by higher and more philosophic knowledge'.[34]

The problem seems to call for more sophisticated explanation. Ordinary members of a Gnostic sect were not expected to read and understand Basilides or Valentinus any more than ordinary members of the orthodox party were expected to read and understand Origen. That both trends had their philosophers and their theorists is adequately attested; it also seems beyond doubt that simple and uneducated adherents were to be found among the Gnostics as among the orthodox. I am inclined to attribute the relative short-term success of each trend to the merits of individuals rather than to the content of the theology preached; in the long run orthodoxy prevailed, not because it was more appropriate to the bulk of the population than Gnosticism, but because it favoured – and its exclusive theology allowed for – a more disciplined and better organized community enjoying the support of the Roman and other powerful churches.

Social and Economic Developments in Rural Egypt

Before considering the spread of Christianity in rural Egypt, I shall attempt a schematic presentation of the principal social and economic developments from the time of the Ptolemies to the early third century. Religious transformations cannot be reduced to either economic or political factors; there do exist, however, factors, which in a sense activate, or at least make possible, religious developments. The present section is concerned with such factors, with the emphasis falling principally on the problem of land, which is of central importance in all agricultural societies. Three main questions will be raised: (a) who were the legal owners of land? (b) who tilled the soil? and (c) how was the surplus exacted from the immediate producers? During the period examined, it is unlikely that the standard of living of the bulk of the peasantry changed substantially: productivity, with all its seasonal and annual variations, did not increase or decrease beyond certain limits, and the surplus exacted, whether in form of tax, rent or compulsory labour was kept fairly constant. The bulk of the peasantry was probably poor, though it must be kept in mind that even villages were often socially stratified. What did change, however, as Egypt passed from one form of legal ownership to another, were the customs and laws of land inheritance, land sales and leases. One effect of the introduction of private landed property was the widening of the gap between the different classes and the transition from a relatively uniform to a more stratified peasantry; also affected was the family structure, its sense of security and some of its practices. I have for convenience divided the period under consideration into four phases.[35]

Phase 1

Agricultural production in Egypt had always been based on a complex system of irrigation, which was centrally supervised and kept functioning or expanded by compulsory labour imposed on peasants. The importance of the irrigation system remained unaltered throughout the history of ancient Egypt. Under the Ptolemies we can distinguish three categories of land ownership. By far the largest area belonged to the kings; next came the land belonging to the priesthoods; last, for the first time in Egyptian history, house- and garden-land was sometimes allocated to private proprietors, usually settled soldiers of Greek origin. To the above we must add the waste land of the later Ptolemaic era, which was either ownerless or dry through the neglect of irrigation. Land belonging to the kings and the temples was cultivated almost exclusively by native peasants. (These natives, though not free in the classical Greek sense, were not chattel slaves – a category almost unknown in Ptolemaic Egyptian agriculture.) Land belonging to private owners was cultivated either by natives or by Greek settlers with or without assistance. All cultivated land was subject to tax according to its legal classification and the type of its cultivation (arable, vineyards, orchards and gardens). Taxation rates on royal land were much higher than those imposed on sacred and private land, though strictly speaking what was paid was more of a rent than a tax. There were also a poll tax, a transfer tax and some other forms of additional taxation.

Phase 2

With the conquest of Egypt by the Romans, several changes took place. The land once belonging to the Ptolemaic kings, together with Cleopatra's private fortune, augmented by her latest confiscations, passed to the Romans. Some historians believe that part of the land was taken over by the emperor and his family as their personal property, but it seems more likely that the confiscated land became *ager publicus* and was brought under the *imperium* of the Roman people – which in effect meant the emperor and the senate; administratively, this land was controlled by the Egyptian *fiscus*. The temples continued to function as religious centres, but were deprived of most of their landed property; it is also possible that they were deprived of the control of some of the land which remained in their possession; control of confiscated land was vested in the *fiscus*. The priesthood thus lost the economic base of its power, which had been an effective means of controlling large numbers of peasants. Over the priests, including those of the Greek and Roman temples, was appointed a High Priest, actually a Roman procurator; in addition, Egyptian priests were now subject to personal taxation. In the circumstances it seems fair to claim that the power of the temples was 'crushed once and for all'.[36] The priesthood did, however, retain control over a part of the former temple land, which it leased and could perhaps sell. Those of the old Greek settlers whose land had not been confiscated were granted full right of ownership; whether Roman veterans were also settled in Egypt under Augustus is unclear. Though it is a matter of dispute, it seems that the two forms of granting land peculiar to the Pharaonic and Ptolemaic kings, gift and allotment, are unlikely to have continued under Roman rule: gifts of land (unknown to Roman law) and allotments were unnecessary for an occupying force.

A large part of confiscated land was sold to investors from Rome, and investment in Egyptian land was encouraged by the opening of a world market for Egyptian products. In this investment we can trace the origins of the large estates later to be found in Egypt; among the first major investors we meet relatives and close associates of Augustus. Efforts were made to reclaim neglected and unproductive land: natives were encouraged to buy such land with the incentive of ownership rights. Sometimes, when it was not possible to find buyers or tenants for unproductive or heavily assessed land, the Roman administration imposed the task of cultivation on tenants and owners of neighbouring parcels, even on whole villages. Enforced cultivation was known in the Ptolemaic period, but under Roman rule it grew into a regular institution. Augustus used troops to help clear some irrigation canals; apart from this, almost all agricultural labour, including the maintenance of the irrigation system, was performed by native peasants. The best land, which remained state property, and most of the privately owned land was leased to tenants; only a small part of privately owned land was cultivated by Greek settlers themselves. Alongside these forms of cultivation, farmers with very small holdings never ceased to exist. Agricultural slavery gradually made its appearance, but never became widespread during the Roman period. Slaves may have made up something like a tenth of the total population; but only a small number of them was employed in cultivation, since free workers both for continual service and for day hire were usually easily available: slaves in numbers and at prices to replace cheap tenants and day workers were difficult to find. This evidence comes mostly from the larger estates, but it cannot have been very different in smaller holdings, though small holdings seem to have employed proportionately more slaves than larger. In Egypt slavery 'appears not so much as a mode of production, but rather as a method of recruiting supplementary labour, particularly to help a family in the medium term through a crisis caused by death or by the needs of dependent children'.[37]

The conclusion to be drawn from this first period of Roman rule is that private owners, whether of large estates or small holdings, largely replaced the Ptolemaic kings and the temples. Though exact calculations cannot be made, it seems that this process continued during the following years. It has thus been justly claimed that the institution of the private ownership of land was 'one of the most radical changes introduced in Egypt by the Romans'.[38] It should also be observed that the area where Christianity later spread most significantly, the Arsinoite (the Hadrianic Antinoopolis was soon to follow), had a heavy concentration of Graeco-Macedonian inhabitants, as of privately owned land. This area (and that surrounding Antinoopolis) also became known in the fourth century for its Christian ascetic movement.

Phase 3

The mid first century AD may be considered as the beginning of a new period in Roman Egypt. Once private ownership of land was introduced in Egypt, it became custom among farmers to bequeath their landed property to all their children. To this fragmentation of land, we must add the measures, inaugurated under Nero, which led to the liquidation of many of the large estates. These measures were meant to favour resident rather than absentee landlords; the motive must have been to facilitate taxation, which had become difficult to administer because many absentee owners were influential senators and members of the imperial families. Evidence from mid-first-century Egypt makes clear that there was an active market in land: in Tebtunis, a village of the Arsinoite nome, roughly one tenth of the agricultural land was either leased or sold in a single year (AD 75/76); although the class of landowners did not cease to expand, no new large estates were formed until the third century. Nero's reign is also known for what has been called an economic crisis in Egypt, which led to complaints from upper and lower classes alike. Peasants responded to the crisis by flight (*anachoresis*), a traditional reaction which became frequent under Nero.

(We may note in passing that the third and fourth century Christian anchorites (*anachoretai*) were following the example of the distressed and oppressed villagers of earlier times.) Edicts from the time of Nerva in AD 104 are known to have ordered peasants to return to their lands; hereditary ties to a locality were originally meant to facilitate the administration and collection of the poll tax.

Phase 4

Our last phase starts with the Jewish War, which accelerated a process of decay already manifest in the previous period. The Jewish War was followed not long after by an insurrection of Egyptian fellaheen which during the reign of Antoninus Pius endangered the corn supply of Rome. Under Hadrian, part of the former royal land was converted into quasi-private holdings; this land was taxed like private property. The intention was to lower the rent – now called tax – and thus help overcome the agricultural difficulties; Hadrian apparently went even further by selling unproductive former royal land to private purchasers. Such measures became necessary because large areas seem to have been left uncultivated and gradually abandoned by farmers. Private ownership of land was also strengthened by the settlement of discharged veterans, some at least of whom received allotments of land in such cities as the newly founded Antinoopolis. Veterans settled under Hadrian and Antoninus Pius, and more systematically under Septimius Severus, are believed to have been recruited from the Greek and Graeco-Egyptian elements of the population. Constant efforts were made to force fugitive peasants to return to their lands. Temples, for their part, continued to possess landed property up to the mid fifth century but in the second century their financial administration was assigned to Roman procurators. The financial administration of temples must have been highly complicated, owing to the different methods of revenue collection from each one. It has been suggested that the reason for employing different methods was the government's desire to foster jealousy between temples. The Bucolic Revolt, which took place in the years of Marcus Aurelius and spread to become a country-wide movement, is proof that such precautions were necessary, since the rising assumed a religious character and was led by a priest. Hadrian's and subsequent reforms had not been totally successful. However, the general tendency which led to the establishment of peasant proprietors was well under way and continued uninterrupted almost until the fifth century. In the early fourth century the bulk of Egyptian land was held by peasant proprietors; it was not until the sixth century that the situation changed much.

The Financial Position of the Christian Churches

The Christian churches of the fifth, sixth and early seventh centuries succeeded the Egyptian temples in their function as landowners and organizers of agricultural production.[39] The question is whether the Christian churches acquired this function before or after the conversion of the empire. We know next to nothing about the landed property of the Egyptian Christian community in the second and third centuries. No extant papyrus of the period gives clear information about the Christian churches' economic activities in Egypt – a few hints apart. But inferences from ancient sources suggest that the churches were involved in agricultural production from an early date. Taking the information provided by ancient authors in close connection with later developments, the following conclusions may be drawn:

1. The Christian churches had an income from New Testament days, the main – for some time the exclusive – source of which was the offerings of the faithful. These offerings, which were in kind or money or both, were administered at first by specially appointed members. Some of the offerings were distributed to those in need, some kept to support the missionaries and the teachers. It is possible that donations included land, though sometimes it may have been sold; land was also bought with the money collected, as it was needed for burial purposes.[40] According to early second-century regulations, officials of the Christian churches were sustained by the brotherhood: these officials were given both money and food. Christian farmers gave their first fruits to this end – a practice which proved an enduring one. The administration of church finance passed to church officials and, when the monarchical episcopate was established, to bishops. From the mid second century at the latest fixed salaries were being paid to some church officials, while from the end of the second century at least one bishop is known to have been paid a fixed salary. Presbyters in Carthage were paid a monthly stipend in the age of Cyprian.[41]

2. The Christian churches quickly developed two further, very important sources of income: banking and urban property. Of banking and the involvement in it of influential Christians, enough has been said in chapter 6. But a few details should be given about the financial significance of urban property. Contrary to standard views, revenue from urban property, Garnsey has demonstrated, was far more important to the Roman economy and to the wealthy classes than their ideology allowed to be revealed in public statements. Urban property brought in a higher return than rural: Cicero's urban property, for example, contributed almost as much as his extensive country estates. The problem with urban property was that it was less secure and brought no prestige, and

so aristocratic funds were usually diverted to the rural sphere. However, as the case of Cicero illustrates, even aristocrats could benefit considerably from urban investments.[42]

The Christian communities moreover were owners of church buildings from an early date. At first, ordinary houses were converted for the purpose, but by the second century special buildings were purchased and sometimes erected. At the time of the great persecutions the Christian communities were in possession of urban estates rented to artisans or lodgers. Although the exact legal titles of church property are not known, it is certain that by the time of the emperor Aurelian, Christians could, as legal owners, appeal to the Roman administration about their property.[43] One of the few early Christian papyri from Egypt gives an idea of what a village church could be expected to possess in the early fourth century. The text was written in the name of a lector of the former church of the village of Chysis near Oxyrhynchus in AD 304; the relevant section reads as follows:

> I reported that the said church had neither gold nor silver nor money nor clothes nor beasts nor slaves nor land nor property either from grants or bequests, excepting only the bronze gate which was found and delivered to the logistes to be carried down to the most glorious Alexandria.[44]

Written during the persecutions and the confiscations, the text is probably insincere: the only thing that the lector admits that the church possesses is the bronze gate, which obviously cannot be hidden. What exactly the church did possess we cannot tell, but the list given includes items that were in fact owned by Christian communities at that date.

3. Landed property used for cemeteries the Christian churches possessed from the earliest days. Christians held assemblies in cemeteries to commemorate their martyrs: at times of persecution prefects took care to forbid them from even entering the cemeteries, where they were known to assemble for prayers; one well known case is that connected with the Alexandrian bishop Dionysius.[45] During the late persecutions, the Christian churches were in possession of land used for agricultural purposes; it was restored to them by Constantine and Licinius. Further information is not available, but from what has already been said it is clear that the churches lacked neither the funds nor the organization to become landowners. With the exception of the periods of severe persecution, they could administer their property according to Roman law without obstruction. If aristocrats always took good care to invest the wealth obtained from banking or urban estates in land, why should it have been any different with the Christian churches? Starting from the fourth century, and with imperial aid, the Egyptian churches

became very important landowners. It is even probable that the Egyptian churches took possession of the same domains which had once belonged to the temples; it is known that as early as the late third century Christian ascetics found shelter in deserted temples of Serapis.[46] The Christian churches must therefore be seen, not only as the religious heirs of the temples, but as their heirs in the process of production as well. How religious and financial interests intermingled we can see from the information given by the Alexandrian bishop Dionysius about the persecutions of Valerian: one of the instigators of the persecutions was 'the master and ruler of the synagogue of the Egyptian magicians', who felt threatened not only in his 'abominable and disgusting incantations' but also in his secular aspirations, for he was a 'minister over the imperial accounts as a whole' and was hoping to see his sons rise still higher.[47]

Christianity in Rural Egypt

The Gnostic Basilides, who was active from the time of Hadrian to that of Antoninus Pius, did not confine himself to cities alone but extended his activities to the surrounding rural areas also: he is reported to have visited, among other places, the suburbs of Prosopitis, Atribis, Sais, Alexandreiopolis and Alexandria. (These places lie on the Delta, between Memphis and the sea.) In the late fourth century, there were still Valentinian Gnostics in these areas as well as in Arsinoe and Thebais[48]. By the late second century, according to Clement, Christianity had spread to 'every nation, and village and town'.[49] Clement, unfortunately, was not interested to write history, and many of his statements suffer from rhetorical exaggeration; furthermore, he had been travelling widely before settling in Alexandria and it is not easy to determine whether or not he had Egypt in mind. By tradition bishop Demetrius was the first to appoint bishops outside Alexandria; this is a clear sign of expansion and penetration into the countryside.

Martyrs from Egypt and the whole of Thebais were brought to Alexandria during the persecutions in the reign of the Severan emperors. Early in the third century the bishop of Jerusalem was corresponding with a Christian community at Antinoopolis.[50] Of greater significance is Origen's distinction between 'Greek' and 'Egyptian' Christians, the latter being the native non-Greek-speaking population. Unquestionable evidence comes from the Alexandrian bishop Dionysius, who was active in the mid third century. In one of his letters, Dionysius describes how a whole company of a marriage feast taking place in a village not far from Alexandria called Taposiris had saved him from arrest during the local

(Decian) persecutions. Referring to a subsequent exile of his in a village called Cephro not far away, he describes how the pagan natives 'left their idols and turned to God'. While at Cephro, he continues, 'a large church also sojourned with us, some brethren following us from the city, others joining us from Egypt'. When removed to another adjacent village, Colluthion, Dionysius is encouraged by the fact that while Cephro brought much more contact with the brethren from Egypt, Colluthion is nearer Alexandria and he can see more frequently those 'really beloved and most intimate and dear'. They will, he expects, come and stay the night, and, as in the more remote suburban districts, there will be sectional assemblies. Finally, when freed, Dionysius visited the Arsinoite nome to settle theological disputes and called together the presbyters and teachers of the brethren in the villages.[51] Not more than forty years after Dionysius' death, in the early fourth century, the Alexandrian bishop Peter ordained fifty-five bishops in Egypt, all of them in cities and villages outside Alexandria; while the contemporary schismatic Melitius was followed by twenty-nine bishops in Egypt, as well as by four presbyters and three deacons in Alexandria, and one country presbyter.[52] It is therefore obvious that by the early fourth century the Christianization of rural Egypt had significantly advanced with bishops responsible for a large part of the country.

Papyrological evidence, though not abundant, suggests that, from the second century on, Christianity had penetrated as far as remote villages of the Egyptian countryside. Private letters by Christians and church documents are particularly sparse, the earliest being dated to the early third century. But fragments of Biblical and other Christian texts are a good illustration of the spread of Christianity from at least the middle of the second century; this subject has several times been investigated by experts and does not need further consideration. More problematic are many third-century certificates of sacrifice (the so-called *libelli*), which have been discovered in Oxyrhynchus and Arsinoe but refer to inhabitants of remote villages. The existence of such papyri does not imply that the people who produced them were Christians. The edict of Decius in the mid third century required of all people to sacrifice. Attempts have been made to distinguish among those who appear in the *libelli*, the *libellatici* and *sacrificati*, that is those Christians who had obtained a certificate either by sending a slave or family member to sacrifice in their place, or by themselves sacrificing. These researches have been rather unrewarding; but it does seem very unlikely (in spite of what many scholars are inclined to accept) that the edict would actively have been enforced in remote villages where there was no suspicion of Christian penetration.[53]

The evidence mentioned, which is scarce for the second century but rather more suggestive for the third and fourth, suffers from an unfortunate drawback. Although villages were explicitly mentioned in the sources, the whole notion 'rural Egypt' is too vague for the needs of the present investigation. Large villages in Egypt cannot easily be distinguished from 'cities'; and, furthermore, there were many villages inhabited, partly at least, by a Greek-speaking population which had, in spite of intermarriages, remained by and large separate from the native peasants. Direct testimonies from ancient authors cannot fill the gap of our knowledge on this subject; to form an idea of the degree of Christianization of the native population we must turn to linguistic considerations. The narratives of the early Christian Acts, canonical and apocryphal, make little mention of linguistic problems. The early missionaries, travelling for the most part from city to city, neglected the countryside. In the cities of the East, most people would have been able to communicate in Greek, even if it was not their native tongue; but peasants, in most areas, never forgot their ancient language even when they fled to the cities for a better life. To speak of Egypt in particular, it is known from an edict of Caracalla, issued in AD 215, that Egyptian peasants who had fled to Alexandria, though dressed like city people, could be easily recognized among the linen weavers by their speech.[54]

Native peasants in Egypt were by far the largest component of the population. Judging from two late-second-century villages in the Nile Delta it can be inferred that the purely or partially Greek population was less than a sixth of the total, the Romans even fewer[55]; up stream peasants were increasingly unhellenized. It should therefore be possible to detect Christianized peasants by their language; but even linguistic considerations have their drawbacks. Wealthy people, even those living in villages, tended to use Greek names and sometimes even to speak Greek though most of them were not actually of Greek descent; on the other hand late antiquity was characterized by important cultural changes such as a revival of the local vernaculars which had retreated somewhat in earlier years. For such reasons the linguistic evidence can only be used with caution: the most I can do is to formulate a number of tentative propositions. Before doing so, it will be helpful to summarize our general information about the writing, reading and translating of sacred texts up to the third century.

Writing, Reading and Translating the Bible

You are asked then to read with sympathetic attention, and make allowances if, in spite of all the devoted work I have put into the translation, some of the expressions appear inadequate. For it is impossible for a translator to find precise equivalents for the original Hebrew in another language. Not only with this book, but with the law, the prophets, and the rest of the writings, it makes no small difference to read them in the original.

(From the Preface to *Ecclesiasticus*, written in Egypt after 132 BC)

Tradition and doctrine in primitive Christianity were transmitted primarily by preaching, teaching and conversing. Writing and reading for religious purposes, though not unknown, were much less valued than oral communication (see 1 Tim. 4:6-16). Attempts to attribute this phenomenon to the scarcity of available copies are not convincing: almost all religions – with the possible exception of Islam – passed through an oral phase during their early development; reading, writing and commenting upon sacred texts only became important when internal controversies reached intolerable intensity. A religion orally transmitted leaves no traces – until the written phase is reached. It cannot be ascertained, therefore, whether or not native languages were used in primitive Christianity alongside Greek. Missionaries and preachers translating the divine message into native vernaculars could have existed from the earliest days – but how can we tell? (The fourth-century 'interpreters' in Egypt could have been their immediate heirs, but this is a mere hypothesis.) A passage at the beginning of Acts (2:4-13) claiming that the Twelve, inspired by the Holy Spirit, began to preach in all native languages, though fictitious, reflects the difficulties which the first missionaries met: inspired or not, Peter is reported to have had not one but two interpreters, Mark and Glaucias.[56] The same impression is given by the first attempts to have the New Testament translated into Latin; the same willingness and weakness is manifest. 'In the early days of the faith', Augustine was to write some centuries later, 'everyone who happened to get possession of a Greek manuscript and who thought that he had any facility in both languages, however slight it might be, ventured to translate it'.[57] With the early translations we come close to the written phase of Christianity. Papias of Hierapolis, who was active before the middle of the second century, may be considered as the last authority of early Christianity to be heard making the claim: 'For I did not suppose that information from books would help me so much as the word of a living and surviving voice.'[58] Fifty years later Irenaeus, who in other respects was greatly influenced by Papias, wrote that the apostles who had at one time proclaimed the Gosel in public, in a later period handed it down in the Scriptures. The apostolic authorship of Scripture was now the major criterion of their authority.[59]

A systematic reading of the Bible was to start in about the middle of the second century. All second-century apologists exhorted their readers to study the Scriptures, which in their terminology meant mostly the Old Testament. At the same time we have the first evidence of a house-to-house visitation by instructors reading Christian texts aloud.[60] 'The God-fearing man should consider it a great loss if he does not go to the place in which they give instruction, and especially if he knows (how) to read', wrote Hippolytus (*c.* AD 217); the view is affirmed in several other texts.[61] I take systematic reading to imply that texts had acquired a central position in Christian congregations. The same period witnessed the emergence of the churches *sine literis*, the barbarian churches who believed in Christ 'having salvation written in their hearts by the Spirit, without paper and ink'. 'Those who, in the absence of written documents', Irenaeus claimed, 'have believed this faith, are barbarians, so far as regards our language; but as regards doctrine, manner, and tenor of life, they are, because of faith, very wise indeed.'[62] In Germany, Spain, Gaul, Egypt, Libya and elsewhere, there were Christians who, though the speakers of different languages, were allegedly keeping 'the same tradition'.[63] At an early stage, however, natives were acutely in need of written translations; though strangely enough, not all areas have left traces of such translations. This has perplexed Peter Brunt:

> Why individuals conceived the idea of producing translations in some verna-
> culars and not in others, and how the Gospel was ultimately conveyed to the
> peasants in (say) Gaul, if they knew little or no Latin and preachers little or no
> Celtic, are questions to which I have found no answer.[64]

To deal with Brunt's problem we have to look into the history of religious translations a little more closely. First of all, translating sacred Scriptures was not a Christian innovation. I am not concerned here with pagan religions; they had no documents of comparable importance. (The closest thing to a religious text that the ancient Greeks had was the Orphic poems, but they probably did not preach anything uniform or systematic.) But the case of Judaism is instructive. Apart from the Greek translations (the Septuagint and others), Jews had translated their Torah only into Aramaic (the Greek translation was made in the third, the Aramaic in the fourth century BC). The first Latin translations of the Hebrew Bible were Christian and based on the Septuagint version highly valued by Christians. The New Testament was first translated into Syriac in the late second century, followed soon by a Coptic translation.

As reading became central to Christianity, Greek and Roman churches parted ways. The former did not hesitate to encourage trans-lations into native languages such as Syriac, Coptic and later Armenian; the Roman church was much more conservative in this respect. Up to the end of the second century, it had itself used the Greek original for liturgical purposes; the first bishop known to have written theological treatises in Latin was Victor at about AD 190. Even so, it seems that the first Latin translations were made outside Italy, possibly in Africa,

Victor's birthplace. They were subsequently introduced into Italy through Milan, where they were probably first adopted for liturgical purposes. When Latin was finally accepted by the Roman see, it was jealously maintained in the whole of the West.[65]

In the fourth and fifth centuries the scriptures were translated, according to John Chrysostom and Theodoret, into a number of eastern languages, including Egyptian, Persian, Indian, Armenian, Scythian and Thracian; but, Latin apart, there is no mention made or trace found of translations into western languages[66]: the vernaculars of Gaul, Spain and North Africa, for example, are never mentioned. It is not quite clear why the churches of East and West behaved in such different ways. Harnack's belief that the motive for the early translations was 'the earnest desire to place the Scriptures in the hands of the faithful for their private use' does not take us an inch further; nor is it correct to assert with Bardy that at that time native languages in the West had perished.[67] In my view, the differences between East and West were related to the policies followed by each church in its attempt to secure dominance through the control of the production and distribution of sacred knowledge. What determined each policy requires further investigation, but it is fairly clear that, on the one hand, the Latin church was not amenable to theological discussions, and that it secured unity by organization and discipline; and on the other, that the Greek church was unable to restrict theological inquiry and attempted (unsuccessfully) to secure unity by doctrinal elaboration. In these circumstances, restricting scripture to one language only had no meaning in the East: theological discussions presupposed a good knowledge of relevant texts. The case of Coptic is quite revealing.

Coptic

The Egyptian aristocracy had been more or less Hellenized since the Ptolemaic era. This did not change with the Roman conquest; Latin was confined almost exclusively to the realm of administration. But the Egyptian language, largely restricted to the countryside (is is unknown to what extent it was still in use in the big cities), survived as the vernacular of the peasantry. In the course of its history, the Egyptian language had passed successively through three forms of writing: Hieroglyphic, Hieratic and Domotic. The three differed considerably from one another, but none was accessible to the bulk of the population. During the first century AD the Greek alphabet was adapted to the Egyptian language and was used in the writing of magical texts. A later and much more successful combination of the Egyptian language with a modified Greek alphabet known as Coptic gradually achieved wide popularity. The earliest surviving Coptic text used by the Christians, a Graeco-Coptic glossary, dates from the late second or early third century.[68]

Coptic and Christianity were soon interwoven in Egypt. The earliest phases of this relationship remain unknown, but a piece of information preserved by Eusebius suggests that it might have existed much earlier than is usually thought. An adversary of the Gnostic Basilides, called Agrippa Castor, who was active before the middle of the second century, accused the Gnostic leader of having 'set up' prophets of his own, inventing for them 'barbarous names' so as 'to astonish those who were influenced by such things'.[69] These barbarous names obviously could not have been Greek or Latin, and Hebrew names were fairly common among Christians (Christians referred to the 'Hebrew dialect' as distinct from 'barbarous languages'[70]). Basilides, then, was either making use of some strange language, such as Persian, or adopting native Egyptian names. It is known from Origen that 'wise men' in Egypt, Persia or India insisted in their religious usages that 'powerful names' should be kept in their original languages. So to an Egyptian native it must have been of great importance to hear names that in Egyptian were religiously important for him. According to Origen if a 'spell is translated into any other language whatever, it can be seen to be weak and ineffective'.[71] The fact that Basilides had visited the native-speaking suburbs of Egyptian cities suggests that he was probably introducing Egyptian names, not to impress, but to make himself understood and believed. It must have been the Greek-speaking population of Alexandria which was astonished – astonished by the emergence of the old Egyptian language into Christian discourse. It is significant that the first native reported to have written biblical studies in Coptic was Hieracas, born in a village called Leontopolis before the middle of the third century. Leontopolis was not far from the villages visited by Basilides, and Hieracas, besides being a Christian, was interested in astronomy and magic.[72] What these fragments of information suggest is that Christianity, on reaching the natives of the Nile valley (and perhaps elsewhere as well) had, as early as the mid second century, to adopt Coptic and to make concessions to Egyptian religious beliefs. Gnosticism, not surprisingly, was not reluctant to make such concessions.

A whole Christian library discovered near the Egyptian city Nag Hammadi consists of Coptic documents. Some of the originals – all of them presumably Greek – date from the second and third centuries, others even earlier. The exact date of the translation cannot be established with certainty, although it is clear that all the Coptic manuscripts were finished before about AD 400, when the whole library was hidden. By the end of the third century there existed a Coptic version of the New Testament, which was being read at Antony's village, while the first original works in Coptic were written by Hieracas and Pachomius in the early fourth century.[73] The Christian village lector mentioned earlier who had signed the legal document in AD 304 was reported as illiterate; what must really have been meant was that he knew no Greek. Some Christians at the lector's village, not far from Oxyrhynchus, were therefore probably listening to Bible readings in Coptic.[74]

If we could rely on names as proof of ethnicity – which I think we cannot, especially in the case of Egypt where, as Hopkins has pointed out, Greek names were being adopted by natives for social purposes – then it would be noteworthy that all the fictitious Alexandrian bishops of the first two centuries have Greek or Roman names.[75] There are, however, some martyrs of the Decian persecutions with clearly indigenous names, and the Coptic calendar mentioned a native Egyptian bishop who suffered martyrdom under Hadrian. Most of the Coptic martyrs in the calendar, however, belong to the early fourth century.[76]

The Gnostics are considered to have been the first to use Coptic in their preaching, and Gnosticism is thought to have enjoyed a privileged relation to Coptic for a long period. The case of the Nag Hammadi library, which was in use up to the fourth century, is suggestive, for it is both Coptic and Gnostic. The connection is plausible but cannot be proved; a further connection is much more problematic. Combining the use of a national language with heresy and monasticism, some scholars have spoken of Coptic as being the language of dissent, and some have suggested the existence of an Egyptian nationalism invested in Coptic Christianity.[77] My own opinion is rather that of Peter Brown, who claims that Egyptian 'isolationism' in the fourth and fifth centuries was pagan, and that 'Coptic, by contrast was a literature of participation' in the culture of the empire.[78] This view finds some support in the so-called *Acta Alexandrinorum*, which testify that from the late first century AD to the beginning of the third it was pagan, Greek-speaking political rebels who struggled 'to preserve Greek culture and law against the barbarism of Roman domination'. In these *Acta*, Roman officials are portrayed as ruthless and venal, whereas in the various Christian *Acts*, Roman officials are presented 'in the main as honest and scrupulous in performance of their duties'.[79]

Gnosticism's relation to Coptic was, after all, not that substantial. The *Gospel of the Egyptians*, a typically Egyptian product, with pronounced Gnostic elements, used in the early second century by Gentile-Christians (it was the *Gospel of the Hebrews* which probably belonged to the Alexandrian Greek-speaking Judaeo-Christians) was Greek, not Coptic. The well-known leaders of the second-century Gnostic schools preached and wrote mostly in Greek: this is true of Basilides and Valentinus with their reputed Greek education, of Carpocrates, who was married to a Greek woman from Cephallenia, and others. The first person known to have used Coptic for ecclesiastical purposes was Hieracas, whom I have already mentioned; Hieracas' orthodoxy was, according to Epiphanius, doubtful, but he had nothing to do with Gnosticism.

The Christian use of Coptic has a further aspect which makes it difficult to draw any definite conclusions. As has already been mentioned, Coptic was principally used in the countryside, Greek in Alexandria and other large cities. But from the first half of the third century, Greek started to decline in the whole of Egypt. The use of Coptic by Christians until the early third century is therefore a clear sign of Christian penetration into the rural population. However, most references to Coptic as used by Christians come from the third century and later, during the period when the prestige of Greek was declining anyway. I mention this as a matter of caution: the use of Coptic in the third and fourth centuries cannot be interpreted in the same terms as its use in the early Roman period.

* * *

Christianity, as is clear from documentary and literary sources, penetrated rural Egypt from the mid second century; by two or three generations later it had spread quite significantly, with organized communities to be found in small villages and bishops being appointed to oversee the rural districts. There is evidence that Coptic was used by Christian missionaries perhaps as early as the first stages of Christian penetration of the countryside. Coptic seems at first to have been used by Gnostics, but orthodox Christians were soon to follow: there are no signs of reluctance on the part of either in communicating directly with peasants in their own language. A large section of the population (probably the largest by far) spoke no Greek, and the antagonism between rival Christian groups was too intense to permit the neglect of so many people. But the evidence for the use of Coptic among Egyptian Christians is exceedingly sparse in relation to the evidence for the spread of Christianity in general, and authoritative information about the use of Coptic comes only from the late third century, when Greek in Egypt was in general decline. The existing evidence, over all, is far too fragmentary to allow general conclusions; but I shall tentatively put forward a proposition which seems at least plausible, if not probable. Christianity penetrated the Egyptian countryside at a fairly early date (earlier than is generally assumed), but was first accepted among the Greek-speaking populations. It could have been mostly the descendants of Greek settlers or Hellenized farmers who were attracted, both privileged groups by comparison with the bulk of the population. Settlers were owners of land, which they either leased or cultivated themselves with the aid of slaves and hired workers; Hellenized farmers were mostly well-to-do farmers in social or administrative contact with the Greek-speaking upper classes of the cities. But my tentative conclusion that it was among such people, above all, that Christianity found its first adherents in the Egyptian countryside needs qualification.

The Social Character of Christianity

Consideration of early Christianity's social character has led to the belief that, whereas in cities the new religion was rather otherworldly, and thus inclined to accept existing social order, it was in the countryside more concerned with this world, often advocating some kind of social reform.[80] The evidence is not conclusive, but the well-attested tension between city and country makes this argument about early Christianity attractive; all sources therefore containing clues should be examined with care. A somewhat neglected incident in the third century gives us useful information about the social character of Christianity in Egypt. As elsewhere, Christianity in Egypt consisted at that time of numerous schools, sects and communities; in spite of the expected element of mutual polemic, however, there is evidence that in Egypt some of these groupings were on speaking terms and often had no clear boundaries to separate them. Recent research seems to confirm once again the existence of some kind of association between Gnostics and orthodox Christians in second-century Alexandria, and suggests that purely Gnostic literature was being read in orthodox monasteries in Upper Egypt as late as the fifth century.[81] Clear boundaries between orthodoxy and heresy were first drawn in Alexandria in the early third century; in the rest of the country they seem to have made their appearance somewhat later. Conflicts between orthodox Christians, heretics and various schismatic groups went on, of course, until the Arab conquest.

It is rather significant that, Basilides apart, nobody is reported to have taken the initiative for the expansion of Christianity outside Alexandria. The Alexandrian bishops, even at the time of Dionysius, were pre-occupied overwhelmingly with their Alexandrian flock, which alone was for them 'really beloved and most intimate and dear'.[82] It looks as if Christianity was spreading to the countryside in a spontaneous, unorganized way, and that the church leaders were limiting their responsibility in the appointment of bishops to organize the movement and subordinate it to Alexandria, especially during the phases of intense antagonism with the Gnostics and later with the Melitians. It was under similar circumstances that Dionysius himself visited the villages of the district of Arsinoe. Eusebius preserves a section of a treatise in which Dionysius dealt with a controversy he had with the Christian villagers there.[83] No information is given about the date of the controversy, but Dionysius' episcopate lasted from AD 248 to 265; internal evidence suggests that the treatise might have been written at a late date within our limits, but the related meeting could have taken place some time earlier. The treatise called *On Promises* consisted of two parts. The first dealt with the controversial doctrine, the second with the Revelation of John, which was highly valued by the doctrine. The most important teacher of the heterodox views had been a certain Nepos, 'a bishop of those in Egypt', who had elucidated his own view in a book he called *Refutation of the Allegorists.* The idea was that 'the promises which had been made to the saints in the divine Scriptures should be interpreted after a more Jewish fashion', 'that there will be a kind of millennium on this earth devoted to bodily indulgence', and 'that the kingdom of Christ will be on earth'. According to Dionysius, certain teachers who had taken over Nepos' doctrine considered 'the law and the prophets of no value and disregard(ed) the following of the Gospels and depreciate(d) the epistles of the apostles'; but these accusations seem to be overstated.

Christians in Arsinoe were under some kind of Gnostic influence. The disregard of the Old Testament by the followers of Nepos was in line with Gnostic beliefs, while it is known that Valentinian sects survived in that area until the fourth century.[84] But the mythological peculiarities of Gnosticism were evidently absent from Nepos' teaching or they would have been pointed out by Dionysius and Eusebius. What is clear is that the Christian villagers were expecting the realization of the divine promises on earth and thus did not emhasize – or perhaps rejected – the idea of the resurrection of the dead. To Dionysius' great contempt, these people were persuaded 'to hope for what is petty and mortal and like the present in the kingdom of God'. But it could of course not have been something exactly like the present which these villagers were expecting; they were looking forward to a better life, only they were hoping to see it in material rather than spiritual terms. Dionysius, on the other hand, was trying to communicate to them 'high and noble thoughts' about a future life in which the faithful would be 'gathered together' and be 'made like Him'. In addition to Nepos the doctrine was taught by a certain Coracion. Among their followers were presbyters and teachers and brethren from the villages of Arsinoe; some were actually present at the meeting with Dionysius. Dionysius claimed that the doctrine 'had long been prevalent, so that schisms and defections of whole churches had taken place'; but those whom he met could not have been schismatics in the technical sense, since the Egyptian bishops and the presbyters mentioned were considered lawful officials of the churches. Nepos in particular was 'in many other respects' approved and loved by Dionysius, 'for his faith and devotion to work, his diligent study of the Scriptures and his abundant psalmody', by which many of the brethren were cheered. When the meeting ended, Coracion assented and publically testified 'that he would no longer adhere to (the doctrine), nor discourse upon it, nor mention it, since he had been sufficiently convinced by the contrary arguments'. Of the rest, however, only 'some rejoiced', while the others evidently clung to their old beliefs. Unfortunately, the quotation from the treatise stops abruptly at this point, and we are not told what happened to those who were not convinced. Were they expelled from the church, or did they continue to be in communion with the Alexandrian orthodox, as they had been until then? There is no way of telling.

The meeting seems to have taken place around AD 250 – or not long after. At that time Nepos was already dead, but Dionysius makes it clear that he had been alive not long before. Nepos' activity then, is to be placed in the first half of the third century. The statement that this doctrine 'had long been prevalent' suggests that it is at the early years of the third century that we must look. We have one further clue to date the doctrine: Nepos' book was entitled *Refutation of the Allegorists*. This means that Nepos was not actually putting forward a new theory, but responding to what seemed new to him, the allegorical interpretation of Scripture. Dionysius did not say how recent the allegorical method was, but he connected the millenarianism of Nepos to that of Cerinthus – which takes us back to the late first century. We learn from Hippolytus, incidentally, that Cerinthus himself had been trained in Egypt.[85] Since the allegorical method of interpretation of Scriptures – in a well-developed form, at least – is attributed to the Alexandrian school, Origen has been put forward as the probable allegorist refuted by Nepos. The suggestion has been discussed in relation to the hypothesis of a Commentary by Origen on the Revelation of John; for lack of further information, the question has been left open. But though Origen cannot be excluded as the opponent attacked in the *Refutation*, the dates suggested above make it rather unlikely: Nepos seems to have been older than Origen, who was born around AD 185. It is more probable that Origen himself has people like Nepos in mind when he defends the allegorical method in his *On First Principles*. Origen's expression about the 'simpler of those who claim to belong to the church ... yet believe such things about (God) as would not be believed of the most savage and unjust of men'[86] is reflected in Dionysius' statement about the 'simpler of our brethren' who are persuaded 'to hope for what is petty and moral and like the present in the kingdom of God'. Origen and his pupil Dionysius were clearly replying to 'refutations'.

If we set Origen aside, we may turn to Clement of Alexandria, who fits the chronology much better. And one of Clement's preserved works, indeed, *The Rich Man's Salvation*, serves as an excellent example of how an earthly (social) commandment in the Gospel can be turned, through allegory, into a spiritual commandment. The passage which most troubled Clement and the wealthy members of the Alexandrian congregation was that about the rich man in the Synoptics (Mk. 10.17-31 and parallels): 'If you would be perfect sell what belongs to thee and give to the poor.' Clement's argument was that 'as we are clearly aware that the Saviour teaches His people nothing in a merely human way, but everything by a divine and mystical wisdom, we must not understand His words literally, but with due inquiry and intelligence we must search out and master their hidden meaning'.[87] After applying the allegorical interpretation, Clement comes up with the conclusion that the idea of selling one's belongings 'is not what some hastily take it to be, a command to fling away the substance that belongs to him and to part with his riches, but to banish from the soul its opinions about riches ...'. In order to support this interpretation Clement has to emphasize the 'If you be perfect' clause of the Matthaean version, not to be found in the old Marcan version he is citing (nor, indeed, is it found in Luke) and to transform the final clause 'and give to the poor' into the notion of caring for one's neighbour. Such details could pass unnoticed. Through this kind of interpretation it was actually possible to turn the Gospel saying around and argue that 'when a man lacks the necessities of life he cannot possibly fall to be broken in spirit and to neglect the higher things, as he strives to produce these necessities by any means and from any source'.[88] We may note here that when Origen was dealing with the same Synoptic passage he claimed that 'not even a stupid person would praise the poor indiscriminately; the majority of them have very bad characters'.[89]

Some Christians in the villages of Arsinoe were obviously expecting different things from their religion than their brethren in Alexandria. Between these two groups a theological controversy clearly reflected class positions and aspirations: in the countryside Christianity appeared with reformist tendencies which, though present in the Gospels, had lost much of their meaning in the large cities where an allegorical interpretation prevailed. But the class antagonism to be seen in the account given above must not be pressed too far. Nepos' treatise in refutation of the allegorists was written in Greek, employing sophisticated arguments which could only be dealt with by Dionysius at a philosophical level. There can be little doubt that the leaders of the anti-allegorist movement were themselves intellectuals; Nepos had written other works as well, and his follower Coracion was won over by the Alexandrian bishop after lengthy and subtle discussions. What is more, numerous 'simple' believers present at the conference showed, according to Dionysius, an admirable ability to follow sophisticated argument – obviously in Greek. I do not, therefore, think that the Christian villagers of Arsinoe can be classified as humble Egyptian peasants or serfs: either the villages mentioned were wholly Hellenized and of some consequence, or else the Christians in those villages were drawn from their upper strata. (It must not be forgotten that disputes over the allegorical interpretation of Scripture were also common among urban church leaders of the period. Hippolytus and Irenaeus, for example, were millenarians, but neither of them represented rural areas or rural aspirations.)

From the late third century onwards evidence for the use of Coptic by Christians in the Egyptian countryside increases greatly; the Eastern churches either had no objection to, or were forced into accepting, the translation of Scripture. But, as has been already mentioned, the Greek language was in general decline in Egypt. The famous ascetic Antony, who was born some time in the mid third century in a village of Heracle-opolis, not far from the Arsinoe villages mentioned earlier, spoke no Greek. A few years after Dionysius' death in 265, Antony was hearing and taking literally the same Dominical saying which Clement had attempted to allegorize: he sold his property, distributed it to the poor and took to the mountains. And yet Antony was known to have been, not a deprived serf, but a wealthy farmer (his property was something like two hundred acres or more).[90] Millenarianism has appeal for people acquainted with suffering rather than with poverty. The persistent perplexity caused by the Dominical saying about the selling of one's possessions points to landowning peasants, not traditional serfs, who had no landed property and no general conception of private ownership. It may be of significance that it was during the Roman period that a landowning peasant population first emerged in Egypt. The development of a new class in the Egyptian countryside created tensions which may have had something to do with the quest for a more suitable religion. (The Christian churches as earlier mentioned had become land-owners through inheriting the lands of pious Christians.) This may be true for Alexandria as well.[91]

There is no way of proving these assertions; they depend on a general impression from the scattered pieces of information known. That, in expanding to the countryside in Egypt, Christianity initially attracted members of the Hellenized population, seems clear enough. Whether the first peasant converts were landowners, better off than the majority of their fellow countrymen, is much more difficult to say – though the evidence points this way. In the countryside, it seems reasonable to assert, Christianity found more supporters of a literal understanding of the Gospels than it did in the cities. The Gospels had originated in the Palestinian countryside, and all the editing which gave them their present form could not wipe out some essential features which betray a peasant mentality. But even in the Palestinian countryside the mission of Jesus did not advocate social reform, despite its evident antipathy to the extravagances of city culture. At any rate, there are not to be found the slightest traces of serfs or other underprivileged agricultural workers among the early Christians in Egypt.

Conclusion

The Social Structure of the Early Christian Communities

Sociological inquiries into early Christianity must begin and end with acknowledgements of the limitations and fragmentary nature of our extant evidence. The first systematic history of Christianity was written in the fourth century, when traces of its early development were already fading away. The piousness of early converts preserved numerous documents that are significant but not necessarily historically informative. The principal literary sources are the New Testament, apologetic and theological tracts, church canons and several letters of church leaders; the anti-Christian literature and the writings of heterodox or heretical Christians have, with a few exceptions, been left to perish – some of them may even have been destroyed. The difficulties arising from the scarcity of the preserved literature, the indifference of the early Christians towards the recording of events for history's sake and the creeping into historical narratives of myths have been partly overcome with the aid of archaeological material. But on the whole, given that a more or less continuous and reliable history of the early Christian movement cannot be reconstructed, there is no solid basis for sociological investigation. To trace the social origins and positions of the early Christians gaps in the evidence have to be filled in by inference and speculation. Details which would have otherwise passed unnoticed are often discussed at length and mined for any possible information. Sometimes it is the combination of many small details which allows conclusions to be drawn. The risks in such an endeavour are doubtlessly great, the outcome of even the most laborious scrutiny often meagre. The foremost methodological guarantee in dealing with the early Christian communities is to have their history placed firmly in the much more reliable context of Roman history; after all, 'the early history of Christianity is Roman history'.[1] Even so, in reconstructing the social structure of the early Christian communities the tentative conjectures put forward at every stage of the inquiry cannot often be tested beyond the broad claim of plausibility in the light of the available evidence.

The present investigation has been conducted on two related but distinct levels: the level of Christians' intentions in their missionary activities and the level of the actual outcome of their endeavour. At the first level, conclusions have been based primarily on the few but more or less reliable explicit testimonies. (Intentions may also be detected from Christians' actions but in this case conclusions should be drawn with caution.) In spite of all-too-obvious limitations the general picture which emerges is rather clear.

1. Slaves were of no importance in the early Christian missionary movement, with two notable exceptions: a small number of slave-favourites and the slaves of the *Familia Caesaris*. These two fractions of the great slave class were viewed by Christians with solicitude – often with affection. But the mass of agricultural and other urban slaves were ignored. When indeed some of them were converted or expressed a desire for conversion, Christians directed them to accept and fulfil their duties as slaves. Christianity, in fact, offered new ideological justifications of slavery. It took the Christian movement more than three centuries to turn its attention to the 'gangs of slaves', but it was already from the seat of power that it addressed itself to them: there could be no question of a general emancipation.

2. The other end of the social scale was viewed by Christians in a very different light. Aristocrats were not only welcomed, they were persistently and warmly encouraged to join the Christian churches. Conversions of aristocrats were recorded with pride, related with joy and set as an example to others. The second- and third-century propagandists of Christianity – the apologists – addressed their works to the educated, to learned members of the upper classes and, potentially, to the emperors as well. It is unthinkable that emperors ever read these ambitious apologies, but it is informative about the Christian mentality that an urge to convert them was felt.

3. Peasants, villagers and the rural population generally seem long to have gone unnoticed by Christians. When circumstances – circumstances almost always beyond their control – led Christian leaders and missionaries to the countryside, they preached and exhorted villagers to join the churches, but in their heart longed to go back to those 'really beloved and most intimate and dear' urban Christians.[2] How remote this

attitude from that of Jesus, who remained at heart a real *campagnard*![3] Peasants were at first converted in a more or less spontaneous and unorganized manner; even later Christians felt no need to invent fictitious missions by important personages as they did with the urban expansion. It must not be forgotten that farmers entered the picture when the time for first-fruits offerings came. Oblations remained for a long time a major source of income of the early churches, but farmers were often city-dwellers.

4. What is left is the great mass of the urban population: day labourers, artisans, merchants, men of letters, artists, athletes; usurers, debtors, the sick, the poor, widows, orphans, Roman citizens, Greeks, Jews natives, officers, soldiers – in short, people who usually appear without special distinction or detailed information, urban masses, hopeless or hopeful, of the Roman world. Early Christian teachers preached and laboured among them all. Church canons in their restrictions and in their ordinances, are concerned with every class of this population. Common Christians there were among these people; but little more can be said about them, for what is common rarely attracts much attention.

So much for early Christian intentions. Turning to the actual outcome of the missionary process, it may be discerned that it did not greatly diverge from the conscious plan. But there were a few exceptions which carried some weight for religious developments. The highly educated and the aristocracy were resistant to Christian efforts over a long period; they proved far harder to convince than other groups which were the object of less interest. Indeed, people belonging to the lower grades of the populations seem to have knocked at Christian doors in larger numbers than the new religion had cared to imagine; and women, of whom Christianity had no high opinion, ignored prejudice against them and spontaneously joined the new movement. By the time of the last persecutions Christians, to put it in Eusebius' words, differed greatly in 'matters which concern the mind' and 'in manner and sphere of life'. In describing the martyrs of Palestine, Eusebius gives the following picture:

> (Presbyter) Pamphilus traced his descent according to the flesh from a noble stock, and played a part with fame and distinction in the public affairs of his own country, while Seleucus had been honoured in a most notable way with positions of high rank in the army; others belonged to the middle and ordinary class in life. The group which they formed contained even slaves. For the attendant in a governor's household was of their number, as also was Porphyry, who outwardly was a slave of Pamphilus, but ... never failed to imitate his master in everything.[4]

From what has been argued in the present work, there could hardly be a better profile of the early Christian communities than the one given above. The majority of the martyrs belonged to the middle and ordinary classes; it may be noted that for these people no names or further details are given. Two prominent members, by contrast are mentioned by name. We are not told whether Seleucus held any significant post in the church, but he was probably mentioned by name because of his rank in the army; Pamphilus, the group's leader, was a presbyter (and a very learned one) of noble descent who had also distinguished himself in secular life. The group of the martyrs contained *even slaves*: this was a feature that caused some surprise. Two slaves are mentioned; the first one belonged to a rather privileged group, being an attendant in a governor's household (we are here reminded of the Christians in the *Familia Caesaris*); the second was a slave-favourite of an influential Christian master. It is interesting to notice once again that, though this second slave imitated his master in everything, including martyrdom, it had not occurred to the master to emancipate his slave. What was really important for the group was its religious devotion and the cohesion was strengthened by confidence in an important leader.

There is no trace of Christians in the countryside before the second century. The initial spread of the new religion among peasants was gradual and more or less spontaneous. When the first communities emerged in villages the urban churches took care to subordinate them to their control. The Christianization of the countryside in the East was well under way in the third and fourth centuries, and in the West perhaps somewhat later; but the case of Egypt suggests that the process may have started earlier. The prevailing general impression of a retarded expansion into rural districts should perhaps be ascribed more to lack of evidence (due to the indifference of the early Christians in recording events in the countryside) than to actual events. The case of Egypt also suggests that it was Hellenized sections of the rural population that were first converted, only later to be followed by native-speaking peasants. Furthermore, it appears that, until the third century, it was, in the main, rather landowning villagers than serf-like farmers who were attracted.

The conversion of the upper classes calls for some further observations. Most scholars agree that only a very small section of the Roman aristocracy had been converted prior to Constantine. This is probably true but it does not exhaust the question. Aristocrats were a small minority in the Roman world, and Christians as a whole were never more than a fraction of the population before the fourth century. What we should like to know is whether there were proportionately many fewer aristocrats in the Christian communities than there were in Roman society at large. Though there is no way of ascertaining precise numbers, it seems that people of education and wealth were fairly well represented in some Christian communities. And, more significantly, these communities drew most of their leaders from among the higher social ranks. These people provided the nucleus of the Christian communities.

* * *

Protestant and Marxist writers in the nineteenth and early twentieth centuries were, for different reasons, inclined to see in early Christianity a social as well as a religious movement. It was thought that the lower classes predominated among the early Christian communities and invested social aspirations in their new religion, and New Testament theology seemed to justify this assertion. Until fairly recently historians were much influenced by the idea of the decline and fall of the ancient world, systematically expounded by Gibbon on the eve of the French Revolution. As part of the process of this decline and fall, Christianity was conceived as the cultural-religious movement which accompanied the birth of a new world. Later in the twentieth century it increasingly came to be realized that the terms 'decline' and, still more, 'fall' were far too problematic adequately to explain the 'passages from antiquity to feudalism': Momigliano has written with a nicely ironic touch that the only fact on which all ancient historians agree is that the Roman empire declined and fell.[5] Christian doctrines and Christian theology too are coming to be seen in a different light. The world of the Gospels is being seen as clearly separate from the world of the Pauline epistles; and whether the Palestinian mission of Jesus can be historically reconstructed or not, most historians today would agree that church history proper begins after the departure of the first missionaries from Jerusalem to the cities of the Graeco-Roman world. The vicissitudes of the socialist movement, moreover, are currently directing Marxists towards a fresh consideration of the great historical transformations. Under this pressure the history of early Christianity has to change, and in the last few decades it seems that a new consensus is emerging. The early Christian communities, it is now accepted, had complex social structures, drawing members of both sexes from all ages and social classes (as Pliny had noticed in the early second century). In the large cities of the Roman empire, such as Rome and Alexandria, there seem to have been many more of the educated and of the upper classes than was once thought. This much is finding increasing acceptance. What is not yet quite clear is the sociological significance of this emerging consensus; instead of drawing a general conclusion I may perhaps be allowed to make a suggestion.

Since Christianity cannot be reduced to class movements, we should perhaps look more carefully into what is called the 'essence of religion'. Following the triumph of Christianity it was religious divisions which dominated the minds of men. The Roman world had fought many wars, but it never thought of dividing society in religious terms: even when the Romans started to persecute the Christians, it was not because of intolerance of their own, but because of the new religion's exclusiveness. With Constantine, it was, along with Christianity, religion that came to power. What requires further investigation, perhaps, is not so much the social character of early Christianity as the social factors which allowed religion to take on such importance in late antiquity.

Notes

Introduction

1. See A. Momigliano, 'Mabillon's Italian Disciples', repr. in *Essays*.
2. Spinoza, *A Theologico-Political Treatise*, pp. 27, 29, 99, 101.
3. On English Deism see W.G. Kümmel, *The New Testament*, pp. 51 ff.
4. See P. Fuller, 'The Christ of Faith and the Jesus of History'.
5. Gibbon, *Decline and Fall*, vol. 2, ch. 15. See Momigliano, 'Gibbon's Contribution to Historical Method', repr. in *Studies*, who also emphasizes Gibbon's debt to the political, moral and religious ideas of Voltaire.
6. This development is emphasized by R.M. Grant, *A Short History of the Interpretation of the Bible*, p. 123.
7. See R. Bultmann, *The Theology of the New Testament*, vol. 2, pp. 242 ff.
8. Hegel, *The Philosophy of History*, p. 328.
9. See Momigliano, 'J.G. Droysen between Greeks and Jews', repr. in *Essays*.
10. On F.C. Baur and D.F. Strauss see Kümmel, *op. cit.*, pp. 120 ff. Kümmel, like many other historians of New Testament scholarship, completely dismisses B. Bauer and 'radical criticism' as unworthy of attention. On B. Bauer see Z. Rosen, *Bruno Bauer and Karl Marx*, The Hague 1977; see also Engels, 'Bruno Bauer and Early Christianity'; interesting remarks on Bauer and Strauss in G. Plekhanov, 'From Idealism to Materialism' (1917), repr. in *Selected Philosophical Works*, vol. 3, pp. 617 ff.
11. Cf. Engels, *Ludwig Feuerbach*, in Marx and Engels, *Selected Works*, vol. 3; see also L. Althusser's 'Note du Traducteur' in Feuerbach, *Manifestes philosophiques*, Paris 1960.
12. Besides the *Life of Jesus*, *The Twelve Apostles* and the other well-known works, see also the selection of Renan's writings called *Leaders of Christian and Anti-Christian Thought*, where he expressed his views on Spinoza, Feuerbach and other German scholars.
13. See G.E.M. de Ste. Croix, *The Class Struggle*, I.iv.
14. Engels, 'Bruno Bauer', p. 182.
15. Engels, 'The Book of Revelation', p. 183.
16. Engels, 'On the History of Early Christianity', p. 281.
17. Engels to Kautsky, May 21, 1895, in Marx and Engels, *Selected Correspondence*, Moscow 1975, p. 463; Kautsky, *Foundations of Christianity*, p. 7.
18. See Ste. Croix, 'Karl Marx and the History of Classical Antiquity'; on Marxism and the study of ancient slavery, see Finley, *Ancient Slavery*, ch. 1.
19. R. Samuel, 'British Marxist Historians', p. 30.
20. A. Harnack, *Mission and Expansion*, vol. 2, p. 337 n. 1. To the sociologists of the

period I should certainly add E. Troeltsch who greatly influenced M. Weber; Troeltsch's most important work, *The Social Teachings of the Christian Churches*, was first published in 1912, but he had been contributing to the study of Christianity since the beginning of the century.

21. M. Weber, 'The Agrarian History of the Major Centers of Ancient Civilization', in *The Agrarian Sociology*, pp. 258-9.

22. Weber, 'The Social Causes of the Decline of Ancient Civilization', *op. cit.*, p. 400.

23. This discussion also attracted F. Mehring and G. Plekhanov. After the 1905 Revolution in Russia, Plekhanov became engaged in a dispute with A. Lunacharsky and other Russian Marxists and wrote a series of articles 'On the So-Called Religious Seekings in Russia' (repr. in *Selected Philosophical Works* vol. 3). After the October Revolution, Lunacharsky returned to the problem of the origins of religions and published several popular pamphlets. In the Soviet Union a number of scholars continued writing on early Christianity, we are told by I. Lenzmann, who in the late fifties gave his own version of the *Origins of Christianity*. The lack of originality since the time of the old Engels is striking.

24. See Bultmann, *The History of the Synoptic Tradition* (second German ed. 1931), Oxford 1972; also *Primitive Christianity in its Contemporary Setting*.

25. G. Vermes, *Jesus and the World of Judaism*, p. 19; see also his *Jesus the Jew*; cf. J. Klausner, *Jesus of Nazareth*, London 1928.

26. Ste. Croix has contributed a number of articles on early Christianity; I shall just mention two which have been very influential: 'Why Were the Early Christians Persecuted?' (1963), and 'Early Christian Attitudes to Property and Slavery' (1975).

27. See the discussion in the next chapter.

28. An important modern work dealing with the first three centuries of early Christianity is H. Chadwick's, *The Early Church*, but it has little to say on the social origins of the early Christians.

29. One of the first works dealing with early Christianity in the first three centuries was written in 1853 by F.C. Baur.

30. Artemidorus, *The Interpretation of Dreams*, New Jersey 1975.

31. See my review in *JRS* 75, 1985.

32. Averil Cameron's review in *JRS* 73, 1983.

33. This is the title of Ste. Croix's influential article.

34. Momigliano, 'Freedom of Speech and Religious Tolerance in the Ancient World' in S.C. Humphreys, *Anthropology and the Greeks*, London 1978, p. 189.

35. Ste. Croix, 'Heresy, Schism and Persecution in the Later Roman Empire' (to be published shortly).

36. Brown, *The Making of Late Antiquity*, ch. 2. Cf. R.C. Smith and J. Lounibos (eds), *Pagan and Christian Anxiety: a Response to E.R. Dodds* (well reviewed by Lane Fox in *JRS* 76, 1986).

37. Dodds, *Pagan and Christian*, p. 103. Cf. Averil Cameron, 'Redrawing the Map: Early Christian Territory after Foucault', *JRS* 76, 1986.

38. See MacMullen, 'What Difference did Christianity Make?', *Historia* 35.3, 1986. See also Henry Chadwick's review of the book in *TLS* April 5, 1985.

39. Lane Fox, *Pagans and Christians*, Viking 1986, p. 23. Cf. the good review by Peter Brown in *The New York Review*, 12 March 1987.

40. Lane Fox, *op. cit.*, pp. 282, 315, 327, 329.

41. *Ibid.*, 265; cf. below, p. 176.

42. Cf. below, p. 40.

43. Cf. the acute observations in Frend's *The Donatist Church* on the social significance of the division between orthodox and Donatists. I have not been able to read W.H.C. Frend's latest book *The Rise of Christianity*, London 1984.

44. Lane Fox, *op. cit.*, p. 319; this view is flatly contradicted a few pages later when it is argued that 'The recruitment of lesser families into civic service might bring existing Christians or their friends into the upper orders of a town', p. 334. On social mobility the arguments of Keith Hopkins in 'Elite Mobility in the Roman Empire' are conclusive.

Chapter 1

1. Gibbon's view is to be found in vol. 2, ch. 15 of *Decline and Fall*.
2. See Engels, 'On the History of Early Christianity', p. 281.
3. Kautsky, *Foundations of Christianity*, p. 460.
4. Lenin, *The State and Revolution*, repr. in *Selected Works* 2, p. 317.
5. Harnack, *What is Christianity?*, London 1901, p. 88.
6. *Ibid.*, p. 100.
7. *Ibid.*, p. 268.
8. Engels, 'Bruno Bauer', pp. 177-8.
9. Engels, 'On the History of Early Christianity', p. 281.
10. This topic has been discussed by Finley, *Ancient Slavery and Modern Ideology*, ch. 1; cf, J. Vogt, *Ancient Slavery and the Ideal of Man*, ch. 9.
11. H. Wallon's *Histoire de l'esclavage dans l'antiquité* was first published in 1847; Marx's comment was made in an article published in the same year, see Marx and Engels, *On Religion*, p. 74.
12. Baur, *The Church History*, vol. 2, p. 251 n.; cf. pp. 148 n., 243 n.
13. P. Allard, *Les esclaves chrétiens*. The contrary view was argued by H. Wiskemann, *Die Sklaverei*, 1866, and F. Overbeek, *Studien zur Geschichte der Kirche*, 1875; but it was above all the Marxist E. Ciccotti who dealt with the topic systematically, attributing the decline of slavery to economic factors; see Ciccotti, *Il tramonto della schiavitù nel mondo antico*, 1899.

Chapter 2

1. The discussion on slavery which follows draws extensively on the work of M.I. Finley, K. Hopkins and G.E.M. de Ste. Croix (see bibliography).
2. This is stressed by B. Hindess and P. Hirst, *Pre-Capitalist Modes of Production*, p. 109.
3. Aristotle, *Politics* I. 13, 1260^a 5.
4. The famous passage runs as follows: 'The truth of the independent consciousness is accordingly the consciousness of the bondsman. This doubtless appears in the first instance outside itself, and not as the truth of self-consciousness. But just as lordship showed its essential nature to be the reverse of what it wants to be, so, too, bondage will, when completed, pass into the opposite of what it immediately is: being a consciousness repressed within itself, it will enter into itself, and change round into real and true independence'; Hegel, *The Phenomenology of Mind* (1807), London 1949, p. 237.
5. Hegel, *Philosophy of Mind* (1830, 1845), Oxford 1971, pp. 174-5.
6. Aristotle, *Politics* I. 7, 1255^b 35-7. There is a long discussion on the problems posed by the notion 'slave society'. P. Garnsey is probably correct in arguing 'at the risk of dogmatism' that 'slave labour was never dominant in agriculture outside Italy and Sicily', *Non-Slave Labour*, p. 35. Recently Ste. Croix has argued that the distinguishing feature of each social formation 'is not so much *how the bulk of the labour of production is done*, as *how the dominant propertied classes*, controlling the conditions of production, *ensure the extraction of the surplus* which makes their own leisured existence possible.' It is in this sense that 'we are justified in saying that the Greek and Roman world was a "slave economy"'; *The Class Struggle*, p. 52.
7. See A.H.M. Jones, 'Slavery in the Ancient World'.
8. Finley, *Ancient Slavery*, p. 86.
9. For details see Hopkins, *Conquerors and Slaves*, ch. 1.
10. Juvenal, 6. 219-222.
11. Pollux, *Onomasticon* 3.83. See also W.L. Westermann, 'Slavery and the Elements of Freedom in Ancient Greece', in Finley, *Slavery in Classical Antiquity*; Finley, 'Between Slavery and Freedom' repr. in *Economy and Society*; Hopkins, *op. cit*, ch. 3. On the

Roman law of slavery see W.W. Buckland, *The Roman Law of Slavery.*

12. Ste. Croix, 'Class in Marx's Conception of History'; Ste. Croix has shown that Marx sometimes referred to class struggles in a way that would exclude slaves, but then always what Marx had in mind were *political* struggles.

13. M. Weber, *Economy and Society,* p. 484.

14. Tacitus, *Annals* 14.44.

15. A. Momigliano, 'Popular Religious Beliefs and the Late Roman Historians', repr. in *Essays,* p. 144.

16. F. Bömer, *Untersuchungen* I, pp. 184 ff.

17. J. Johnson, *Excavations at Minturnae* 2, Inscriptions, Part I, Roma 1933. A.D. Nock in his review of the above observes that 'While the great civic cults were the affair of the city as a political unit, and authority could therefore be delegated only to citizens and in some cases only to patricians, (at Minturnae) on the other hand the unit was geographical, and social status was irrelevant', review repr. in *Essays* I, p. 412. See also pp. 49 ff.

18. Livy 39.8 ff.

19. F. Cumont, *The Mysteries of Mithra,* pp. 63 ff., 70 f., 78, 189; *The Oriental Religions,* p. 106. See also A.D. Nock, *Conversion,* pp. 131-2.

20. For a discussion of the literature on the subject see J. Vogt, *Ancient Slavery,* ch. 9; Finley, *Ancient Slavery,* ch. 1.

21. In what follows, I am heavily indebted to Ste. Croix 'Early Christian Attitudes', and *The Class Struggle,* ch. 7 ii and iii; for references to slavery in the New Testament and relevant discussion, see C.J. Cadoux, *The Early Church and the World,* pp. 131-5.

22. Aristotle's view is presented in Book I of the *Politics.*

23. Seneca, *Ep.* 91; cf. *De Beneficiis.*

24. *Ep.* 47; see K.R. Bradley, 'Seneca and Slavery' *CM* 37, 1986.

25. Thus Ste. Croix, *op. cit.,* p. 420.

26. M. Goguel, *The Primitive Church,* pp. 554-7. J. Chrysostom's exegesis in *MPG* 62, 704; cf. p. 193 n26 below.

27. Clement *Strom.* 4.3, p. 411. Early traces of the theory are to be found in Xenophon *Oeconomicus* 1.21-2. Cf. Augustine *City of God* 4.3: 'The good man, though a slave, is free ...'

28. Clement, *Paed.* 3.12. In Clement's view slaves should be corrected by their masters, *ibid.* 3.11.

29. Origen, *C. Cels.* 3.54.

30. Chrysostom, *NPNF,* f.s. 12, pp. 108-9.

31. John Chrysostom writes that 'if the unbeliever sees slaves conducting themselves insolently on account of their faith, he will blaspheme, as if the Doctrine produced insubordination', *NPNF,* f.s. 13, pp. 465, 533.

32. Hippolytus, *Apost. Trad.* 16. 3-5, 23-4; cf. *Apost. Const.* 8.32.

33. *Apost. Const.* 8.33. For the observance of feast days in the pagan world see Cato, *De Agri Cultura* 5.

34. *Apostolic Canons* 82, in C.J. Hefele, *A History of the Christian Councils,* p. 490; also *Apost. Const.* 8.47.82, p. 505. Cf. Canon 4 of the Council of Chalcedon.

35. Canons 5, 8, 41 in Hefele, *op cit.,* pp. 140, 141, 154. Ste Croix is probably right in believing that the flogging to death of the slave girl was due to the fact that she 'had accepted the sexual attentions of the woman's husband'; *The Class Struggle,* p. 420.

36. Ste. Croix 'Early Christian Attitudes', p. 23; on the sexual exploitation of female slaves by free men see S. Treggiari 'Questions on Women Domestics in the Roman West', in *Schiavitù,* Roma 1979, pp. 192 ff; see also A. Dalby 'On Female Slaves in Roman Egypt', *Arethusa* 12, 2, 1979; Finley *Ancient Slavery,* pp. 95-6.

37. Paulinus of Pella *Eucharisticus* 162-8. That this mentality was common throughout the Roman period we may infer from such works as Petronius' *Satyricon,* Horace's *Satires* and Seneca the Elder's *Controversies*; see Finley *op. cit.*

38. See references in Cadoux *op. cit.,* pp. 199-200.

39. Vogt *op. cit.,* p. 145.

40. Chrysostom, *NPNF,* f.s. 13, p. 465. In the well-known New Testament parable on 'The Unmerciful Servant' (Mt. 18:23 ff.) which is supposed to portray the Kingdom of

Heaven, not only are slaves at the mercy of their master (God), but a strict hierarchy among slaves is observed.

41. Athanasius *The Life of Antony* 18, p.45.
42. Eusebius, *HE* 5.1.14, vol. I, p. 413.
43. Irenaeus, fragment 13, in *ANF* 1, p. 574.
44. Tertullian, *Apol.* 7.3; 27.5, 7.
45. Literally 'betrayed by those of their own houses'; Hefele, *op. cit.*, p. 203.
46. Origen, *C. Cels.* 6.13.
47. This was how John Chrysostom understood the situation, *NPNF*, f.s. 11, p.74.
48. See discussion in M. Hengel, *Property and Riches*, ch. 4. Hengel believes that 'social distinctions were virtually abolished ...', p. 34.
49. Hegel, *Early Theological Writings*, pp. 87-8.
50. Renan, *The Apostles*, ch. 5.
51. This passage from *Anti-Dühring* is reprinted in Marx and Engels, *On Religion*, p. 129.
52. Kautsky, *Foundations of Christianity*, p. 415.
53. Troeltsch, *The Social Teachings*, vol. 1, p. 62.
54. Harnack, *The Mission and Expansion*, vol. 1, p.151 n. 2.
55. The expression 'a passing phase of early Church life' belongs to Cadoux, *The Early Church*, p. 131 n. 5.
56. Lucian, *Peregrinus* 13.
57. Renan, *op. cit.*; Kautsky, *op. cit.*
58. Hippolytus, *Comm. in Daniel* 4.19; translation of the text in Harnack, *op. cit.*, vol. 2, pp. 204-5.
59. See J. Allegro, *The Dead Sea Scrolls*, p. 111; G. Vermes, *The Dead Sea Scrolls in English*, p. 29. The Essenes may also have owned slaves, see Vermes, *The Dead Sea Scrolls*, p. 128.
60. W.M. Ramsay, *The Church*, pp. 56 f., 133. f., 147; *The Cities*, p.72; the two quotations are taken from R.H. Barrow, *Slavery*, p. 163, and W.H.C. Frend, *Martyrdom and Persecution*, p. 189 respectively.
61. Cyprian, *Ep.* 80.1.
62. Canons 40 and 49 of the Council of Elvira.
63. Weber, *The Agrarian Sociology*, p. 400.
64. See Cato, *De Agri Cultura* 56; Columella, *De Re Rustica* 1.8.16.
65. See Finley, *Aspects of Antiquity*, p. 154; J. Kolendo, 'Eléments pour une enquête sur l'iconographie des esclaves dans l'art Hellénistique et Romain', in *Schiavitù*, Roma 1979, pp. 162 f. Chained slaves were common in the days of Chrisostome, *On Virginity* 41.2.
66. Pliny, *Ep.* 3.19.
67. See the discussion in R. MacMullen, *Christianizing the Roman Empire*, p. 65, and p. 148 n. 20.
68. See W.W. Buckland, *The Roman Law of Slavery*, p. 76.
69. Plutarch, *Marcus Cato* 21.3; Varro, *De Re Rustica* 1.17.5; 2.1.26; 2.10.6-7; Columella, *De Re Rustica* 1.8,19. K.J. Dover in his *Greek Homosexuality*, Cambridge, Mass., 1978, p. 97, observes that 'There is a certain tendency in comedy to treat masturbation as behaviour characteristic of slaves, who could not expect sexual outlets comparable in number or quality with those of free men'; further information on this topic in Ste. Croix, *The Class Struggle*, pp. 235-6.
70. The translation is given as 'appendix 4' in Josephus, *The Jewish War*, Penguin, p. 400.
71. Athenagoras, *Legatio* 11.4: 'In our ranks, however, you could find common men, artisans and old women ...'; Tatian, *Oratio* 32, 33.
72. Minucius Felix, *Octavius* 8.4, p. 335. I cannot see how Barrow, *op. cit.*, p. 163 takes the expression 'ultima faece' to refer to slaves. How could slaves 'gather together' and 'organize a rabble of profane conspirators, leagued by meetings at night' etc.? The Christian reply in 36.3 ff., refers to 'reputed poor' and leaves no place for slaves.
73. Tertullian, *Apol.* 39.6, p. 177; *Idol.* 17.
74. Origen, *C. Cels.* 3.44, p. 158; also 3.55.

75. Pliny, *Ep.* 10.96; Ignatius, *Polycarp* 4; Eusebius, *Passio* 3.18.

76. Ignatius, *Polycarp* 4; Eusebius, *HE* 5.1.17 ff.; *The Martyrs of Lyons, The Martyrdom of Perpetua and Felicitas, The Martyrdom of Pionius* in H. Musurillo, *The Acts*, pp. 66 ff., 106 ff., 147; Eusebius, *Passio* 3.18; Hippolytus, *Ref.* 9.12.1.

77. This passage is probably an addition to the Greek original of Aristeides' *Apology* 15.6-7, found in the Syrian version; translation in *NE*, p. 57.

78. Diodorus Siculus, 3.13.3; for conditions in the mines of Spain see 5.38. Cf. Lucretius, *De Rerum Natura* 6.813-5.

79. See A.S. Barnes, *Christianity at Rome*, pp. 163 ff.

80. *Acts of Paul* 6, in James, *ANT*, p. 287.

81. Eusebius, *HE* 4.23.10; cf. Tertullian, *Apol.* 39.6.

82. Hippolytus, *Ref.* 9.12.1-13.

83. *The Epistle of Phileas*; *Mosaicarum et Romanorum Legum Collatio* XV. iii; Eusebius, *HE* 8.13.5; Epiphanius, *Panarion* 68.2.

84. Cyprian, *Ep* 76; Eusebius, *Mart. Pal.* 8.1, 9.1; *Apost. Const.* 5.1.

85. *Cod. Theod.* 9.40.2.

86. J.B. Mullinger, 'Slavery', in *DCA*, vol. 2, p. 1904; de Rossi, *Boll. di Arch. Christ.*, 1866, p. 24; O. Marucchi, *Christian Epigraphy*, p. 223.

87. Harnack, *The Mission and Expansion*, vol. 1, p. 168 n. 1; also vol. 2, pp. 33-4.

88. I. Kajanto, *Onomastic Studies*, pp. 6-9.

89. Lactantius, *The Divine Institutes* 5.16, p. 151.

90. Hegel, *The Phenomenology of Mind*, London 1977, p. 236.

91. I have made use here of S. Ferenczi's work *Sex in Psycho-Analysis*, New York 1956; quotation from p. 66.

92. Varro, *De Re Rustica* 1.17.7.

93. Juvenal, 14.19.

94. Details are given in Ste Croix, *The Class Struggle*, pp. 409 f.

95. Juvenal, 9. 120.

96. Phaedrus 3.

97. See J. Liebeschuetz, *Continuity and Change*, pp. 70-1; J. Johnson, *Excavations at Minturnae*, p. 8; A.D. Nock, *Conversion*, pp. 72-3, 285; J.G. Frazer, *The Golden Bough* (1922), London 1957, pp. 208, 764; F. Cumont, *The Oriental Religions*, p. 106.

98. Hermas, Vis. 2.3.1.

99. Only the slave leader Eunus, so far as we know, may have been inspired by religious revelation to his revolutionary actions; see the discussion in Vogt, *Ancient Slavery*, pp. 51 ff.

100. In C.J. Hefele, *History*, p. 154.

101. Justin, *Apol. 2*, 12.4; Athenagoras, *Legatio* 35.3 and 3.1; Eusebius, *HE* 5.1.14; Irenaeus, frag. 13; the *Martyrdom of Polycarp* 6; the case of the slave volunteer, afterwards executed, is given in Eusebius, *HE* 5.21.2-3; for a slave public executioner during the persecutions see *The Martyrdom of Saints Agape, Irene, and Chione* 6.

102. *Acts of John* 63 ff., in *NTA* 2, pp. 245 ff.

Chapter 3

1. Tacitus, *Annals* 13.27. Cf. Seneca, *Ep.* 47. The discussion of manumission which follows draws mainly on the works of A.M. Duff, W.L. Westermann, W.W. Buckland, M.I. Finley and K. Hopkins cited below.

2. Tacitus, *Annals* 11.36 f.; 15.72; Pliny, *Ep.* 3.14; Statius, *Silvae* 3.3, lines 85-108; Historia Augusta, *Pertinax* 1.1 etc.

3. See W.L. Westermann, *The Slave Systems*, p. 18.

4. See A.M. Duff, *Freedmen*, p. 12; Finley (ed.), *Slavery*, p. 58; D. Whitehead, *The Ideology of the Athenian Metic*, Cambridge 1977, p. 114.

5. See Ste Croix, *The Class Struggle*, pp. 507 f; for a different view, H. Kreissig,

'L'esclavage dans les villes d'Orient pendant la période hellénistique', in *Actes du Colloque*, 1973.

6. See I. Bieżuńska-Malowist, 'L'esclave à Alexandrie dans la période Gréco-Romaine', in *Actes du Collogue* 1973; J.A. Strauss, 'La terminologie de l'esclavage dans les papyrus Grecs d'époque Romaine trouvés en Egypte', in *Actes du Colloque* 1973.

7. See B. Nadel, 'Slavery on the North Shore of the Euxine', in *Actes du Colloque*, 1973.

8. Westermann, *op. cit.*, p. 9, discussing E. Meyer's *Die Sklaverei im Altertum.*

9. Finley, *The Ancient Greeks* (1963), London 1977, p. 72.

10. Ste. Croix, review of Westermann, *op. cit.*, *CR* n.s. 7, 1957, p. 56.

11. P. Brunt, 'Free Labour and Public Works at Rome', *JRS* 70, 1980, p. 90.

12. Finley, *op. cit.*, p. 72.

13. See A.M. Duff, *op. cit.*, pp. 19, 103, 196 f.

14. Suetonius, *Augustus* 40. See also Westermann, *op. cit.*, pp. 89 f.; Buckland, *The Roman Law of Slavery*, pp. 537-51; M.L. Gordon, 'The Freedman's Son', pp. 65 f.; T. Frank, 'Race Mixture', p. 50.

15. Suetonius, *Augustus* 42; Dion. Hal., *Ant.* 4.24.5. See discussion in Duff, *op. cit.*, pp. 20 f.; L.R. Taylor, 'Freedmen and Freeborn', pp. 128 f.; S. Treggiari, *Roman Freedmen*, pp. 11 ff.; Hopkins, *Conquerors and Slaves*, pp. 115 ff.

16. Westermann, 'The Paramone as General Service Contract', *JJP* 2, 1948, p. 9; cf. Ste. Croix, *The Class Struggle*, p. 169.

17. Duff, *op. cit.*, pp. 36 f., 44; Brunt, *art. cit.*, p. 89.

18. See Finley, 'Between Slavery and Freedom', (1964) repr. in *Economy and Society*; Hopkins, *op. cit.*, ch. 3.

19. See Frank, *art. cit.*; Treggiari, *op. cit.*, pp. 31 ff.; Taylor, *art. cit.*, pp. 117-23; Gordon, *art. cit.*, p. 70. More recently, calculations based on sepulchral inscriptions have fallen into disrepute, see Hopkins, *op. cit*, pp. 115ff.

20. See P.R.C. Weaver, *Familia Caesaris.*

21. Livy. 39.9.

22. Cf. F. Cumont, *Oriental Religions*, p. 28; E.R. Dodds, *Pagan and Christian*, p. 137.

23. See Duff, *op. cit.*, p. 132; Hopkins, *op. cit.*, pp. 211 ff.

24. Tacitus, *Annals* 2.85; Josephus, *Jewish Antiquities* 18. 65-8, 81-4.

25. Canon 3, in *SEC*, p. 93; the Synodical Letter in p. 91.

26. J. Chrysostom, *NPNF*, f.s. 13, p. 533; for a discussion of the Pauline passage see p. 546: '... Now we are not ignorant that some say, the words "use it rather", are spoken with regard to liberty: interpreting it, "if thou canst become free, become free." But the expression would be very contrary to Paul's manner if he intended this.'; see also *NPNF*, f.s. 12, p. 108; Theodoret, *Comm. on 1 Cor. 7.21.*

27. Ignatius, *Polycarp* 4, p. 273.

28. W. Bauer, *Orthodoxy and Heresy*, pp. 64, 69.

29. *Acts of Peter* 28; in *NTA* 2, p. 312.

30. *Acts of Philip* 80; in James, *ANT*, p. 445.

31. *Acts of Thomas* 83; in *NTA* 2, p. 487.

32. See Cadoux, *The Early Church*, p. 454; R.M. Grant, *Augustus to Constantine*, p. 301. The views of these scholars have been rejected by Ste. Croix in his 'Early Christian Attitudes', p. 22.

33. Cyprian, *Ad Demetrianum* 8.

34. Tertullian, *Apol.* 39.6; Cyprian, *Ep.* 35.

35. Seneca, *Ep.* 47.

36. Eusebius, *HE* 4.15.46; for the date see H. Musurillo, *The Acts*, pp. xxviii f.; the text of the *Martyrdom* in pp. 136 ff.

37. See Grant, *Early Christianity*, p. 93.

38. See Cadoux, *op. cit.*, p. 606.

39. *Apost. Const.* 4.2.12.

40. See Musurillo, *op. cit.*, pp. 150, 164.

41. W.H.C. Frend, *Martyrdom and Persecution*, p. 411.

42. *Apost. Const.* 4.1.9, p. 435.

43. This is what Cadoux understood from the passage, *op. cit.*, p. 609.

44. *1 Clem.* 55, p. 51.

45. Eusebius, *HE* 6.42.4, vol. 2, p. 110; Cyprian, *Ep.* 59.

46. *Apost. Const.* 2.7.62, p. 424.

47. *Ibid.*, p. 424 n. 9.

48. See C.K. Barrett, *The New Testament Background*, p. 53.

49. W.W. Buckland, *The Roman Law of Slavery*, pp. 449-51; W.L. Westermann, *The Slave Systems*, pp. 130, 154-5; T.D. Barnes, *Constantine and Eusebius*, pp. 50-1, 311 n. 76.

50. A.M. Duff, *Freedmen*, p. 197.

51. Sozomen, *HE* 1.9, p. 246.

52. See Westermann, *op. cit.*, pp. 154-5.

53. Sozomen, *HE* 1.9, p. 246.

54. *Cod. Theod.* 4.7.

55. Canons 64 (Greek 67) and 129 (Greek 130) of the African Code of AD 419 (in *SEC*, pp. 474, 504).

56. Firmicus Maternus, *Mathesis* 7.4.12, 14, pp. 239 f.

57. Dodds, *Pagan and Christian*, p. 137; W.A. Meeks, *The First Urban Christians*, pp. 22-3, 191.

58. See Finley, 'Aulos Kapreilios Timotheos, Slave Trader', repr. in *Aspects of Antiquity*, pp. 154 ff.

59. For a discussion of the topic see Ste Croix, *The Class Struggle*, pp. 174 ff.

60. However, the much-quoted passage in 1 Cor. 7:22 according to which slaves receiving the call to become Christians are Lord's freedmen, brings us close to the problem of emancipation. In spite of its theological/metaphorical usage, the expression becomes intelligible primarily among people who have faced or are in the prospect of facing actual manumission; cf. Ignatius, *Romans* 4.

61. This seems to be the implication of the opening paragraph of *The Shepherd*. See discussion in W.J. Wilson, 'The Career of the Prophet Hermas'. If Hermas had been the slave of a Christian master, the same must have been true for his brother Pius who became 'bishop' of Rome.

62. See Harnack, *The Mission and Expansion*, vol. 2, p. 46; Cadoux, *The Early Church*, p. 180; Frend, *Martyrdom and Persecution*, p. 242.

63. For a very interesting discussion of the case of Erastus, see Meeks, *op. cit.*, pp. 58-9.

64. Meeks has gone through most of the material discussed in this paragraph from a rather different angle and has provided valuable information and suggestions. For slave names in the Roman Empire see A.M. Duff, *Freedmen*; T. Frank, 'Race Mixture'; M.L. Gordon, 'The Nationality of Slaves'; L.R. Taylor, 'Freedmen and Freeborn'.

Chapter 4

1. Tacitus, *Hist.* 5.9.

2. I shall just mention W.M. Ramsay, *St. Paul the Traveller*, pp. 352 f. and Cadoux, *The Early Church*, pp. 392, 389. More recently attention has been drawn to the subject by J.G. Gager, 'Religion and Social Class' and Meeks, *The First Urban Christians*, pp. 21 f., 63, 73, 75 f.

3. In what follows I have drawn upon the work of P.R.C. Weaver (see bibliography); P. Garnsey, *Social Status and Legal Privilege*, pp. 87 ff., 258; G. Boulvert, *Domestique et Fonctionnaire*, pp. 200, 205, 259 and L.R. Taylor, 'Freedmen and Freeborn', p. 122.

4. Hopkins, 'Elite Mobility', p. 113; also Jones, 'The Roman Civil Service', *JRS* 39, 1949.

5. See Jones, 'Taxation in Antiquity', repr. in *The Roman Economy*, p. 166.

6. See Tacitus, *Annals* 14.39.

7. See I. Bieżuńska-Malowist, 'Les esclaves impériaux dans l'Égypte Romaine' (1976), in *Schiavitù*, Roma 1979.

8. Jones, 'The Caste System', repr. in *op. cit.*, p. 404.

9. Suetonius, *Claudius* 25.

10. *Acts of Paul* 11, in *NTA* 2, p. 383. Much of the evidence discussed in the present section has been collected by Harnack, *The Mission and Expansion*, vol. 2, pp. 44 ff., and Cadoux, *The Early Church*, pp. 114 f., 391 ff.

11. *Acts of Peter* 1.3; 2.4-6, in *NTA* 2, pp. 282 ff. If the story about Narcissus is a pious invention, then it is striking that the second-century compilers of the *Acts* knew that the household of Narcissus belonged to the *Familia Caesaris*; Paul himself did not make this connection.

12. *1 Clem.* 63, 65; *Clementine Homilies* 12.8.

13. *The Martyrdom of Justin*, Recensions B, 4 and C, 3 in H. Musurillo, *The Acts*, pp. 51, 57. Another companion of Justin's is reported to have said that his earthly parents were dead and that he came to Rome being 'dragged off' from Iconium in Phrygia; were he and Euelpistus slave-captives?

14. Irenaeus, *AH* 4.30.1, p. 503.

15. *Acts of Peter* 4, in *NTA* 2, pp. 289 f.

16. Eusebius, *HE* 5.20.5.

17. Hippolytus, *Ref.* 9.

18. Tertullian, *Apol.* 37; *Ad Scapulam* 4.

19. Eusebius, *HE* 6.28; 7.10.3, vol. 2, pp. 81, 151.

20. Cyprian, *Ep.* 80.1.

21. Eusebius, *HE* 7.32.3; 8.6.1-7.

22. Eusebius, *HE* 8.1.3; 8.6.1-7; 8.11.2; Lactantius, *De Mortibus Persecutorum* 11.3; *Acta Maximiliani* 2; see also E.R. Barker, *Rome of the Pilgrims and Martyrs*, pp. 185 f. There is a translation of the Epistle of Theonas in *ANF* 6, pp. 158 ff.

23. Hopkins, 'Elite Mobility in the Roman Empire'; Ste. Croix, *The Class Struggle*, pp. 380 f.

24. Eusebius, *HE* 8.6.1, vol. 2, p. 265.

25. Lactantius, *De Mortibus Persecutorum* 11.1-3; cf. Eusebius, *HE*, a section given as 'Appendix to Book 8' in p. 323 of the Loeb edition vol. 2.

26. Cumont, *The Mysteries of Mithra*, p. 75.

27. Meeks, *The First Urban Christians*, p. 22; Weaver, 'Social Mobility in the Early Roman Empire', p. 123.

Chapter 5

1. See W. Bauer, *Orthodoxy and Heresy*.

2. H. Chadwick, *The Early Church*, p. 85.

3. W.H.C. Frend, 'Early Christianity and Society', p. 71.

4. See the works of Engels cited in the bibliography. According to Kautsky the early Christian movement consisted of 'the free urban proletarians, workers and idlers (who) did not feel that society was living on them; they all strove to live on society without giving any return'; Kautsky, *Foundation of Christianity*, pp. 464-7.

5. M. Weber, *Economy and Society*, pp. 439, 452 ff.

6. A. Harnack, *The Constitution and Law of the Church*, pp. 23 ff., 121 ff. The theory of prophet–priest opposition in the early church was continued by Harnack's successor at Berlin, H. Lietzmann; see his *The Foundation of the Church Universal*, pp. 193 ff.

7. The same idea concerning the religious history of the Jews is recently repeated by Frend: '... one can detect the thinly disguised tensions between the priestly and the prophetic parties in Israel. The priests served the temple of the Lord in an orderly,

urbanised environment. The prophets, as Elijah and Elisha or Amos, were countrymen, often itinerant ... denouncing the crimes of the rich'; 'Town and Countryside in Early Christianity', repr. in *Town and Country*, I, p. 29.

8. W.M. Ramsay, *The Church in the Roman Empire*, pp. 56 f.

9. Ramsay, *St. Paul the Traveller*, pp. 133 f.

10. This observation has been made several times by Frend; besides the article mentioned above, see also 'The Winning of the Countryside', repr. in *op. cit.* The subject has also been given detailed treatment by Ste. Croix, 'Early Christian Attitudes' and *The Class Struggle*, pp. 425 ff.; quotation from p. 430. According to G. Vermes' vivid account Jesus was not only confined to the Palestinian countryside, but was in particular a *Galilean* Jew, impressing his countrymen 'chiefly as a charismatic teacher, healer and exorcist', in *Jesus and the World of Judaism*, p. 5.

11. A.T. Kraabel, 'Synagoga Caeca', in J. Neusner and E.S. Frerichs (eds.), *To See Ôurselves as Others*, California 1985, p. 225.

12. Ste. Croix, from whom I borrow these arguments, has seen this transformation of early Christianity 'as the transfer of a whole system of ideas from the world of the *chōra* to that of the *polis*', *op. cit.*, p. 433; see also his foreword above.

13. On the topic, see the work of Vermes, *Jesus the Jew*.

14. See the remarks made by Kraabel, *art. cit.*

15. Eusebius, *HE* 5.16.

16. Athanasius, *The Life of Antony* 2, p. 31.

17. Besides the articles by Frend and Ste. Croix mentioned above, I would like to add two articles by Brown, 'The Rise and Function of the Holy Man in Late Antiquity', and 'Town, Village and Holy Man: The Case of Syria', both now repr. in *Society and the Holy*.

Chapter 6

1. See M. Hengel, *Property and Riches in the Early Church*, p. 36.

2. On the social structure of the Pauline communities, see Meeks, *The First Urban Christians.*

3. Jones, 'The Social Background of the Stuggle Between Paganism and Christianity'; Brown, 'Aspects of the Christianization of the Roman Aristocracy', repr. in *Religion and Society*, p. 181.

4. See R. von Haehling, *Die Religionszugehörigkeit der hohen Amtsträger des Römischen Reiches*, 324-450/5, Bonn 1978; I have only been able to see a good review of this work by J.R. Martindale in *JRS* 69, 1979.

5. Brown, *art. cit.*, p. 164.

6. R.L. Wilken, *The Christians as the Romans Saw Them*, p. 58. In this recent book most of the extant pagan evidence has been collected and discussed.

7. On Synesius see now J.A. Bregman, *Synesius of Cyrene: Philosopher-Bishop*, Berkeley, Los Angeles, London 1982.

8. On the complex topic of divisions among the upper classes in Roman Egypt, with which I shall be mostly concerned in the present chapter, see the discussion in H.I. Bell, *Egypt*, pp. 65 ff.

9. Clement, Fragment from the Latin translation of Cassiodorus 1 *ANF* 2, p. 573. The well-dressed man with the golden ring mentioned in James 2:2 is certainly an equestrian. The epistle of James, however, favours the poor in the congregations, recalling that the oppressors of Christians were the rich. The passage is self-contradictory; but it is of course clear that the persecutors in high administrative posts were always members of the upper classes. *Acts of Peter* 2, 4.

10. Cadoux, *The Early Church*, p. 266, on the *Acts of Paul*; Harnack, *The Mission and Expansion*, vol. 2, p. 43 n. 4, wrote something similar of the *Acts of Peter*.

11. Eusebius, *HE* 5.21.2.

12. *The Martyrdom of Apollonius* 11, in H. Musurillo, *The Acts*, p. 93. Jerome's account in *De Viris Illustribus* 42.

13. Tertullian, *Apol.* 37.4, p. 169.

14. The rescript is recorded in Cyprian, *Ep.* 80.1.

15. Eusebius, *HE* 7.16.1.

16. *Ibid.*, 8.1.2.

17. Hippolytus, *Apost. Trad.* 16.17-18. In his Commentary on Daniel (4.18), Hippolytus reported the case of a Christian wife of a governor of Syria who was able to save Christians by influencing her husband; this story must refer to the reign of Commodus or Septimus Severus. There are many other such stories reported by various authors.

18. See among others Harnack, *op. cit.*, vol. 2, pp. 33-42, and Cadoux, *op. cit.*, pp. 389 ff., 555. Numerous other scholars have dealt with particular periods and especially with the first century; such are E.A. Judge, *The Social Pattern of Christian Groups in the First Century* and Meeks, *op. cit.* A recent very important work dealing with AD 100-400 is R. MacMullen's *Christianizing the Roman Empire.*

19. Eusebius, *HE* 8.9.6. The martyrs of Lyons in the second century had their own slaves, they numbered members of the liberal professions and some of them were Roman citizens (*ibid.*, 5.1).Some further details will be considered later in the present chapter.

20. Introductory note to Clement of Alexandria in *ANF* 2, p. 167.

21. M. Hengel, *op. cit.*, p. 76.

22. F.C. Burkitt, 'The Christian Church in the East', in *CAH* 12, p. 480.

23. Harnack, *op. cit.*, vol. 2, p. 37 n. 4.

24. E.R. Dodds, *Pagan and Christian*, p. 134 n. 3.

25. See his introduction to the *Sources Chrétiennes* edition of *Le Pédagogue*, Paris 1960, vol. 1, pp. 7, 64.

26. To facilitate references to the *Paedagogus* in the present section and the next, I have given in parenthesis the book, the paragraph and the page number of the quotation.

27. In *The Rich Man's Salvation*, perhaps alluding to his own vocation, Clement, addressing himself to the Christian who was 'haughty and powerful and rich', calls him to appoint for himself 'some man of God as trainer and pilot'; 'Let there be at all events', he adds, 'one whom you respect, one whom you fear, one whom you accustom yourself to listen to when he is outspoken and severe, though all the while at your service.' (41, p. 355). So, according to Clement, an important catechist should be at the service of the rich.

28. This statement needs to be substantiated by a much wider investigation of the extant evidence. I can only add at this point, that in about the same period, according to the evidence of Tertullian, the Christian communities in Carthage had also penetrated into the upper classes; 'what cause have you for appearing in public in excessive grandeur', Tertullian asks Christian women in his congregation; *On the Apparel of Women* 2.9, p. 24.

29. G.W. Butterworth, Introduction to *The Rich Man's Salvation* in Clement of Alexandria, Loeb, pp. 265 ff.

30. *The Rich Man's Salvation* 3, p. 275.

31. *Ibid.* 26, p. 325.

32. *1 Clement* 38, p. 43.

33. *Paed.* 2.13, p. 268.

34. *The Rich Man's Salvation* 12-3, p. 295.

35. Clement, *Strom.* 2.1, p. 347.

36. R. Browning, *Medieval and Modern Greek*, p. 50.

37. See E.L. Bowie, 'Greeks and their Past in the Second Sophistic', repr. in Finley (ed.), *Studies in Ancient Society.*

38. Jones, *The Later Roman Empire*, vol. 2, p. 1006.

39. Browning, *op. cit.*, p. 54.

40. P. Brown, 'Aspects of the Christianization of the Roman Aristocracy', repr. in *Religion and Society*, p. 178.

41. P.D. Scott-Moncrieff, *Paganism and Christianity in Egypt*, pp. 99-132. Many mummies, however, were discovered after the publication of this work. On the practice of mummification by Christians in Egypt, see Athanasius, *Life of Antony* 90.

42. See the valuable discussion by E.A. Judge and S.R. Pickering, 'Papyrus Documentation of Church and Community in Egypt'.

43. In his *Strom.* 1.21, Clement mentioned the death of Commodus (A.D. 192); the

Paedagogus seems to have been written shortly before.

44. On the election of Demetrius, see Eusebius, *HE* 5.22; on the predominance of Gnosticism in Egypt see W. Bauer, *Orthodoxy and Heresy.*

45. On liturgies see H.I. Bell, *Egypt,* pp. 84 f.

46. M. Rostovtzeff, *The Social and Economic History of the Roman Empire,* vol. 1, p. 374.

47. For a brief but comprehensive description of the general military situation, see Jones, *The Decline of the Ancient World,* pp. 10 ff.

48. Rostovtzeff, *Rome,* p. 276.

49. On taxation, see Jones, 'Taxation in Antiquity', repr. in *The Roman Economy;* on debasement and inflation, see Hopkins, 'Taxes and Trade'.

50. Hopkins, *art. cit.,* p. 122.

51. On inflation, see also Jones, 'Inflation Under the Roman Empire', repr. in *The Roman Economy.* The suggestion that Callistus may have been broken because of the falling interest rate of the age of Commodus was made by P. Petit, *Historie Générale de l'Empire Romain,* pp. 315 ff.

52. These propositions have been demonstrated by Hopkins, *art. cit.*

53. Jones, *The Decline of the Ancient World,* p. 21.

54. P. Garnsey, 'Aspects of the Decline of the Urban Aristocracy', p. 241; see also the discussion in Ste. Croix, *The Class Struggle,* pp. 469 ff.

55. R. MacMullen, 'Nationalism in Roman Egypt', *Aegyptus* 44, 1964, p. 190.

56. Jones believed that the stratified and stable Roman society started to break down during the late second and the third century; 'The Caste System in the Late Roman Empire', repr. in *The Roman Empire,* pp. 408 f.

57. The papyri mentioned, four of which came from Oxyrhynchus and one from the Great Oasis, are, along with several others of the fourth century, presented and discussed in E.A. Judge and S.R. Pickering, 'Papyrus Documentation of Church and Community in Egypt'. An earlier but still valuable discussion of the papyrological evidence is found in H.I. Bell, 'Evidences of Christianity in Egypt During the Roman Period'.

58. Clement, *The Rich Man's Salvation* 26, p. 325.

59. *Ibid.* 3, p. 275. Needless to add, of course, that several Acts of Christian martyrs demonstrate exactly the opposite: the army officer Marinus, for example, was about to be promoted centurion, when a rival candidate denounced him as a Christian. So as not to forsake his faith Marinus preferred death rather than promotion (Eusebius, *HE* 7.15). In the present discussion, however, I am interested, not in martyrdom, but in much more common everyday practices, which, as a rule, did not attract the attention of church historians.

60. On the expectation of gaining the favour of the emperor Constantine after conversion, see Jones, 'The Social Background'.

61. Hermas, Sim. 8.9.1, p. 211.

62. *Didache* 15, p. 331.

63. Polycarp, 11.2.

64. On Hermas See W.J. Wilson, 'The Career of the Prophet Hermas'.

65. Tatian, *Address to the Greeks* 32, p. 78.

66. Irenaeus, *AH* 4.30.1, pp. 502 f.

67. Cyprian, *De Lapsis* 5.6, translation as corrected in *NE,* pp. 299 f.

68. Eusebius, *HE* 7.30, vol. 2, pp. 217, 221, 223. On Paul see F. Millar, 'Paul of Samosata, Zenobia and Aurelian'.

69. W.M. Ramsay argued that this detail, omitted in some manuscripts, 'is a gloss, which crept from the margin into the text. It is doubtless very early, and perfectly trustworthy: its vitality lies in its truth, for that was not the kind of detail that was invented in the growth of the Pauline legend'; *St. Paul the Traveller,* p. 253.

70. Meeks, *The First Urban Christians,* p. 65.

71. See p. 191n 70 above.

72. Justin, *2 Apol.* 10, pp. 191 f.

73. Athenagoras, *Legatio* 11.4, p. 25.

74. *Didache* 12.

75. Origen, *C. Cels.* 3.55, p. 165.
76. Hippolytus, *Apostolic Tradition* 16.11; cf. *Apost. Const.* 8.4.32; Tertullian, *Idol.* 8.
77. See Jones, 'The Caste System in the Later Roman Empire', repr. in *The Roman Economy*, pp. 408-11.
78. The present notes are based on the extensive review of Fikhman's work by E. Wipszycka (see bibliography).
79. *Acts of Thomas* 17, in *NTA* 2, p. 451.
80. Cf. *P. Antin* 1.38.
81. I owe this suggestion to Professor R. Browning.
82. See Eusebius, *HE* 5.28.
83. Eusebius, *HE* 5.18.7, 11.
84. See *NTA* vol. 1, p. 83, vol. 2, p. 120. Eusebius, *HE* 8.7.3.
85. Pliny, *Ep.* 10.96.
86. Lucian, *Peregrinus* 12-3.
87. Tatian, *Address to the Greeks* 25, p. 75: '(Philosophers) though they say that they want nothing, yet, like Proteus, they need a currier for their wallet ...'
88. Hippolytus, *Ref.* 9.21.1, 6, translation as given in *NE*, pp. 160 f.
89. F. Cumont, *The Mysteries of Mithra*, p. 76.
90. See A. Deissmann, *Licht vom Osten*, Tübingen 1923, pp. 172-9; *P. Amh.* 3(a) provides evidence of the involvement of Maximus in financial dealings.
91. A translation of the letter in *ANF* 6, pp. 158 f. But see Harnack, *The Mission and Expansion*, vol. 2, p. 51 n. 5.
92. Origen, *C. Cels.* 3.9; Justin, *1 Apol.* 67.
93. Cyprian, *De Lapsis* 6, translation as given in *NE*, p. 230.
94. Translation as given in *NE*, p. 307. Almost all the important Councils of the early churches dealt with the problem of usury exacted by clerics; besides Elvira, Nicaea, Arles, Carthage and Tours condemned usury.
95. M.L. Gordon, 'The Freedman's Son in Municipal Life', p. 70.
96. Finley, *The Ancient Economy*, p. 77.
97. See the remarks made by Ste. Croix, *The Class Struggle*, pp. 174 f.
98. Jones, *The Greek City*, p. 298.
99. See discussion in Meeks, *op. cit.*, pp. 58 f.
100. Eusebius, *HE* 6.41.11.
101. Suetonius, *Otho* 5; *Vespasian* 23.
102. Tacitus, *Annals*, 11.38.5; 12.53.2-5.
103. Weaver, 'Social Mobility', pp. 126 f.
104. I.B. de Rossi, *Inscriptiones Christianae*, Rome 1857, vol. 1, 5, p. 9; see also Harnack, *op. cit.*, vol. 2, pp. 48 f.; Cadoux, *The Early Church*, p. 392; O. Marucchi, *Christian Epigraphy*, p. 225.
105. E. Wipszycka, 'Remarques sur les lettres privées chrétiennes', p. 205.
106. G.W. Clarke, 'Two Christians in the Familia Caesaris'; the inscription, to which little attention had been paid before Clarke's article, was also classified as Christian by Marucchi, *op. cit.*, p. 224.
107. Weaver, *Familia Caesaris*, p. 121; Clarke, *art. cit.*, p. 122.
108. See Hopkins, 'Structural Differentiation in Rome', in I.M. Lewis (ed.), *History and Social Anthropology*, London 1968, pp. 70 ff.
109. See discussion in Harnack, *op. cit.*, vol. 2, pp. 81 ff.; and Cadoux, *op. cit.*, pp. 126, 444. Valuable information and discussion may be found in the recent article of E. Pagels, 'Adam and Eve, Christ and the Church: A Survey of Second Century Controversies Concerning Marriage' in A. Longan and A.J.M. Wedderburn (eds.), *The New Testament and Gnosis*, London 1983.
110. A. Cameron, 'Neither Male nor Female', p. 63.
111. *1 Clem.* 30; Tertullian, *De Corona* 13; Cyprian, *Adv. Judaeos* 3.62; *De Lapsis* 6.
112. Justin, *2 Apol.* 2; the story of Pomponia, who is thought by some to have been a Christian, is reported by Tacitus, *Annals* 13.32.
113. See *Apost. Const.* 8.32.
114. See P.E. Corbett, *The Roman Law of Marriage*, Oxford 1930, pp. 24-34; W.W.

Buckland, *A Text-Book of Roman Law,* pp. 114 f.

115. Hippolytus, *Ref.* 9.12.24; translation as given in *NE,* p. 166.

116. See *Apost. Const.* 8.32.

117. Council of Elvira, Canons 15, 16, 17; Council of Arles, Canon 11.

118. See E.A. Judge, *The Social Pattern of Christian Groups,* pp. 35 ff.

119. Clement, *Strom.* 6.18; Eusebius, *HE* 5.21.1.

120. Hermas, Sim. 5.3.9.

121. *Apost. Const.* 4.11, p. 436.

122. Eusebius, *Mart. Pal.* 4.5.

123. Clement, *The Rich Man's Salvation* 22, p. 317.

124. *Apost. Const.* 5.6, p. 439.

125. See N. Baynes, *Constantine the Great and the Christian Church;* Jones, *Constantine and the Conversion of Europe;* and recently T.D. Barnes, *Constantine and Eusebius.*

126. Jones, *op. cit.,* p. 85.

127. Lactantius, *De Mortibus Persecutorum* 44.5; this work was probably written before 318.

128. Eusebius, *Vita Constantini* 1.28.1.

129. Eusebius, *HE* 1.13, vol. 1, pp. 84 ff.; for an introduction and discussion see W. Bauer, *Orthodoxy and Heresy,* pp. 2 ff. and his chapter in *NTA* 1, pp. 437 ff. According to Bauer the legend was created during Eusebius' lifetime.

130. *Acts of Thomas,* in *NTA* 2, pp. 454 f.

131. Eusebius, *HE* 2.2; 6.36; 7.10.3 (this last passage clearly implied, without mentioning by name, Alexander Severus and Philip Arab).

132. Origen, *C. Cels.* 8.68 ff.

133. Sozomen, *HE* 2.7, 8.

134. Origen, *C. Cels* 1.29; p. 28.

135. M. Weber, *Economy and Society,* pp. 444 ff.

136. Eusebius, *HE* 5.10.1 f.

137. E. Pagels, 'The Demiurge and his Archons: A Gnostic View of the Bishop and Presbyters?' *HTR* 69.3-4, 1976.

138. Clement, *Strom* 6.13.

139. *Ibid.* 6.13, p. 504.

140. *Ibid.* 2.11.

141. For the early stages of organized Christianity in Alexandria our sole source is Eusebius, who gives a highly incomplete and in many respects self-contradictory account. For the present section the following works have been consulted: Bauer, *Orthodoxy and Heresy;* W. Telfer, 'Episcopal Succession in Egypt'; E.R. Hardy, *Christian Egypt;* R.M. Grant, 'Early Alexandrian Christianity', repr. in *Christian Beginnings;* much older but still valuable is C. Bigg, *The Christian Platonists of Alexandria.*

142. Eusebius, *HE* 5.9.1; 5.22.1; 6.2.2; from then onwards Alexandria is presented as having one community or church; *ibid.* 6.8.3; 6.26; 6.31.2; etc.

143. See W.H.C. Frend, 'Open Questions' and 'A Severan Persecution?', repr. in *Town and Country.*

144. Eusebius, *HE* 6.4.

145. H. Chadwick, *The Early Church,* p. 100.

146. Eusebius, *HE* 6.2.

147. *Ibid.* 7.32. See also J. Quasten, *Patrology,* vol. 2, pp. 101 ff., 109 f., 111 f., 113 f.; and the biographical notices in *ANF* 6, pp. 155 ff.

148. Eusebius, *HE* 7.32.

149. Pontius, *Vita Cypriani;* Gregory of Nyssa, *Vita Greg. Thaumaturgus;* about Rome see Eusebius, *HE* 6.29.3; Gilliard, 'Senatorial Bishops', *HTR* 77, 1984.

150. In the previous section, while examining the evidence about the involvement of Christians in the banking business, I mentioned that bishops were often accused of being usurers; it may be added that control over church funds often led clerics to grave temptations; bishops and presbyters were constantly reminded that they should be 'far from all love of money'; cf. Polycarp. 6.1.

151. See my review of Meeks, *The First Urban Christians, JRS* 75, 1985.

Chapter 7

1. As further evidence of this conjecture modern scholars have pointed to the word *paganus* (peasant, villager) which came to be used as synonymous with heathen; M. Weber, *The Agrarian Sociology*, p. 336; *Economy and Society*, p. 471; A.H.M. Jones, *The Greek City*, p. 298; K. Hopkins, 'Economic Growth in Towns', p. 39. But A. Harnack showed that at first Christians as *milites* were distinguished from all other people who were *pagan*, i.e. civilians, and therefore in Christian usage *pagani* had nothing to do with peasants; *Militia Christi*, pp. 84, 105. Cf. H. Chadwick, *The Early Church*, p. 152 n. l.

2. Pliny, *Ep.* 10.96; Justin, *1 Apol.* 67. In his mission to India, the apostle Thomas is reported to have preached in towns and villages (*Acts of Thomas* 19), but there does not seem to be any historical truth in the account.

3. M. Weber, *The Agrarian Sociology*, p. 400; *Economy and Society*, p. 469.

4. Discussion in E.L. Woodward, *Christianity and Nationalism*, opposed by Jones, 'Were Ancient Heresies National or Social Movements in Disguise?', repr. in *The Roman Economy*; cf. W.H.C. Frend, 'Heresy and Schism'; P. Brown, 'Christianity and Local Culture in Late Roman Africa', repr. in *Religion and Society*; R. MacMullen, 'Nationalism in Roman Egypt', *Aegyptus* 44, 1964.

5. This remark has been forcefully made by F. Braudel, who has argued, after Marx, that 'town-country confrontation is the first and longest class struggle history has known'; *Capitalism and Material Life*, Fontana 1974, p. 373. Ste. Croix has given the fullest account to date of this confrontation in the ancient Greek world in his *Class Struggle*.

6. M. Rostovtzeff, *The Social and Economic History of the Roman Empire*, vol. 1, pp. 297 f.

7. H.I. Bell, 'Egypt, Crete and Cyrenaica', in *CAH* 11, p. 650.

8. K. Hopkins, 'Economic Growth in Towns', p. 59.

9. P. Brown, 'Town, Village and Holy Man', repr. in *Society and the Holy*, pp. 159 f.

10. Eusebius, *HE* 8.9, 10, 13; *Codex Veronensis* 60; *Passio Phileae* (in a Greek and a Latin version); Jerome, *De Viris Illustribus* 78.

11. Eusebius, *HE* 8.9.7; *Acts of Phileas* 1.2.

12. From the Latin version of the *Acts of Phileas* in Musurillo, *op. cit.*, pp. 350 f.

13. Irenaeus, *AH* 1.24.6.

14. For the papyrological evidence see H.I. Bell, 'Evidence of Christianity in Egypt'; B.M. Metzger, *The Early Versions of the New Testament*, pp. 101 ff.; C.H. Roberts, *Manuscript, Society and Belief in Early Christian Egypt*; E.A. Judge and S.R. Pickering, 'Papyrus Documentation of Church and Community in Egypt'.

15. See J. Daniélou and H. Marrou, *The Christian Centuries*, pp. 45 f.; Roberts, *op. cit.*, pp. 56 n. 3 and 57 f.

16. Roberts, *op. cit.*, p. 58.

17. Clement, *Strom.* 2.1.

18. See discussion in Roberts, *op. cit.*, pp. 47, 75 f.; and his 'Book in the Graeco-Roman World and in the New Testament' in *CHB* 1, pp. 57, 60 f.

19. T.C. Skeat, 'Early Christian Book Production', in *CHB* 2, pp. 72 f.

20. This story was put forward by Bauer, *Orthodoxy and Heresy* pp. 44-60.

21. Metzger, *op. cit.*, p. 101.

22. Roberts, *Manuscipt, Society and Belief*, pp. 51 f.; also his Review of Bauer, in *JTS* n.s. 16, 1965.

23. The books of Basilides are mentioned by Eusebius, *HE* 4.7.7; the quotation is from Irenaeus, *AH* 1.24.6.

24. See H. Jonas, *The Gnostic Religion*, p. 33.

25. The letter of Hadrian in *Historia Augusta* 3, pp. 399 ff. is probably a forgery but it may reflect in this respect a historical reality. The quotation is from Scott-Moncrieff, *Paganism and Christianity in Egypt*, p. 127 and ch. 5.

26. Irenaeus, *AH* 1.24.5.

27. Eusebius, *HE* 2.16.1.

28. *Clementine Homilies* 1.8. f.

29. See discussion in Bauer, *op. cit.*, p. 60; Roberts, *Manuscript*, p. 54; Chadwick, *The*

Early Church, p. 64; and Daniélou, *op. cit.*, p. 45.

30. C. Bigg, *The Christian Platonists of Alexandria*, p. 67.

31. Eusebius, *HE* 6.14.10.

32. Irenaeus, *AH* 1.25.6.

33. Plotinus, *Against the Gnostics* 6, in the Loeb edition, vol. 2, pp. 243, 247.

34. Chadwick, 'Philo and the Beginnings of Christian Thought', in *CHLGEMP*, p. 167; cf. J.G. Gager, 'Religion and Social Class', p. 114.

35. The discussion which follows draws on W.L. Westermann, *Upon Slavery in Ptolemaic Egypt* and *The Slave Systems*; S. Wallace, *Taxation in Egypt*; H.I. Bell, *Egypt*; M. Rostovtzeff, *The Social and Economic History of the Roman Empire*; a number of articles has also been consulted, among them M. Bloch, 'The Rise of Dependent Cultivation'; A.H.M. Jones, 'Taxation in Antiquity', 'The Roman Colonate', 'The Caste System in the Later Roman Empire' (all repr. in *The Roman Economy*); P. Brunt, 'The Fiscus and its Development', *JRS* 56, 1966. A very useful work which I read after writing this book is N. Lewis, *Life in Egypt under Roman Rule*, Oxford 1983.

36. G. Parassoglou, *Imperial Estates in Roman Egypt*, p. 4.

37. Hopkins, 'Brother-Sister Marriage in Roman Egypt', p. 331.

38. Parassoglou, *op. cit.* p. 6.

39. See E.R. Hardy, *The Large Estates of Byzantine Egypt*, pp. 44 ff.

40. On the financial organization of the primitive church see M. Goguel, *The Primitive Church*, pp. 247 ff.

41. Evidence about financial administration in the early churches is plentiful; among other sources see *Didache* 13, 15; Polycarp 4; the *Apostolic Tradition* of Hippolytus and the *Apost. Const.* 8.30, 31, 39. On salaries of bishops Eusebius, *HE* 5.18.2 and 5.28.10; Cyprian, *Ep.* 27.

42. P. Garnsey, 'Urban Property Investment'.

43. Eusebius, *HE* 7.13.1; 7.15.4; 7.30.19; 8.1.5; 8.2.1.

44. *P. Oxy.* 33.2673.

45. Eusebius, *HE* 7.11.10.

46. See Jones, 'Church Finance in the Fifth and Sixth Centuries', repr. in *The Roman Economy*; E. Wipszycka, *Les Ressources et les Activités Economiques des Eglises en Egypte*.

47. Eusebius, *HE* 7.10.4-9.

48. Epiphanius, *Panarion* 24.1, 31.2, 31.7.

49. Clement, *Strom.* 6.18.

50. Eusebius, *HE* 6.1.1, 6.11.3.

51. *Ibid.* 6.40, 4 ff., 7.11.4 ff., 7.24.6.

52. *Acta Petri Sincera*, English translation in *ANF* 6, pp. 261 ff.; Athanasius, *Apol. contra Arian* 71.

53. See discussion in P.D. Scott-Moncrieff, *Paganism and Christianity in Egypt*, pp. 82 ff.; J.R. Knipfing, 'The Libelli'; H.I. Bell, 'Evidence of Christianity in Egypt'.

54. *P. Giess* 40, quoted and discussed in R. MacMullen, *Roman Social Relations*, p. 46.

55. R. MacMullen, 'Nationalism in Roman Egypt', *Aegyptus* 44, 1964, p. 188. The two villages considered by MacMullen contained no Roman names.

56. Eusebius, *HE* 3.39.15; Clement, *Strom.* 7.17. On the importance of reading the Scriptures see A. Harnack, *Bible Reading in the Early Church*.

57. Augustine, *De Doct. Christ.* 211.16, quoted in C.S.C. Williams, 'The History of the Text and Canon of the New Testament to Jerome', in *CHB* vol. 2, p. 38.

58. Eusebius, *HE* 3.39.4, vol. 1, p. 293.

59. Irenaeus, *AH* 3.1.1.

60. Cf. Hermas, Vis. 1.3.3.

61. Hippolytus, *Apost. Trad.* 35.2; cf. Clement, *Paed.* 3.11.

62. Irenaeus, *AH* 3.4.2, p. 417.

63. *Ibid.* 1.10.2, p. 331.

64. P.A. Brunt, 'The Romanization of the Local Ruling Classes in the Roman Empire', in *Travaux*, p. 172.

65. See B.M. Metzger, *The Early Versions of the New Testament*, pp. 285 ff.

66. See G. Bardy, *La Question de langues dans l'Eglise Ancienne*; A.H.M. Jones, *The Greek City*, pp. 288 f.; Harnack, *op. cit.*, p. 91.

67. Harnack, *op. cit.*, p. 46; Bardy, *op. cit.*, pp. 72 f.

68. Bell, *art. cit.*, p. 203.

69. Eusebius, *HE* 4.7.7, vol. 1, p. 317.

70. Cf. *ibid.* 3.39.16.

71. Origen, *C. Cels.* 24, 25.

72. Epiphanius, *Panarion* 67.

73. Antony must have heard a Coptic translation of the Bible at about AD 270; see Athanasius, *Life of Antony* 2.

74. *P. Oxy.* 33.2673.

75. K. Hopkins, 'Brother-Sister Marriage', p. 351; cf. MacMullen, 'Provincial Languages in the Roman Empire', *AJP* 87, 1966, p. 9.

76. Eusebius, *HE* 6.41; see D.L. O'Leary, *The Saints of Egypt*, pp. 14 f.; E.R. Hardy, *Christian Egypt*, pp. 24, 34 ff.

77. See discussion in the works mentioned on p. 201n.4 above.

78. P. Brown, *The World of Late Antiquity*, p. 94.

79. H. Musurillo, 'Christian and Political Martyrs', pp. 337 f.

80. Cf. the views expressed by Frend in 'Town and Countryside in Early Christianity', repr. in *Town and Country*.

81. See W. Bauer, *Orthodoxy and Heresy*; M. Smith, *Clement of Alexandria* (the evidence of the letter in pp. 446 ff.); T. Orlandi, 'A Catechesis against Apocryphal Texts by Shenute and the Gnostic Texts of Nag Hammadi', *HTR* 75, 1982.

82. Eusebius, *HE* 7.11.17.

83. The information and quotations below are from Eusebius, *HE* 7.24, vol. 2, pp. 191 ff.

84. According to Epiphanius, *Panarion* 31.2, Valentinus was from the coast of Egypt; there were Valentinians at Arsinoe until his own days in the late fourth century.

85. Hippolytus, *Ref.* 7.7; 10.21.

86. Origen, *On First Principles* 4.2.1, p. 180.

87. Clement, *The Rich Man's Salvation* 5, pp. 281-3.

88. *Ibid.* 11, 12, pp. 291, 295. The observation that Clement, while giving Mark's account, inserts Matthew's qualification ('If you would be perfect') has been made by Ste. Croix, *The Class Struggle*, p. 434.

89. Origen, *C. Cels.* 6.16.

90. Athanasius, *Life of Antony* 2.

91. Cf. the observations made by J. Liebeschuetz, 'Problems Arising from the Conversion of Syria', in *SCH* 16, 1979.

Conclusion

1. R.M. Grant, 'Christian and Roman History', in S. Banko and J. O'Rourke (eds.), *Early Church History*, p. 24.

2. Eusebius, *HE* 7.11.17, vol. 2, p. 163.

3. The expression is that of G. Vermes, *Jesus the Jew*, p. 49.

4. Eusebius, *Passio Pamphili* 3.8, translation from *The Martyrs of Palestine*, vol. 1, p. 380.

5. A. Momigliano, 'Christianity and the Decline of the Roman Empire', p. 1, in *The Conflict*.

Bibliographical Acknowledgements

The author and publishers are grateful to the following for permission to include copyright material:

The Oxford and Cambridge University Presses (*The New English Bible*, second edn, © 1970); the Cambridge University Press (Origen, *Contra Celsum*, translated by Henry Chadwick); the Harvard University Press (the Loeb Classical Library editions of *Ausomius*, translated by H.G. Evelyn-White; Eusebius, *Ecclesiastical History*, translated by Kirsopp Lake and J.E.L. Oulton; *Lucian*, vol. 5, translated by A.M. Harmon; *Minucius Felix*, translated by G.H. Rendall; *Diodorus Siculus*, vol. 2, translated by C.H. Oldfather; *Barbius*, translated by Ben E. Perry; *The Apostolic Fathers*, translated by Kirsopp Lake; *Clement of Alexandria*, translated by G.W. Butterworth); Penguin Books Ltd (Josephus, *The Jewish War*, translated by G.A. Williamson, revised by E. Mary Smallwood, Penguin Classics, 1959, revised edition 1969, 1981, copyright © G.A. Williamson, 1959,1969, editorial matter copyright © E.M. Smallwood, 1981; Tacitus, *The Annuals of Imperial Rome*, translated by Michael Grant, Penguin Classics, 1956, revised edition 1959, 1971, copyright © Michael Grant Publications Ltd, 1956, 1959, 1971; Seneca, *Letters from a Stoic*, translated by Robin Campbell, Penguin Classics 1969, copyright © Robin Alexander Campbell, 1969); the Paulist Press (Althanasius, *The Life of Antony*, translated by Robert C. Gregg © The Missionary Society of St Paul the Apostle in the State of New York, 1980).

Bibliography and Abbreviations

The abbreviations listed below include journals, series of texts, dictionaries and a few works which appear often in the notes. Abbreviations that are more or less self-evident have been omitted.

In the first part of the Bibliography I give the ancient sources in the English translations used in the present work. In the notes, when quoting longer passages of particular interest, I have also given the page numbers of the translations. Passages from the Bible are quoted from *The New English Bible*, Penguin 1974. The translations in the *Anti-Nicene Fathers* series, which were made in the ninteenth century, almost always give 'servant' for 'slave'; in quoting from these translations I have silently changed the word to 'slave' whenever it is clear from the original that non-free persons are meant.

In the second part of the Bibliography I give a selection of modern works which have been consulted. Books, and in particular articles, appearing only once or twice in the notes have not been listed unless they are of more general interest for the subject of this book. Full details of works not listed in the bibliography are given in the notes where they appear. In cases where the date of a book's first publication, or of publication in the original language, may be of some interest, I have given it in parentheses after the title.

Abbreviations

AB	*Analecta Bollandiana.*
Actes du Colloque	*Actes du Colloque 1973 sur l'esclavage*, Paris 1976.
AF	*Apostolic Fathers*, LCL 1912-13 (two vol.).

AJP	*American Journal of Philology.*
ANF	*Ante-Nicene Fathers*, American reprint of the *Ante-Nicene Christian Fathers*, Edinburgh 1867-72.
ANRW	*Aufstieg und Niedergang der römischen Welt*, Ed. H. Temporini, Berlin-New York, 1972 ff.
CAH	*Cambridge Ancient History*, 2nd ed. 1966 ff.
CHB	*Cambridge History of the Bible*, 1970.
CHLGEMP	*Cambridge History of Later Greek and Early Medieval Philosophy*, 1967.
CM	*Classica et Mediaevalia.*
CQ	*Classical Quarterly.*
CR	*Classical Review.*
CSSH	*Comparative Studies in Society and History.*
DCA	*Dictionary of Christian Antiquities*, London 1875, 1880.
ECW	*Early Christian Writings*, Penguin 1968.
Eusebius *HE*	*Ecclesiastical History.*
Mart. Pal.	*The Martyrs of Palestine.*
GR	*Greece and Rome.*
Hippolytus *Ref.*	*Refutation of all Heresies.*
HTR	*Harvard Theological Review.*
HWJ	*History Workshop Journal.*
Irenaeus *AH*	*Against Heresies.*
JAC	*Jahrbuch für Antike und Christentum.*
James *ANT*	M.R. James (ed.), *The Apocryphal New Testament*, Oxford 1953.
JEH	*Journal of Ecclesiastical History.*
JJP	*Journal of Juristic Papyrology.*
JRS	*Journal of Roman Studies.*
JTS	*Journal of Theological Studies.*
MPG	*Patrologia Graeca*, ed. J.P. Migne.
NE	J. Stevenson (ed.), *A New Eusebius*, London 1968.
NLR	*New Left Review.*
NTA	E. Hennecke, *New Testament Apocrypha*, ed. W. Schneemelcher (1959, 1964), London 1963, 1974 (two vol.).
NPNF	*Nicene and Post-Nicene Fathers.*
Origen *C. Cels.*	*Contra Celsum.*
PP	*Past and Present.*
SCH	*Studies in Church History*, ed. D. Baker.
Schiavitú	*Schiavitú Manomissione e Classi Dependenti nel Mondo Antico*, Roma 1979.
SEC	*The Seven Ecumenical Councils*, in *NPNF* s.s 14.

Sozomen *HE*   *Ecclesiastical History.*
Travaux   *Travaux du VIe Congrès International d'Etudes*
                  Classiques, Madrid 1974.
VC   *Vigiliae Christianae.*

Bibliography

Apostolic Constitutions, in *ANF* 7.
Aristotle, *The Politics,* Penguin 1962.
Athanasius, *Contra Gentes* and *De Incarnatione,* Oxford 1971.
—— *The Life of Antony* and *The Letter to Marcellinus,* SPCK, London 1980.
Athenagoras, *Legatio* and *De Resurrectione,* Oxford 1972.
Barnabas, *The Epistle,* in *AF* 1.
Cato and Varro, *On Agriculture,* LCL 1934.
Clement of Alexandria, *The Exhortation to the Greeks* and *The Rich Man's Salvation,*
    LCL 1919.
—— *The Instructor, The Stromata,* Fragments, in *ANF* 2.
Clement of Rome, *The First Epistle* and *The Second Epistle,* in *AF* 1.
Columella, *De Re Rustica,* LCL, vol. 1, 1941.
Didache, in *AF* 1.
Diodorus Siculus, *Library of History,* LCL, vol. 2, 1935.
Eusebius, *The Ecclesiastical History,* LCL, 1926, 1932 (two vol.).
—— *The Martyrs of Palestine,* London 1927 (two vol.).
—— *Passio Sanctorum Pamphili et Sociorum,* in *AB* 16, 1897.
Firmicus Matermus, *Ancient Astrology Theory and Practice,* New Jersey 1975.
Hermas, *The Shepherd,* in *AF* 2.
Hippolytus, *Apostolic Tradition* (eds. Dix, Chadwick), London 1968.
Ignatius, *The Epistles,* in *AF* 1.
Irenaeus, *Against Heresies,* in *ANF* 1.
Josephus, *The Jewish War,* Penguin 1970.
Justin, *The First Apology* and *The Second Apology,* in *ANF* 1.
Juvenal, *The Sixteen Satires,* Penguin 1974.
Lactantius, *The Divine Institutes* and *Of the Manner in Which the Persecutors Died,* in
    ANF 7.
Livy, *Rome and the Mediterranean,* Penguin 1976.
Lucian, *The Passing of Peregrinus,* LCL, vol. 5, 1936.
Minucius Felix, see Tertullian.
Origen, *Contra Celsum,* Cambridge 1980.
—— *An Exhortation to Martyrdom, Prayer, First Principles* etc, SPCK, London 1979.
Papias, Fragments, in *ANF* 1.
Pliny the Younger, *The Letters,* Penguin 1969.
Plotinus, *Against the Gnostics,* LCL, vol. 2, 1966.
Polycarp, *The Epistle to the Philippians,* in *AF* 1.
Seneca, *Letters from a Stoic,* Penguin 1969.
Socrates, *Church History,* in *NPNF* s.s. 2.
Sozomenus, *Church History,* in *NPNF* s.s. 2.
Suetonius, *The Twelve Caesars,* Penguin 1957.
Tacitus, *The Annals of Imperial Rome,* Penguin 1977.
—— *The Histories,* Penguin 1975.
Tatian, *Address to the Greeks,* in *ANF* 2.
Tertullian, *Apology, De Spectaculis*; and Minucius Felix, *Octavius,* LCL 1931.
—— *On the Apparel of Women,* in *ANF* 4.
Theophilus of Antioch, *Ad Autolycum,* Oxford 1970.
Varro, see Cato.

* * *

210

Allard, P., *Les esclaves chrétiens* (1876), Paris 1914.
Allegro, J., *The Dead Sea Scrolls*, Penguin 1964.
Anderson, P., *Passages from Antiquity to Feudalism*, London 1974.
—— *Considerations on Western Marxism*, London 1976.
—— 'Class Struggle in the Ancient World' *HWJ* 16, 1983.
Bardy, G., *La question des langues dans l'église ancienne*, tome I, Paris 1948.
—— *The Church at the End of the First Century*, London 1938.
Barker, E.R., *Rome of the Pilgrims and Martyrs*, London 1913.
Barnes, A.S., *Christianity at Rome in the Apostolic Age*, London 1938.
Barnes, T.D., *Constantine and Eusebius*, Harvard 1981.
Barrett, C.K. (ed.), *The New Testament Background: Selected Documents*, London 1956.
Barrow, R.H., *Slavery in the Roman Empire*, London 1928.
Bauer, W., *Orthodoxy and Heresy in Earliest Christianity* (1934), London 1972.
Baur, F.C., *The Church History of the First Three Centuries* (1853), London 1978-9.
Baynes, N.H., *Constantine the Great and the Christian Church*, London 1931.
Bell, H.I., *Jews and Christians in Egypt*, Oxford 1924.
—— 'The Economic Crisis in Egypt under Nero' *JRS* 28, 1938.
—— 'Evidences of Christianity in Egypt During the Roman Period' *HTR* 37, 1944.
—— *Egypt. From Alexander the Great to the Arab Conquest*, Oxford 1948.
Benko, S. and J.J. O'Rourke (eds.), *Early Church History*, London 1972.
Bigg, C., *The Christian Platonists of Alexandria*, Oxford 1913.
Bloch, M., 'Comment et pourquoi finit l'esclavage antique', repr. in M.I. Finley (ed.), *Slavery in Classical Antiquity*.
Bömer, F., *Untersuchungen über die Religion der Sklaven in Griechenland und Rom*, vol. 3, Mainz 1961.
Boulvert, G., *Domestique et Fonctionnaire sous le Haut-Empire Romain. La Condition de l'Affranchi et de l'Esclave du Prince*, Paris 1974.
Brown, P.R.L., *The World of Late Antiquity*, London 1971.
—— *Religion and Society in the Age of Saint Augustine*, London 1972.
—— *The Making of Late Antiquity*, Harvard 1978.
—— *Society and the Holy in Late Antiquity*, London 1982.
Browning, R., *Medieval and Modern Greek*, London 1969.
Buckland, W.W., *The Roman Law of Slavery*, Cambridge 1908.
—— *A Text-Book of Roman Law. From Augustus to Justinian*, Cambridge 1921, 1966 (revised by P. Stein).
Bultmann, R., *Theology of the New Testament* (1948), London 1955 (two vol.).
—— *Primitive Christianity in its Contemporary Setting* (1949), New York 1956.
Cadoux, C.J., *The Early Church and the World*, Edinburgh 1925.
Cameron, Averil, 'The Theotokos in Sixth-Century Constantinople' *JTS* n.s. 29, 1978.
—— 'Neither Male nor Female' *GR* s.s. 27, 1980.
Chadwick, H., *Early Christian Thought and the Classical Tradition*, Oxford 1966.
—— *The Early Church*, Penguin 1967.
Ciccotti, E., *Il tramonto della schiavitù nel mondo antico* (1899), Bari 1977 (two vol.).
Clarke, G.W., 'Two Christians in the Familia Caesaris' *HTR* 64, 1971.
Coulanges, N.D.F. de, *The Ancient City* (1864), Gloucester 1979.
Cumont, F., *The Mysteries of Mithra* (1902), New York 1956.
—— *The Oriental Religions in Roman Paganism* (1906), New York 1959.
Daniélou, J. and Marrou, H., *The Christian Centuries. The First Six Hundred Years*, London 1964.
Dodds, E.R., *The Greeks and the Irrational*, London 1951.
—— *Pagan and Christian in an Age of Anxiety*, Cambridge 1965.
Duff, A.M., *Freedmen in the Early Roman Empire*, Oxford 1928.
Engels, F., 'Bruno Bauer and Early Christianity' (1882), in K. Marx and F. Engels, *On Religion*.
—— 'The Book of Revelation' (1883), in K. Marx and F. Engels, *On Religion*.
—— 'On the History of Early Christianity' (1894-5), in K. Marx and F. Engels, *On Religion*.

Feuerbach, L., *The Essence of Christianity* (1841), New York 1957.
—— *Manifestes Philosophiques*, French translation with introduction by L. Althusser, Paris 1960.
Finley, M.I. (ed.), *Slavery in Classical Antiquity*, Cambridge 1960, 1968.
—— *The Ancient Economy*, London 1973.
—— (ed.) *Studies in Ancient Society*, London 1974.
—— *Aspects of Antiquity*, London 1977.
—— *Ancient Slavery and Modern Ideology*, London 1980.
—— *Economy and Society in Ancient Greece*, London 1981.
Finn, T.M., 'Social Mobility, Imperial Civil Service and the Spread of Early Christianity', in *Studia Patristica* 17.1, Oxford 1982.
Foerster, W., *Gnosis. A Selection of Gnostic Texts* (1969), Oxford 1972.
Frank, T., *Roman Imperialism*, New York 1914.
——'Race Mixture in the Roman Empire' (1916), in D. Kagan (ed.), *Decline and Fall of the Roman Empire*, Boston 1962.
Frend, W.H.C., *The Donatist Church*, Oxford 1952.
—— *Martyrdom and Persecution in the Early Church*, Oxford 1965.
—— 'Heresy and Schism as Social and National Movements' *SCH* 9, 1972.
—— *The Rise of the Monophysite Movement*, Cambridge 1972.
—— 'The Monks and the Survival of the East Roman Empire in the 5th Century' *PP* 54, 1972.
—— 'Open Questions Concerning the Christians and the Roman Empire in the Age of the Severi' *JTS* n.s. 25, 1974.
—— *Town and Country in the Early Christian Centuries*, London 1980.
—— 'Early Christianity and Society: A Jewish Legacy in the Pre-Constantinian Era' *HTR* 76, 1983.
Fuller, P., 'The Christ of Faith and the Jesus of History' *NLR* 146, 1984.
Gager, J.G., 'Religion and Social Class in the Early Roman Empire', in S. Benko and J.J. O'Rourke (eds.) *Early Church History*.
Garnsey, P., *Social Status and Legal Privilege in the Roman Empire*, Oxford 1970.
—— 'Aspects of the Decline of the Urban Aristocracy in the Empire', in *ANRW* 2.1, Berlin 1974.
—— 'Urban Property Investment', in M.I. Finley (ed.), *Studies in Roman Property*, Cambridge 1976.
—— (ed.) *Non-Slave Labour in the Greco-Roman World*, Cambridge 1980.
Gibbon, E., *The Decline and Fall of the Roman Empire* (1776) (ed. J.B. Bury) London 1897-1900.
Goguel, M., *The Primitive Church* (1947), London 1964.
Gordon, M.L., 'The Nationality of Slaves under the Early Roman Empire' (1924), in Finley (ed.), *Slavery in Classical Antiquity*.
—— 'The Freedman's Son in Municipal Life' *JRS* 21, 1931.
Grant, R.M., *Second-Century Christianity. A Collection of Fragments*, London 1946.
—— *A Short History of the Interpretation of the Bible*, London 1948, 1965.
—— *Gnosticism and Early Christianity*, New York 1959.
—— *Augustus to Constantine: The Thrust of the Christian Movement into the Roman World*, London 1970.
—— *Early Christianity and Society*, London 1978.
—— 'Early Christians and Gnostics in Graeco-Roman Society', in A. Logan and A Wedderburn (eds.), *The New Testament and Gnosis*, London 1983.
—— *Christian Beginnings:Apocalypse to History*, London 1983.
Hardy, E.R., *The Large Estates of Byzantine Egypt*, New York 1931.
—— *Christian Egypt: Church and People*, Oxford 1952.
Harnack, A., *History of Dogma* (1894-9), London 1910.
—— *What is Christianity?* (1900), London 1901.
—— *Monasticism: Its Ideals and History* (1901), London 1901.
—— *The Mission and Expansion of Christianity in the First Three Centuries* (1903), London 1908 (from the second German edition) (two vol.).

—— *Militia Christi* (1905), Philadelphia 1981.
—— *The Constitution and Law of the Church in the First Two Centuries* (1910), London 1910.
—— *Bible Reading in the Early Church* (1912), London 1912.
Hefele, C.J., *A History of the Christian Councils from the Original Documents to the Close of the Council of Nicaea AD 325*, Edinburgh 1971.
Hegel, G., *Early Theological Writings*, Chicago 1948.
—— *The Philosophy of History*, New York 1956.
Hengel, M., *Property and Riches in the Early Church* (1973), Philadelphia 1974.
Hindess, B. and P. Hirst, *Pre-Capitalist Modes of Production*, London 1975.
Hopkins, K., 'Elite Mobility in the Roman Empire' *PP* 32, 1965, repr. in M.I. Finley (ed.), *Studies in Ancient Society.*
—— 'Economic Growth in Towns in Classical Antiquity', in P. Abrams and E.A. Wrigley (eds.), *Towns in Societies*, Cambridge 1978.
—— *Conquerors and Slaves*, Cambridge 1978.
—— 'Taxes and Trade in the Roman Empire' *JRS* 70, 1980.
—— 'Brother-Sister Marriage in Roman Egypt' *CSSH* 22, 1980.
Jaeger, W., *Early Christianity and Greek Paideia*, Oxford 1969.
Jolowicz, H.F. and Barry Nicholas, *Historical Introduction to the Study of Roman Law*, Cambridge 1932, 1972.
Jonas, H., *The Gnostic Religion*, Boston 1958, 1963.
Jones, A.H.M., *The Greek City: From Alexander to Justinian*, Oxford 1940.
—— *Constantine and the Conversion of Europe* (1948), Toronto 1978.
—— 'Slavery in the Ancient World' (1956), in M.I. Finley (ed.), *Slavery in Classical Antiquity.*
—— 'The Social Background of the Struggle Between Paganism and Christianity' (1958-9), in A. Momigliano (ed.), *The Conflict.*
—— *The Later Roman Empire* (1964), Oxford 1973 (two vol.).
—— *The Decline of the Ancient World*, London and New York 1966.
—— *The Roman Economy*, Oxford 1974.
Judge, E.A., *The Social Pattern of Christian Groups in the First Century*, London 1960.
—— 'Antike und Christentum: Towards a Definition of the Field', in *ANRW* 2.23.1, Berlin 1979.
Judge, E.A. and S.R. Pickering, 'Papyrus Documentation of Church and Community in Egypt to the Mid-Fourth Century' *JAC* 20, 1977.
Kajanto, I., *Onomastic Studies in the Early Christian Inscriptions of Rome and Carthage*, Helsinki 1963.
Kautsky, K., *Foundations of Christianity* (1908), New York 1972.
Keresztes, P., 'The Imperial Roman Government and the Christian Church' *ANRW* 2.23.1, Berlin 1979.
Knipfing, J.R., 'The Libelli of the Decian Persecution' *HTR* 16, 1923.
Konstan, D., 'Marxism and Roman Slavery' *Arethusa* 8, 1975.
Kreissig, H., 'Zur sozialen Zusammensetzung des frühchristlichen Gemeinden im ersten Jahrhundert u.Z.' *Eirene* 6, 1967.
Kümmel, W.G., *The New Testament. The History of the Investigation of its Problems*, London 1973.
Laistner, M.L.W., *Christianity and Pagan Culture in the Later Roman Empire*, New York 1951.
La Piana, G., 'The Roman Church at the End of the Second Century' *HTR* 18, 1925.
Leach, E. and D.A. Aycock, *Structuralist Interpretations of Biblical Myth*, Cambridge 1983.
Lee, C.L., 'Social Unrest and Primitive Christianity', in S. Benko and J.J. O'Rourke (eds.), *Early Church History*
Lenzmann, I., *L'origine du christianisme* (1958), Moscou 1961.
Liebeschuetz, J.H.W.G., *Continuity and Change in Roman Religion*, Oxford 1979.
Lietzmann, H., *The Beginnings of the Christian Church* (1932), London 1953.
—— *The Founding of the Church Universal* (1936), London 1953.

MacMullen, R., *Enemies of the Roman Order*, Oxford 1967.
—— *Roman Social Relations*, New Haven and London 1974.
—— *Paganism in the Roman Empire*, New Haven and London 1981.
—— 'Two Types of Conversion to Early Christianity' *VC* 37, 1983.
—— *Christianizing the Roman Empire*, New Haven and London 1984.
Malherbe, A.J., *Social Aspects of Early Christianity*, Baton Rouge and London 1977.
Marucchi, O., *Christian Epigraphy*, Cambridge 1912.
Marx, K. and F. Engels, *On Religion*, Moscow 1957.
—— *Pre-Capitalist Socio-Economic Formations*, Moscow 1979.
Meeks, W.A., *The First Urban Christians. The Social World of the Apostle Paul*, New Haven and London 1983.
Meeks, W.A. and R.L. Wilken, *Jews and Christians in Antioch in the First Four Centuries of the Common Era*, 1978.
Metzger, B.M., *The Early Versions of the New Testament*, Oxford 1977.
Millar, F., 'Paul of Samosata, Zenobia and Aurelian' *JRS* 61, 1971.
Momigliano, A., (ed.) *The Conflict Between Paganism and Christianity in the Fourth Century*, Oxford 1963.
—— *Studies in Historiography*, London 1966.
—— *Essays in Ancient and Modern Historiography*, Oxford 1977.
Musurillo, H., *The Acts of the Christian Martyrs*, Oxford 1972.
—— 'Christian and Political Martyrs in the Early Roman Empire: A Reconsideration', in *Travaux* 1974.
Nag Hammadi Library in English, The, Leiden 1977.
Nock, A.D., *Conversion*, Oxford 1933.
—— *Essays on Religion and the Ancient World*, Oxford 1971 (two vol.).
Norris, F.W., 'Paul of Samosata, Procurator Ducenarius' *JTS* n.s. 35, 1984.
O'Leary, De Lacy, *The Saints of Egypt*, London 1937.
Pagels, E.H., *The Gnostic Gospels*, London 1979.
—— 'Adam and Eve, Christ and the Church: A Survey of Second Century Controversies Concerning Marriage', in A. Logan and A. Wedderburn (eds.), *The New Testament and Gnosis*, London 1983.
Parassoglou, G., *Imperial Estates in Roman Egypt*, Amsterdam 1978.
Petit, P., *Histoire Générale de l'Empire Romain*, Paris 1974.
Plekhanov, G., *Selected Philosophical Works*, vol. 3, Moscow 1976.
Quasten, J., *Patrology*, Utrecht-Antwerp 1950-60 (three vol.).
Ramsay, W.M., *The Church in the Roman Empire Before AD 170*, London 1893.
—— *St. Paul the Traveller and the Roman Citizen* (1895), London 1925.
—— *The Cities of St. Paul*, London 1907.
Renan, F., *The Life of Jesus* (1863), London 1864.
—— *The Apostles* (1866), London 1888.
—— *Leaders of Christian and Anti-Christian Thought*, London (a selection of articles) n.d.
Roberts, C.H., *Manuscript, Society and Belief in Early Christian Egypt*, Oxford 1979.
Rostovtzeff, M., *The Social and Economic History of the Roman Empire*, Oxford 1926, second edition 1957 (two vol.).
—— *Rome*, Oxford 1928.
Ste. Croix, G.E.M. de, 'Why Were the Early Christians Persecuted?' *PP* 26, 1963, repr. in M.I. Finley (ed.), *Studies in Ancient Society*.
—— 'Early Christian Attitudes to Property and Slavery' *SCH* 12, 1975.
—— 'Karl Marx and the History of Classical Antiquity' *Arethusa* 8, 1975.
—— *The Class Struggle in the Ancient Greek World*, London 1981.
—— 'Class in Marx's Conception of History, Ancient and Modern' *NLR* 146, 1984.
Samuel, R., 'British Marxist Historians, 1880-1980: Part One' *NLR* 120, 1980.
Schlaifer, R., 'Greek Theories of Slavery from Homer to Aristotle', in M.I. Finley (ed.), *Slavery in Classical Antiquity*.
Schweitzer, A., *The Quest of the Historical Jesus* (1906), London 1922.
Scott-Moncrieff, P.D., *Paganism and Christianity in Egypt*, Cambridge 1913.

Skeat, T.C., 'Early Christian Book Production: Papyri and Manuscripts', in *CHB* 2, 1970.
Smith, M., *Clement of Alexandria and a Secret Gospel of Mark*, Harvard 1973.
—— *The Secret Gospel*, Wellingborough 1985.
Spinoza, B. de, *A Theologico-Political Treatise* (1670), New York 1951.
Taylor, L.R., 'Freedmen and Freeborn in the Epitaphs of Imperial Rome' *AJP* 82, 1961.
Telfer, W., 'Episcopal Succession in Egypt' *JEH* 3, 1952.
Treggiari, S., *Roman Freedmen During the Late Republic*, Oxford 1969.
Troeltsch, E., *The Social Teachings of the Christian Churches* (1911) London 1931 (two vol.).
—— 'Adolf von Harnack and Ferdinand Christian von Baur' (1921), in W. Pauk, *Harnack and Troeltsch*, Oxford 1968.
Vermes, G., *Jesus the Jew*, London 1973.
—— *The Dead Sea Scrolls in English*, Penguin 1975.
—— *The Dead Sea Scrolls*, London 1977.
—— *Jesus and the World of Judaism*, London 1983.
Vogt, J., 'Pagans and Christians in the Family of Constantine The Great', in A. Momigliano (ed.), *The Conflict*.
—— *Ancient Slavery and the Ideal of Man*, Oxford 1974.
Wallace, S.L., *Taxation in Egypt from Augustus to Diocletian*, Oxford 1938.
Wallon, H., *Historie de l'esclavage dans l'antiquité* (1847), Paris 1879 (three vol.).
Weaver, P.R.C., 'Social Mobility in the Early Roman Empire: The Evidence of the Imperial Freedmen and Slaves' *PP* 37, 1967, repr. in M.I. Finley (ed.), *Studies in Ancient Society*.
—— *Familia Caesaris*, Cambridge 1972.
Weber, M., *The Agrarian Sociology of Ancient Civilizations* (1896, 1909), London 1976.
—— *Economy and Society*, Berkeley-Los Angeles-London 1978 (two vol.).
Westermann, W.L., *Upon Slavery in Ptolemaic Egypt*, New York 1929.
—— *The Slave Systems of Greek and Roman Antiquity*, Philadelphia 1955.
Wilken, R.L., *The Christians as the Romans Saw Them*, New Haven and London 1984.
Wilson, W.J., 'The Career of the Prophet Hermas' *HTR* 20, 1927.
Wipszycka, E., Review of I.F. Fikhman *L'Egypte entre deux époques*, Moskva 1965 (original in Russian) *JJP* 16-7, 1971.
—— *Les ressources et les activités économiques des églises en Egypte, du IVe au VIIIe siècle*, Brusseles 1972.
—— 'Remarques sur les lettres privées chrétiennes des IIe-IVe siècles' *JJP* 18, 1974.
Woodward, E.L., *Christianity and Nationalism in the Later Roman Empire*, London 1916.

Index of Names and Places

Index of Modern Authors

(Only modern authors mentioned in the main text have been included)

Allard, P. 23-4
Anderson, P. 10

Bardy, G. 170
Barnes, T.D. 14, 70
Bauer, Bruno 4, 5, 21
Baur, F.C. 4, 23
Bell, H.I. 149
Benko, S. 15
Bloch, Marc 30
Bolland, John van 2
Bömer, F. 29
Brown, P. 15, 98, 111, 150, 172
Browning, R. 109-10
Brunt, P. 169
Bultmann, R. 9, 10
Burkitt, F.C. 103

Cadoux, C.J. 11, 67
Calvin, 33
Cameron, Averil 131
Chadwick, H. 90
Ciccotti, E. 7, 30
Clarke, G.W. 129
Cumont, F. 29, 84, 125

Dodds, E.R. 15, 71, 103

Engels, F. 5-7, 9, 22-3, 39, 90
Erasmus 2, 33

Feuerbach, L. 5
Fikhman, I.F. 122
Finley, M.I. 10, 26-7, 30, 127
Frend, W.H.C. 90

Garnsey, P. 163
Gibbon, E. 3, 8, 21-2, 114, 185
Goguel, M. 33
Gordon, M.L. 127
Grant, R.M. 41, 67

Haehling R. von 98
Harnack, A. 7, 9, 11, 22, 39, 48, 91,
    103, 106, 125, 170
Hefele, C. J. 35
Hegel 3-5, 26, 39, 51
Hengel, M. 103
Hobbes 2
Hopkins, K. 27, 83, 172

Jones, A.H.M. 10, 98, 127, 136
Judge, E.A. 41

Kajanto, I. 48
Kautsky, K. 7-9, 22, 39, 90
Kreissig, H. 41

Lane Fox, R. 16-7
Lenin 22
Locke, John 2
Luther, Martin 2, 5, 6, 33

223

LYONS

ROME

ELVIRA

CARTHAGE

THE ROMAN WORLD